Routledge Phil

MW00657149

Derrida on Deconstruction

Jacques Derrida is one of the most influential and controversial philosophers of the last fifty years. *Derrida on Deconstruction* introduces and assesses:

- Derrida's life and the background to his philosophy
- The key themes of the critique of metaphysics, and the development of new positions in language, consciousness, aesthetics and ethics that characterise his most widely read works
- The continuing importance of Derrida's work to philosophy

This is a much-needed introduction for philosophy or humanities students undertaking courses on Derrida.

Barry Stocker is Assistant Professor in Philosophy at Yeditepe University, Istanbul, Turkey, and Senior Honorary Research Fellow in Philosophy at University College London.

ROUTLEDGE PHILOSOPHY GUIDEBOOKS

Edited by Tim Crane and Jonathan Wolff,
University College London

Routledge Philosophy Guidebook to

Derrida on Deconstruction

Barry
Stocker

Routledge
Taylor & Francis Group

LONDON AND NEW YORK

First published 2006
by Routledge
2 Park Square, Milton Park, Abingdon, Oxon OX14 4RN

Simultaneously published in the USA and Canada
by Routledge
270 Madison Avenue, New York, NY 10016

*Routledge is an imprint of the Taylor & Francis Group, an informa
business*

Typeset in Aldus and Scala by Taylor & Francis Books
Printed and bound in Great Britain by
TJ International Ltd, Padstow, Cornwall

British Library Cataloguing in Publication Data
A catalogue record for this book is available from the British Library

Library of Congress Cataloging in Publication Data
Stocker, Barry, 1966-
  Routledge philosophy guidebook to Derrida on deconstruction /
Barry Stocker.
     p. cm. -- (Routledge philosophy guidebooks)
  Includes bibliographical references.
  ISBN 0-415-32501-3 (hardback : alk. paper) -- ISBN 0-415-32502-1
(pbk. : alk. paper) 1. Derrida, Jacques. 2. Deconstruction. I. Title.
II. Series.
  B2430.D484S76 2006
  194--dc22

                            2005026150

ISBN10: 0-415-32501-3   ISBN13: 978-0-415-32501-1 (hbk)
ISBN10: 0-415-32502-1   ISBN13: 978-0-415-32502-8 (pbk)

CONTENTS

Acknowledgements

Excerpts from Jacques Derrida, *Speech and Phenomena and Other Essays on Husserl's Theory of Signs*, Translated by David B. Allison, Evanston: Northwestern University Press, 1973. Reproduced with kind permission of Northwestern University Press.

Excerpts from Jacques Derrida, *Writing and Difference*, London: Routledge, 1978. Reproduced with kind permission of Routledge.

Excerpts from Jacques Derrida, *Margins of Philosophy*, Chicago: University of Chicago Press, 1984. Reproduced with kind permission of University of Chicago Press.

1

INTRODUCTION

DERRIDA'S LIFE AND THE BACKGROUND TO HIS PHILOSOPHY

LIFE

Jacques Derrida was born in 1930 in El-Biar, near Algiers, in French colonial Algeria. Like most French families, the Derridas returned to metropolitan France on Algerian independence in 1962. He came from a prosperous background, but as a Jew he suffered from discrimination during the Second World War. For three years Algeria was under the control of the Vichy government in France, which collaborated with Nazi Germany to the extent of persecuting French Jews. Derrida suffered exclusion from high school in 1941, which was a minor event compared with the horrors of the Holocaust, but was clearly bad enough in itself. From 1943 he completed his studies at the *lycée* developing an interest in philosophy. He went to Paris in 1950 for the *khâgne* at the particularly famous *Lycée Louis-le-Grand*. The *khâgne* is a peculiar French institution, referring to a period of study in high school after the normal school leaving exam, in order to prepare for the entrance exams to the *grandes écoles*, another very specific French institution. The *grande école* is a superior university, whose graduates usually enter the higher echelons in their profession; leading graduates have traditionally been guaranteed a distinguished career in a state institution or a private company. In 1952, Derrida

secured entry to the *École normale supérieure* (ENS), which spe-
cializes in training academics and provides a high proportion of
French university lecturers, particularly at the better-known institutions. From 1953 to 1954 he studied the Husserl archives at the
University of Louvain in Belgium, the university with the most
elevated tradition in the study of Phenomenology. He wrote the
equivalent of an MA thesis on Husserl, which was published after
Derrida became famous (Derrida 2003). After a period preparing
lycée students for the *khâgne*, he taught at the Sorbonne (now
properly known as the University of Paris I Sorbonne-Panthéon)
from 1960 to 1964, and then returned to the ENS as a lecturer. He
stayed there until 1984 when he transferred to the *École des
hautes études en sciences sociales* (a *grande école* specializing in
graduate studies in the humanities), where he was director of
philosophical studies. In 1983, at the invitation of the then French
President, François Mitterrand, he became the founding director of
the *Collège international de philosophie*, which does not have full-
time teaching staff or offer qualifications. Instead, open lecture
courses are given by a volunteer body of philosophers, in various
languages. From early in his publishing career, Derrida made a
strong impression. He won a prize for his first major publication, a
translation of, and a long introduction to, Husserl's short essay,
'The origin of geometry' (Derrida 1989a). His fame in the United
States goes back to 1966 when he participated in a conference at
Johns Hopkins University on Structuralism, presenting what has
since become one of his most widely read papers, 'Structure, sign
and play in the discourse of the human sciences'. In 1967, his
international reputation was secured by the publication of three
important and original books: *Speech and Phenomena* (Derrida
1973), *Writing and Difference* (Derrida 1978), *Of Grammatology*
(Derrida 1976). These early successes set him on the road to exceptional fame and influence, in philosophy and in other disciplines.

When Derrida died in October 2004, the sad event was
announced by the office of the President of the Republic of France.
This was something of a specifically French occasion. There are few
other countries in the world where the head of state would be connected with such an announcement. Even by French standards
though it was an extraordinary act of recognition for an academic

philosopher, particularly when we consider that Derrida is not easy to read and that he had no political connections with the President of that time. Jacques Chirac is a politician on the right, while Derrida was always firmly on the left. Not only was Derrida distinct from Chirac in politics, he had campaigned for Chirac's left-wing rival François Mitterrand in presidential elections.

PHILOSOPHICAL REPUTATION

Long before his death, Derrida had become famous as a contemporary thinker throughout the world. His work has proved of interest not only to philosophers, but also to people working across the humanities. Large amounts of work referring to Derrida have appeared particularly in literary studies and cultural studies, but also in many other areas. In the United States, his main institutional connections were with programmes in literature and cultural studies, though he was also a regular visitor to departments of philosophy. The weight of interest in Derrida outside philosophical circles has proved something of a problem for his philosophical reputation. For some, it confirms the claim that Derrida is not a 'real' or 'serious' philosopher. Some of Derrida's predecessors in the history of European philosophy, and who are important for his own work, were attacked in similar terms for many years but are now being recognized as central figures in philosophy by an increasing number of philosophers from different backgrounds. That applies in particular to G.W.F. Hegel, Friedrich Nietzsche, Martin Heidegger, Jean-Paul Sartre and Maurice Merleau-Ponty, along with more recent figures contemporary with Derrida such as his teacher Michel Foucault and his friend Emmanuel Lévinas. Derrida is likely to undergo the same process, and there are already signs that it is under way.

While the interest in Derrida outside philosophical circles has produced much important and valuable work, it does mean putting Derrida's work in a frame other than the philosophical one with which he was concerned. The fact that some (but only some) people in these fields resort to political gestures, and superficial use of 'theoretical' slogans, as a substitute for argument, has also been used to attack Derrida on a guilt by association basis. Derrida certainly emphasized that philosophy always occurs in a context, but nevertheless it is always the philosophical questions that are most important for him; there is certainly no question of asserting a position without arguing for it, and even less of resorting to arguments from political purity. Derrida did write about literary texts and art works, but the discussions are essentially philosophical and should be distinguished from the use made of Derrida in literary theory and literary criticism. Derrida made philosophical remarks about literature, and put aesthetic aspects at the centre of philosophy, but he did not produce a literary or cultural theory. There is nothing wrong with using Derrida to construct such theories, but that was not what he was doing.

It is the interdisciplinary reception of Derrida that marks a distinction between the way Derrida is seen in France and the way Derrida is seen in the English-speaking world. Despite the influence of French figures in interdisciplinary work in the humanities, such as literary theory, cultural studies, social theory, art theory and legal theory, these are mostly areas of influence for Derrida outside France. Within France, the academic disciplines are still much more segregated and are still more guided by notions of disciplinary purity. The result of this was that Derrida was a well-known philosopher in France, with all the dubious benefits of celebrity and journalistic coverage, but less of a general star across the humanities.

The manner in which Derrida's death was announced confirms his status as a celebrity intellectual, who stood as a symbol of cultural achievement for those who had no knowledge of his writings. This status is at least as much of a burden as a benefit in establishing Derrida's real achievements. The name has come to be a symbol for those with little knowledge of his texts who nevertheless think he ought to be defended as a symbol of 'radical' intellectual culture, or who like to use the word Deconstruction with little knowledge of its philosophical content. The name Derrida is equally a symbol for those who think of him as an example of relativism, postmodernism, nihilism, scepticism or even just as an example of confusing senseless pretentiousness, and who regard Derrida as a charlatan. Most of the latter group show little knowledge of Derrida's texts, or they would have noticed that Derrida never argues for relativism, postmodernism, nihilism or scepticism; or if they do show any knowledge, their reading is so polemical and so obviously designed to attack rather than understand that it lacks any intellectual credibility. The latter group of people like to claim that Derrida was better known in the United States and the rest of the English-speaking world than in France, though that of course does not establish anything about his philosophical worth and seems odd coming from people who claim to defend intellectual rigour. Despite persisting strident claims that Derrida is despised by all 'real' philosophers in well-established academic departments of philosophy, there has been a growth of interest in Derrida in such places, along with a longstanding interest in those departments that specialize in the relevant European schools of philosophy. Although some would like to pretend otherwise, there has been a distinct downturn in polemical attacks on Derrida. Philosophers from very different backgrounds from that of Derrida himself have either commented appreciatively on his works, or at least criticized them in a respectful way, or in some cases show signs of indirect influence.

Derrida's celebrity in the English-speaking world did not impress everyone in France, where many are used to defining France's place in the world by rivalry with the United States, but the fact that some people were disturbed by this suggests he did have an impact in France. After all, it is hardly likely that the French presidency would announce the death of someone who does not matter in France. All of this is of little relevance to real discussions of Derrida's place as a philosopher, and all the international publicity, including a film about Derrida, tended to reduce him to the category of 'fashionable' thinker. Derrida's work has already endured long enough for it to have transcended fashion; it is now forty-four years since his first major publication. In any case, the 'fashion' has now passed to Gilles Deleuze and Emmanuel Lévinas, and those who still attack Derrida as 'fashionable' have missed the point. They just have not made the necessary effort to follow the field that would justify them intervening in any way. There was a time when Ludwig Wittgenstein had such a status, as the 'in' reference for those who wished to show off their supposed intellectual sophistication, but few would doubt that Wittgenstein was a philosopher of great seriousness and enduring importance.

Unlike those who seize various opportunities to launch polemical attacks on him, Derrida was a man with a deeply civilized attitude to intellectual debate, and who was never aggressive except in reaction to very aggressive, and sometimes downright insulting, criticism. In all circumstances, he made a genuine effort to reconstruct the position of his opponent, and maintained the most generous attitudes towards his rivals and colleagues in the French philosophical scene. Derrida's importance as a philosopher is not affected one way or the other by his attitude to dialogue and polemics; nevertheless it is worth noting his exemplary qualities from that point of view.

Derrida's commitment to an ethics of intellectual dialogue and communication was matched by a commitment to increasing the role of philosophy in society and public access to philosophy, through the International College of Philosophy and his participation in a campaign for philosophy in French schools. He also showed strong commitment to promoting political and social justice. Though he was clearly on the left, and identified himself as a critic of the right, many of his causes would appeal to members of the genuinely liberal and libertarian right. He participated in campaigns against apartheid, the imprisonment of Nelson Mandela, and racism; and in campaigns for immigrants' and refugees' rights. He also strongly opposed totalitarian Communism, particularly in Czechoslovakia, where he participated in a group campaigning for solidarity with intellectual dissidents. As a consequence he was arrested in Prague on absurd charges of drug trafficking in 1981 and was only released after diplomatic protests. Some of his later writings refer to the Czechoslovak Phenomenological philosopher Jan Patochka (Derrida 1995), who was a major inspiration for anti-totalitarian dissidents such as Václav Havel. Derrida's willingness to give time and energy, and even risk imprisonment, for his principles should surely preclude claims that his philosophy is irresponsible, subordinating moral and political principles to individual selfishness and self-serving scepticism. Nevertheless, absurd and nonsensical though they are, such claims are sometimes made.

DERRIDA'S PHILOSOPHY

This book aims to explain Deconstruction on the basis of Derrida's earlier philosophy. Derrida's earlier philosophy is an odd phrase in the sense that there is no widely recognized distinction between different stages of Derrida's philosophy, as there is in various other philosophers. In the twentieth century Ludwig Wittgenstein and Martin Heidegger are the best examples of philosophers whose career can be usefully divided into stages, according to general agreement. Nevertheless, it is widely recognized that Derrida's philosophy as put forward in his first six books is generally written in a more philosophically direct style than later works. The six books are: *Introduction to the Origin of Geometry* (IOG) (Derrida 1989a [first published in 1961]), *Speech and Phenomena* (SP) (Derrida 1973 [first published in 1967]), *Of Grammatology* (OG) (Derrida 1976 [first published in 1967]), *Writing and Difference* (WD) (Derrida 1978 [first published in 1967]), *Margins of Philosophy* (MP) (Derrida 1982 [first published in 1972]), *Dissemination* (D) (Derrida 1981 [first published in 1972]). A new stage can be said to begin with *Glas* (Derrida 1990 [first published in 1974]). The word *Glas* is not translated in the English edition, because of the importance of word play on the title in Derrida's text, though 'Knell' would be quite adequate as a translation, and maybe should have been used to avoid the general air of mystification around Derrida. It is the case that *Glas* is composed and written in a quite extraordinary manner. The very large book is divided on each page into parallel columns. The first column is largely a discussion of the philosophy of G.W.F. Hegel and the second column is largely a discussion of the French dramatist, poet and essayist Jean Genet. There is much more going on in each column than can be summarized here, and the columns overlap in some respects, which suggests the challenge that its reading provides. Some of Derrida's earlier texts play with the form of an academic text, most notably 'Tympan' (MP), the first essay in *Margins of Philosophy*, which is also divided into parallel columns; and two essays in *Writing and Difference*, 'La parole soufflée' (WD 6)[1] and 'Ellipsis' (WD XI), which intersperse quotations from Edmond Jabès with compressed related comments by Derrida on law, literature and religion. However, nothing ever compares with the hundreds of pages of text in *Glas*, which are deliberately at the limits of recognizably philosophical discourse and which are both playfully allusive and conceptually difficult. For some advocates of Derrida as an important philosopher and thinker, this marks *Glas* as the highpoint of Derrida's philosophical career; for others, including the present author, there is a suspicion that Derrida's style has taken over in a book that, though fascinating and compelling to read, does not add to what was established in the earlier books.

In some respects *Glas* is a watershed text for Derrida, as afterwards the Derridean style is often to the fore in an extreme way; and more pieces appear that are very oblique or very slight or both. For these reasons alone, even for those who find *Glas*, or possibly some later texts by Derrida, to be more important, it is surely reasonable to suggest that the earlier texts provide the best introduction. Additionally, in the later texts, there is more emphasis on psychoanalysis and less on the Phenomenological tradition in philosophy from which he emerged. The average level of writing drops, though many important works appeared after *Glas* and we are comparing with the extraordinarily high level achieved throughout the first six books. There is no disgrace in falling below that extraordinary high early level, and many later texts can be mentioned that are extremely important and written to the highest standard, which include: on aesthetics, *The Truth in Painting* (Derrida 1987b); on ethics and politics, *The Politics of Friendship* (Derrida 1997); on law and jurisprudence, 'Force of law' (Derrida 1990); readings of philosophical classics in *Of Spirit* (Derrida 1989b) on Heidegger, and *Spurs* (Derrida 1979) on Nietzsche; on philosophy and literature, 'Two words for Joyce' (Derrida 1984), 'Ulysses gramophone' (Derrida 1992), amongst others. However, a good deal of weaker work also appeared, partly as a result of the enormous publication demand for any text that Derrida wrote after he became an intellectual celebrity; partly because of the diminishing returns of restating his positions when defending his works against criticism; partly because of the impossibility of keeping to the same very high level when Derrida showed such an inexhaustible appetite for writing, and for speaking at conferences, which leads us back to the first reason mentioned.

While Derrida's work is never easy, as it is never written in the most direct style and is never written as a direct answer to textbook philosophical questions, we do get as close we ever do to these things in Derrida's early texts. Certainly, though Derrida never tries to engage with answers to standard philosophical questions, it is much easier to think of the earlier texts in terms of established questions in metaphysics, knowledge, language and mind. The later texts tend to say more about core themes in ethics, aesthetics, political and legal philosophy, but these issues are also present in the earlier texts in a context where Derrida is developing themes within metaphysics, knowledge, language and mind, though Derrida never explicitly approached philosophy in such a compartmentalized way. The most clearly argumentative texts, and the texts most clearly connected with a philosophical tradition, are IOG and SP, both of which are concerned with Husserl's Phenomenology, which is itself clearly a body of work in mainstream philosophy trying to answer standard classical philosophical questions. Derrida's readings of Phenomenology are closer to that approach even compared with the other texts under consideration in the present book. That raises the question of why this book is not focused on those two books on Phenomenology. One reason is that the interest in Phenomenology is also found in '"Genesis and structure" and Phenomenology' (WD 5) and later in 'Form and meaning: a note on the phenomenology of language' (in MP), so it would not be possible to discuss Phenomenology in Derrida without bringing in those texts. Given the amount of ground covered in this book, the two later essays on Phenomenology get little separate attention, but they would have to be covered in any book on Derrida and Phenomenology. This cannot be a book on Phenomenology in any case: it must be on Derrida's distinct contribution, usually known as Deconstruction. Another reason is there is just far too much going on in the two 'Phenomenological' books, which is developed further in other books under consideration here. It would be very difficult, for example, to get into any discussion of Derrida's position on speech and language featured heavily in the two Phenomenological books, which did not refer to parts of the other books, most obviously the whole of OG along with 'Plato's pharmacy' (in D).

The most obvious choice for a single book as the topic of this book would be OG as that is the biggest Derrida seller and is maybe the most cited of all his texts. Isolating it from the discussion of the same themes in the other books would be very artificial though, particularly when we consider that it was published in the same year as WD and SP. It would be difficult, even absurd, to introduce Derrida's place in philosophy to the reader without both fully bringing in the 'Phenomenological' texts and the two essays in MP that are the most widely discussed by those philosophers who come from a different philosophical background from that of Derrida: 'White mythology' and 'Signature event context'. Much more could be said about the overlaps between the six books, but these should become evident in the thematic chapters of the present book. The coverage of six books means that not every part of every book is equally represented. Some chapters are discussed in more detail, while others are relegated to brief indications of their relevance to themes discussed through analysis of passages in selected chapters. Every effort is made to ensure that the reader knows which chapters and sections to look at in relation to each theme, so the present book should serve as a guide through the six early texts under consideration. The aim is to give as far as possible a way of reading these books as part of a whole Derridean philosophy, and this takes priority over differences between the texts, which are not great enough to preclude the approach of a book like the present one that introduces the reader to Derrida by focusing on the general themes and claims.

ANALYTIC AND CONTINENTAL PHILOSOPHY

Considerations of Derrida's ways of approaching philosophy bring us to another issue in the present book, which is the distinction between Analytic and Continental European philosophy. Derrida seems so strange to so many people working in the Analytic philosophical manner prevalent in the Anglophone world, and increasingly influential outside it, that there is a definite need to explain to such people how Derrida might fit in with what they are doing. Some of these people react with outright hostility to Derrida, questioning his credentials as a serious philosopher, so it is also necessary to acknowledge and reply to these criticisms, and to establish Derrida as an important philosopher, addressing questions of interest to all philosophers.

These purposes of explaining, and justifying, Derrida as a significant philosopher with important arguments also require us to define the terms used to name the traditions. This is something of an issue in itself. How can philosophy be separated between a tradition that names a geographical area (Continental European philosophy), and a tradition that names a mode of doing philosophy (Analytic philosophy)? The geographical name has reality in that the important philosophers so named were indeed from Continental Europe (taken to exclude the British Isles): Germany (Immanuel Kant, J.G. Fichte, F.W.J. Schelling, Arthur Schopenhauer, Friedrich Nietzsche, Edmund Husserl,[2] Martin Heidegger, Theodor Adorno, Hans-Georg Gadamer, Jürgen Habermas); France (Henri Bergson, Jean-Paul Sartre, Maurice Merleau-Ponty, Georges Canguihelm, Gaston Bachelard, Emmanuel Lévinas,[3] Michel Foucault, Louis Althusser, Gilles Deleuze, Maurice Blanchot, Paul Ricoeur, as well as Derrida); Denmark (Søren Kierkegaard).

Various complications arise however. Many of the key Analytic philosophers were Austrian, German or Polish (Gottlob Frege, Hans Reichenbach, Alfred Tarski, Ludwig Wittgenstein, Rudolf Carnap, Moritz Schlick, Hans Neurath, Carl Hempel, Karl Popper). The majority of the important early figures were from Continental Europe, in addition to British and American philosophers, such as: Charles Peirce, G.E. Moore, Bertrand Russell. Many of the European Analytic philosophers came to Britain or the United States after the Second World War, assisting in the great growth of Analytic philosophy after the war.

There are figures who are very hard to classify like Alexius Meinong, an inspiration both for Husserl and for Analytic philosophers like Roderick Chisholm. Husserl himself is difficult to classify since his early work included correspondence with Frege, and, though he is placed at the origin of the Phenomenological strand in Continental European philosophy, *Logical Investigations* (Husserl

2001), in particular, has had influence in Analytic philosophy and some Analytic philosophers would claim it as a book in their own tradition. Habermas studied in the United States and brought a great deal of Analytic philosophy into his work, though he is rooted in the Frankfurt School associated with Theodor Adorno. Though Adorno's philosophy seems far removed from the Analytic style, he himself was in the United States during the Second World War and left a huge legacy in many disciplines, including philosophy, though, as with Derrida and many of the Continental style philosophers, recognition came quicker in sociology, art theory, literary studies and cultural studies than in philosophy. The great founding figure of American philosophy, Charles Peirce, was deeply interested in Hegel, and the Hegelian influence continued after Peirce in William James and then Wilfrid Sellars. Ludwig Wittgenstein spent most of his philosophical career in Britain and was deeply interested in Kierkegaard, Schopenhauer, Nietzsche and Heidegger. Though there was a period in which Analytic philosophy largely defined itself as opposed to Continental European philosophy, and regarded the whole history of philosophy as a merely secondary field, there has been a major evolution. History of philosophy has been rehabilitated, and a growing interest in Kant inevitably led to a greater respectability for German Idealist philosophy, particularly Hegel, and everything that flowed from that in European philosophy. Increasingly important work at the centre of Analytic philosophy makes reference to aspects of the other tradition.

There has been an equivalent movement in Continental Europe, as Analytic philosophy has become more and more influential in recent years. This can happen in a manner antagonistic to the 'Continental European' style, and Derrida suffered from this, feeling isolated in France towards the end of his life because of the Analytic shift. Its most prominent representative, Pascal Engel, is one of those disposed to polemical aggression against Derrida and related work. Nevertheless, many in the new wave of European Analytic philosophers wish to find ways of connecting the traditions and in this way Analytic philosophy is increasing the influence of European Continental philosophy. Certainly in countries where history of philosophy has been very dominant, there has been a tendency to think that it is philosophy up to Kant which matters, so interest in all the currents in philosophy that have emerged since Kant, and the interest in the new and in originality, can converge in promoting a view of philosophy less orientated to translating and commentating on old classics.

The distinction between Analytic and Continental European philosophy is not an easy one to make, but the following points are pertinent. Analytic philosophy attaches great importance to formal logic, which hardly ever appears in Continental texts. Analytic philosophy tends to resolve paradoxes, while Continental philosophy tends to arrive at paradoxes. Analytic philosophy frequently takes natural science as a model, while Continental philosophy is more orientated towards aesthetics and subjective experience. Analytic philosophy aims for a neutral clear style for presenting problems, while Continental philosophy aims to find a style of writing that indicates the movement of philosophical argument. Analytic philosophy aims at very contemporary debates, leaving aside history of philosophy, while Continental philosophy brings the history of philosophy into its contemporary debates. Analytic philosophy tends to treat texts in the history of philosophy as if they were contemporary Analytic texts, while Continental philosophy tends to emphasize the literary qualities and historical context of texts in the history of philosophy. Analytic philosophy tends to take philosophy as given and does not give primary importance to discussions of what philosophy is, while Continental philosophy tends to reflect on the status of philosophy at every point. Analytic philosophy tends to describe and define everything explicitly, while Continental philosophy tends to use indirectness, context and style to describe and define. These distinctions are not absolute at all, but as a whole they clearly show what we are more likely to find in each school of thought.

We can suggest Derrida's place in philosophy through the points above with regard to what is most typical of Continental European philosophy, but since none of these points make absolute distinctions, we can also suggest that Derrida has another approach to issues which are present in Analytic philosophy, and that therefore he cannot be fully understood without reference to that approach. However, Derrida's direct knowledge of that approach is very limited and J.L. Austin is the only Analytic philosopher who makes much of an appearance in Derrida's work. One counterweight to that is that

Derrida begins with Husserl, who has been taken up by many Analytic philosophers, particularly with regard to his earlier work.

Placing Derrida in the specific context of those writers and texts that have importance in his own writing is a difficult task in that his range of reference is so vast that it does not lend itself to summary. The most important context is that which comes from his place in the history of Continental European philosophy. References to Hegel, Nietzsche, Husserl and Heidegger are particularly important, and he is largely situating himself with reference to them. The most important issue there is overcoming metaphysics. This is an issue for Nietzsche and Heidegger rather than Hegel and Husserl. Part of what Derrida is doing is a mediation between, or combination of, the ways in which Nietzsche and Heidegger try to bring metaphysics to an end, which is a goal that was also pursued in early Analytic philosophy. Hegel is important because the exhaustive nature of his attempts to establish the metaphysical goals of absolute being, and absolute spirit, reveal the limits of metaphysics and philosophical system. Husserl is important because his attempts to describe experience in a pure way detached from metaphysics and theory reveal the persistence of metaphysical approaches in any attempt to define pure appearances and the pure contents of consciousness. There are various contexts in which earlier figures in the history of philosophy appear, particularly Plato, Aristotle, Plotinus, Descartes, Leibniz and Kant. The main point of these references is to constitute metaphysics, and also the tensions in metaphysics, where it tends to contradict itself. After Heidegger, Derrida is concerned with French philosophy. He was clearly familiar with the work of Sartre and Merleau-Ponty, but he has very little to say about it directly in the early stage of his career with which this book is concerned and tended only to refer to Sartre as someone who had misinterpreted Heidegger. The work on the theory of knowledge in Gaston Bachelard and Georges Canguilhelm has some bearing on Derrida's work on Husserl and Rousseau. George Bataille's work on sociology, poetics and philosophy, Michel Foucault's work on the structures and history of thought, Emmanuel Lévinas's work on Phenomenology and ethics, and Maurice Blanchot's work on writing and literature all have a very significant place for Derrida, though in the earlier texts Blanchot gets little direct attention.

After outlining Derrida's place in the history of philosophy, we should consider the large role that texts of a kind not usually classified as core philosophical texts play in his work. In the history of thought, Jean-Jacques Rousseau's work on society and language have a very significant place for Derrida, which he ties in with the Structuralist linguistics of Ferdinand de Saussure and the Structuralist anthropology of Claude Lévi-Strauss. Structuralism claims to be non-metaphysical in a pure scientific approach to language and society. For Derrida, Structuralism is full of metaphysical assumptions; indeed it expresses something essential about pure metaphysics. He suggests that these metaphysical concerns come into Structuralism from Rousseau, who is transmitting them from Descartes and ultimately from Plato. Foucault is often included in discussions of Structuralism, though Derrida does not do so, because, while Foucault's early work has some things in common with Structuralism with regard to the emphasis on structures of thought, Foucault does not follow the strict Structuralist approach. Structuralism proper takes Saussure's description of language, in which nature is opposed to the social and pure system is opposed to historical facts, as its model. Structuralism also comes up in Jacques Lacan's version of psychoanalysis, though that was only one aspect of Lacan's complex body of work. It is not really dealt with in Derrida's earlier texts, though psychoanalysis is, so Lacan is not discussed in the present book. Sigmund Freud does feature in the early texts, and becomes more important over time for Derrida. His interest in the unconscious aspects of the mind provides Derrida with a way of challenging any claim that the mind is a rational thing perfectly clear to itself, while also critically discussing metaphysical elements of Freud's theories.

Derrida's relation with Saussure, Lévi-Strauss, Lacan and Foucault means that he is often placed under the label of 'Post-Structuralism', though it is a label used by literary and cultural theorists more than philosophers. The phrase 'Post-Structuralism' is too limited, though it is useful in certain contexts. Derrida is not just reacting to Structuralism, and his real starting point is in philosophical Phenomenology, and he certainly never talked about 'Post-Structuralism'. The other label often applied to Derrida, and his contemporaries, is 'postmodernism'. Again Derrida never used the phrase, and in origin it is used to describe certain kinds of literature. That is literature which is very concerned with referring to its own fictionality, and fictional strategies, as a main part of the fiction. There is an element of that in Derrida's philosophical style, but then that goes back a long way in philosophy. When applied to philosophy, 'postmodernism' is often taken to refer to relativism and scepticism of some kind. Those positions go back to the beginning of the history of philosophy, and do not really single out Derrida or any other recent philosophers.

The literary definitions, alluded to above, bring us to the role of literature in Derrida. Some of what he was interested in is 'postmodern', but for Derrida it all belonged to the category of Symbolist and Modern going back to the nineteenth century. The poetry and poetics of Stéphane Mallarmé are fundamental for Derrida, along with various mostly French writers since. Lautréamont, Paul Valéry, Marcel Proust, James Joyce, Jorge Luis Borges, Edmond Jabès and Philippe Sollers feature significantly in the early texts, though Sollers is clearly the least important of these as a writer. What interests Derrida in these writers is that their concern with the limits of language, experience and rationality connects with what is going on in philosophy since Hegel.

All these strands come together in a philosophy that works on rigorous arguments about concepts, but in a way in which the style of writing is always important. For Derrida, since philosophy exists in language, there is no escaping from language as the medium of philosophy. As the medium, it cannot just be like a pure transparency; it must condition philosophy; and that can only be shown by emphasizing the medium of philosophy. Like both Heidegger and Wittgenstein, Derrida thought that philosophy must show as well as say, because the most basic assumptions of philosophy and language cannot be adequately explained in explicit definitions. Context, and the stylistic resources of language, must be used to draw attention to the most basic assumptions of philosophy and features of language. What Derrida does is no more a mystification, or an irresponsible play with language, than what Heidegger and Wittgenstein do. Within Derrida's style, there are positions and arguments on the basic issues of philosophy as the following chapters aim to demonstrate.

2

METAPHYSICS

PARADOX AND BEING

We are starting the detailed work of Derrida on metaphysics, which is a negative moment for Derrida, and ending with a chapter on Deconstruction which will confirm the affirmative aspects of Derrida's philosophy. The attack on metaphysics is something very familiar in the history of philosophy. Arguments of that kind can probably be traced back at least to the criticisms Aristotle makes of Plato's theory of forms in the *Metaphysics*, so that it can be said that metaphysics begins with the criticism of metaphysics. It is sometimes maintained that Aristotle did not provide the title *Metaphysics*, or that the title only means the volume *after physics*; even if either or both is the case, it certainly remains the case that this is the first text *why?* which anyone thought could be labelled a treatise on metaphysics, and could be taken as the starting point of extended discussion of what we call metaphysics. What is interesting from a Derridean point of view, here, is that we can take the criticism of metaphysics back to the first book with that name, and which inaugurated the idea that there is a branch of philosophy which is metaphysics, and that this branch is not so much the branch as the root of philosophy, since it is the first philosophy. Metaphysics was, and still is, often taken as a synonym for philosophy. And in its beginning, it is the criticism of metaphysics in the naming of metaphysics.

Despite the existence of misleading claims that Derrida tries to dismiss previous philosophy and that he is only concerned to attack it, under the heading of the general claim that 'Derrida is an intellectual terrorist', Derrida goes to enormous trouble to reconstruct the positions of particular philosophical classics. He quotes extensively from them, reads carefully often line-by-line, and refers in full to the relevant scholarship by French commentators. Despite equally misleading claims that Derrida's approach is cavalier and easily refuted, very little serious work has been done to establish refutations of his readings of the philosophical classics from Plato to Husserl; and there is at least as much work using and endorsing Derrida's analyses. The 'refutation' of Derrida is generally extremely cavalier and lacking in the rigorous intellectual virtues Derrida's denouncers claim to be defending.

Returning to Aristotle, his *Metaphysics* is focused on the critique of the metaphysics of his teacher Plato who was writing before metaphysics was recognized as a sub-discipline of philosophy, or as another name for philosophy. There were more radical attacks than that on metaphysics in the Ancient World, in sceptics like Sextus Empiricus or the school of the 'Cynics'. In Medieval philosophy, Nominalists attacked the idea of universal concepts as anything more than names to group things together. Philosophical tradition is full of attacks on Metaphysics. In that sense, Derrida is part of a sceptical tradition; he defines his goal as confronting the philosophical with the empirical in order to question the philosophical. However, Derrida is not a sceptic in the strict sense. The 'strict' sense of scepticism must include at least two positions: first, the complete denial of knowledge of reality itself, usually on the grounds that no knowledge claims have guaranteed certainty; second, in the sense that we deny a large part of what is taken as evidence of the nature of reality, and this sceptical move is often followed by the constructive move in which something better is offered as evidence of reality. The first sense goes back to the Sophists, and certainly earlier Ancient Greek philosophers, such as Heraclitus and Parmenides, offered arguments that could be taken as denying the possibility of knowing reality itself. The second sense may go back to Heraclitus and Parmenides and certainly appears in Plato, where the evidence of the senses is rejected in favour of pure ideas or forms, which are the origin of copies in the senses. Descartes provides a later example of the constructive version of the second kind of scepticism, which is often taken as the beginning of modern philosophy, though Kierkegaard suggested problems with such a claim, along with problems in the sceptical position, which are rather deconstructive in spirit in *Johannes Climacus or De omnibus dubitandum est* (in Kierkegaard 1992b). Derrida himself tackles Descartes in 'Cogito and the history of madness' (WD 2) in a manner very relevant to Kierkegaard.

The questions of scepticism are leading us into issues of epistemology (theory of knowledge), which will be tackled in Chapter 5. However, in scepticism metaphysical issues arise about whether we have any truths about reality, whether there is any reality outside the contents of our experience, and what reality in its most general sense is. Going back to Plato, we find that the earliest metaphysical discussions include discussion of a paradox. In his dialogue the *Sophist*,[1] Plato suggests that we cannot refer to what is not, to non-being, without the danger of paradox and therefore of self-contradiction. The paradox is that, when we refer to what is not, we must in some way be attributing something to it and therefore assuming that it is, that it exists. Even if all I say of the thing that does not exist is that 'the thing does not exist', I seem to have said that there is a thing and it has a property, and that property is that it does not exist. This could lead to self-contradiction because, if I make a statement that assumes the existence of something and says that it does not exist, then we have a contradiction. A contradiction has tended to be something that philosophers regard as the greatest possible danger, because if the statements of our philosophy can lead to a contradiction then either that statement, and all statements that can lead to that statement, are eliminated; or we are left with a statement that is both true and false, undermining any claim to have a way of philosophizing that distinguishes between truth and falsity. It is also true that, for various reasons, philosophers have often suggested that contradiction is inevitable. The inevitability can take two forms: we inevitably produce

contradictions but we can and should eliminate them in a completely consistent discourse; or we inevitably produce contradictions and cannot eliminate them. Very early in the history of
philosophy, Heraclitus seems to have said something like the second version, though anything we say about Heraclitus can only be
a hazardous interpretation of the fragments of his writings that
have survived. Plato and a very long list of philosophers support
forms of the first version. Generally it is philosophical sceptics
who supported the second version, and arguments about contradiction, particularly contradiction in the notion of Being, are related
with arguments about scepticism in knowledge.

Since the time of Kant, though, contradictions have appeared to
many philosophers, who are not sceptics in a strong sense, as not
easily eliminated. Either contradictions are eliminated by restrict-
ing the kind of language we use, introducing artificiality; or, they
cannot be eliminated and we have to live with logical impurity. For
Kant pure reason, out of touch with experience, is always disposed
to get into contradictions, which he called dialectic. Clearing up
these dialectical problems was a major question for Kant. Even
before Kant, in the seventeenth century, Blaise Pascal had suggested that any attempt at philosophical first principles is self-contradictory since we cannot explain where these principles come
from, or how they can be justified, except by reference to a kind of
pure invention that Pascal called 'reasons of the heart'.[2] This and
other similar thoughts in Pascal seem to anticipate Derrida, though
Derrida only directly acknowledges Pascal with reference to law
and justice (Derrida 1990). The problems of contradiction, and
their unavoidability, even their constitutive status in any kind of
metaphysics, was taken up by the German Idealists who came after
Kant: J.G. Fichte, F.W.J. Schelling and G.W.F. Hegel, and then by
those reacting to, transforming and criticizing German Idealism:
Sørren Kierkegaard, Friedrich Nietzsche and Martin Heidegger.
However, the interest in contradiction is not unique to this kind of
Continental European philosophy. Bertrand Russell, one of the
principal figures in the Analytic approach to philosophy, was
deeply concerned with this issue, on at least two fronts. On one
front he was concerned with sentences about things that do not
exist, and how we eliminate the possibility of interpreting these

sentences as assuming the existence of what does not exist (Russell 1992a); on the other front he was concerned with classes of things, and the status of the class of things which do not exist (Russell 1992b: 73–9). The second problem in itself is clearly a version of the first one, but it also leads into an important paradox when we are talking about classes. The paradox is the status of the class of classes that are not members of themselves. If this class is a member of itself then it cannot be a member of itself, because if it is a class that is a member of itself it cannot be a member of the class of classes that are not members of themselves. If this class is not a member of itself, then it must be a member of itself, since it is the class of classes that are not members of themselves. We cannot say it is either true or false that the class of classes which are not members of themselves is a member of itself, without getting into a contradiction. This is an unacceptable situation for a logical purist like Russell. It is undeniable that talk about classes can lead to Russell's paradox, and the only solution for Russell, as with the problem of sentences that refer to what does not exist, where the solution is known as the 'Theory of Descriptions', is to revise natural language, or the apparatus of mathematics, which is also what is at stake, in a solution known as the Theory of Types. In this instance the revision is to stipulate that sentences cannot refer to themselves, and classes cannot be members of themselves. It must be noted that Russell does not so much solve the paradox, as stipulate that we should avoid getting into it. Russell's paradox is not just a paradox for classes. As he points out (Russell 1992b: 73), it is a version of Plato's paradox of non-being. It is also a version of a paradox in language, originally known as the Cretan Liar, and formulated more recently as the 'Liar Paradox'. This paradox can be expressed in many ways, but the essential form is 'This statement is false'. Is the statement true or false? If it is true to say that the statement is false, then the statement is false and it is true to say that it is false. If it is false to say that the statement is false, the statement is true, and it is false to say that it is false. There is no way to say that the statement is true or that it is false, another problem for any attempt at logically pure philosophy. The normal solution is a version of Russell's solution to Russell's paradox; we stipulate that no sentences should be formulated that refer to themselves, and particularly not to their relations with truth or falsity. Though the Liar Paradox has been an issue for Analytic rather than Continental European Philosophy, 'The paradox of the Cretan' (in Benjamin 1996) is a very incisive short contribution by the aesthetic and cultural theorist Walter Benjamin, who is closely linked with Continental European philosophy, and who is discussed by Derrida at various points.

This diversion into a brief sketch of some fundamental work in Analytic philosophy is necessary to situate Derrida within twentieth-century philosophy. Like Russell, Derrida referred to Plato's paradox (OG I, 2). The reference is oblique but significant:

> Henceforth it is not to the thesis of the arbitrariness of the sign that I shall appeal directly, but to what Saussure associates with it as an indispensable correlative and which would seem to me rather to lay the foundations for it: the thesis of *difference* as the source of linguistic value. What are from the grammatological point of view, the consequences of this theme that is now so well-known (and upon which Plato already reflected in the *Sophist*)?
>
> (OG 52–3)

[handwritten margin note: Conclusion: because language (signs) exist, differences/contradictions are created — pragmatism???]

Derrida gives a full quotation, and contextual discussion of other Plato dialogues, in 'Plato's pharmacy' (D 163–5). However, it is the passage quoted from OG that puts it in a broader context, useful for present purposes. For Plato in the *Sophist*, avoiding the paradox of being means a full account of the dialectic that leads from differences in kinds of being to the forms of things. This is supposed to avoid the Sophistical tendency to say that what we mention always exists. It is the Sophists who raise the issue of the paradox by claming that everything that can be said must refer to what exists, including non-being. Only a full account of the kinds of being and their differences can enable us to avoid getting into the Sophistical paradox of being. What we call Plato's paradox of being is for him the consequence of Sophistical pseudo-reasoning. What Derrida refers to is the method of Saussure that is in some measure a repetition of Plato, though Saussure's idea of full being is distinct from Plato, in appearance, though not in the structure of the argument. Plato's paradox or the Sophistical paradox has remained an issue for twentieth-century philosophy, as in W.V.O. Quine's influential paper 'On what there is' (Quine 1980), which refers to it on the first page as 'Plato's beard'.

METAPHYSICS OF STRUCTURALISM

How does Plato's beard relate to Derrida's discussion of Saussure, an influential figure in linguistics rather than philosophical ontology? A discussion and explanation of the oblique and compressed excerpt from Derrida above will help answer that question, and will also give an idea of how to read Derrida's famously elusive style. It would be more appropriate to say apparently elusive style. Derrida's more scrupulous critics have conceded that clear arguments exist in Derrida if we have the patience to untangle them, which is what reading philosophical texts is all about in any case. There is nothing more obviously difficult about reading Derrida for those who are new to his philosophy, than there is about reading many other philosophers for those who are new to the philosophy at issue.

On the passage above, first of all, we need to say something about Ferdinand de Saussure, discussed by Derrida at length in OG and in the related essay 'The linguistic circle of Geneva' (in MP). Derrida always explains his own philosophy through commentary on, and discussion of, other work. This means that there is little chance of explaining Derrida successfully without a particularly large amount of contextual explanation of his references. Careless readers, critics and followers alike, are in danger of confusing Derrida's own philosophy with the positions he is putting into question. Saussure had a revolutionary impact on linguistics through his book *Course in General Linguistics* (Saussure 1995), constructed after his death from notes taken at his lectures on that topic. Saussure has been superseded as a dominant figure in linguistics, particularly by Noam Chomsky, though that is not say that everyone now follows Chomsky.[3] Nevertheless what Saussure has to say is still of interest in linguistics, and had an enormous impact of continuing importance in various branches of the humanities and social sciences. Saussure's key ideas are: that we should distinguish between language as a system (*langue*) and language as an individual using language at a particular moment (*parole*); that we should distinguish between language as a static abstract system (synchrony) and language as a system changing over time; that within the linguistic sign (sounds of speech or marks of writing) we should distinguish between the material signifier (the spoken phoneme or written grapheme) and the concept signified; that we should distinguish between the linguistic sign and its referent. We should see the sign as arbitrary, that is its relation with the concept signified, or the thing that is its referent, is accidental. Because the sign is arbitrary its linguistic value is dependent not on the concept or referent, but on a system of differences with the other signs. That is words can only be defined through their relation with other signs, which means the differences between signs that determine when and how individual signs are used. Not only did Saussure have a bold theory for linguistics, he thought that linguistics could provide a model for a general theory of signs, which he called semiology. Linguistics is not just concerned with word signs, but with the sign as a general institution. Derrida looks at Hegel in this light in 'The pit and the pyramid: introduction to Hegel's semiology' (in MP).

Saussurean linguistics had a very decisive effect on the French humanities and social sciences in the 1960s, that is when Derrida started publishing, and then beyond France through the appeal of Structuralism. Structuralism was the name given to Saussurean linguistics and the work it influenced. Structuralism has also been used in a broader sense, with regard to work that is not at issue here, or has been extended to work that was not strictly Structuralist in the Saussurean sense, but analogous, and influential in Derrida's formation as a philosopher. That includes the early work of Michel Foucault, who was one of Derrida's lecturers at the *École normale supérieure*, particularly his early books *The Order of Things* (Foucault 2001b) and *The Archaeology of Knowledge* (Foucault 2002); and the work of Louis Althusser, also a lecturer at ENS, who achieved great influence in Marxist philosophy through *For Marx* (Althusser 1990) and *Reading Capital* (Althusser 1997). Those who were Structuralist more strictly speaking, for at least some part of their career, include the psychoanalyst Jacques Lacan, the literary critic and semiologist Roland Barthes, Julia Kristeva who has similar interests to Barthes, and the anthropologist Claude Lévi-Strauss. Saussure, Lévi-Strauss and Lacan all have an important place in Derrida, though in the texts we are concerned with it is Saussure and Lévi-Strauss who are most significant.

In his account of Saussure, Derrida finds the claims to a metaphysically neutral science of linguistics to be highly open to doubt. In particular, he considers that Saussure follows Rousseau and that Rousseau is full of Platonic and Cartesian metaphysical assumptions. The doubt Derrida casts on the metaphysical neutrality of Structuralism, and also philosophical Phenomenology as we shall see, resembles earlier criticisms of philosophical Positivism. Positivism is a term coined by Auguste Comte in the nineteenth century for a science that has gone beyond the earlier stages of human history, religion and metaphysics. Comte claimed that there could be a science, and a whole organization of society based on Positive knowledge, derived from pure facts. Such claims of nineteenth-century Positivism are one of the main targets of Nietzsche. Nietzsche emphasized that the claim to have a science, and whole way of thinking, based on pure facts is self-refuting. Science and empirical method undermine what is not empirical and that must include any metaphysical posit about the universe, including causality, law-governed events, continuously existing physical objects, general laws beyond the contents of observation and the presupposition of the unity of laws. Such rigorous empirical refutation must follow from Positivism, according to Nietzsche, ✍ but the list of what it undermines in the last sentence comprise the basic assumptions of scientific method and Positivist thought. Comte's positivism is a precursor of Saussure's linguistics, and of Lévi-Strauss's anthropology, partly via the great French classical sociologist Émile Durkheim. Positivism appeared in a new form in the early twentieth century in the Vienna Circle of Logical Positivists. This is not something that enters into Derrida's work at all. However, it is worth thinking about the parallels between Derrida's criticisms of Structuralism and the philosophical critique of Logical Positivism. Where that critique begins is highly ambiguous since Wittgenstein's *Tractatus Logico-Philosophicus* (Wittgenstein 1961) is often taken as a manifesto of that tendency

where in nietzsche is this ??

but could equally well be regarded as exposing tendencies in Logical Positivism towards solipsism, a metaphysics of logical form, and a collapse of all laws and theory into nonsense. As has been noticed more and more recently, these aspects of the *Tractatus* reflect Wittgenstein's interests in the philosophies of Schopenhauer, and Kierkegaard, and in religious mysticism. These aspects all connect with aspects of deconstructive philosophy. Wittgenstein's later philosophy provides clear denunciations of Logical Positivist positions, partly through a critical stance towards the *Tractatus*. Works from this time, such as the most famous *Philosophical Investigations* (Wittgenstein 2001), also connect with deconstructive strategies, as we shall see. It is certainly not just Wittgenstein who criticized the Logical Positivists. The Vienna Circle texts themselves are full of stresses with regard to their claims to have eliminated metaphysics while taking positions on the status of our statements of observation, the contents of our sensation, the nature of physical objects and scientific laws, which have unavoidable metaphysical consequences. The Vienna Circle members themselves gave up on pure Logical Positivist positions after a few years, and the history of their evolution from that initial position is a large part of the history of Analytic philosophy. Again some of that connects with deconstruction.

After providing some context for Derrida's philosophical criticisms of Structuralism, we can consider his criticisms of Saussure. When we say that Derrida had a philosophical critique of Structuralism, the words are being chosen very deliberately. Derrida very clearly states that he was defending philosophy as a field against any kind of claim in linguistics to have superseded philosophy as merely metaphysical, as is indicated by the title of his essay 'The supplement of copula: philosophy before linguistics' (in MP). The reference to Derrida's Deconstruction as critique is to emphasize the continuity with Kant's claims to have undermined the illusions of pure reason. From the point of view of this critique, Saussure's major theoretical claims above are full of metaphysics, which does not detract of course from his enormous work in putting linguistics on organized theoretical grounds. It is the way in which Saussure claims to be putting linguistics on scientific grounds that is essentially metaphysical.

What Saussure saw without seeing, knew without being *able* to take into account, following in that the entire metaphysical tradition, is that a certain model of writing was necessarily but provisionally imposed (but for the inaccuracy in principle, insufficiency of fact, and the permanent usurpation) as instrument and technique of representation of a system of language. And that this movement, unique in style, was so profound that it permitted the thinking, *within language*, of concepts like those of the sign, technique, representation, language. The system of language associated with phonetic-alphabetic writing is that within which logocentric metaphysics, determining the sense of being as presence, has been produced.

(OG 43)

Saussure is said to rely on an absolute opposition between the natural and the social in which language marks the emergence of the social, in a break with nature. Such complete breaks, and oppositions, are what Derrida regards as metaphysics. Despite the claim to a pure scientific method, Saussure, according to Derrida, is clearly repeating the assumptions that Jean-Jacques Rousseau made in his *Essay on the Origin of Language* (Rousseau 1980). There, Rousseau refers to language as what marks the separation of the human social world from the natural physical world. This in itself repeats Descartes's metaphysical separation between spirit as substance and matter as substance. Like all metaphysical oppositions it is an attempt to overcome contradictions that cannot be eliminated. As with all metaphysical oppositions, one term is placed above the other, though particular instability in this hierarchy is notable in Rousseau. The social is placed above the natural in language, for Rousseau, since this is what language is. This in itself leads into a Platonist position in which the pure ideas contained in language are opposed to the empirical forces of linguistic acts: the force of the voice in the air in speech, and the force of material inscription in writing.

One could push the inventory of analogies a long way, far beyond the programmatic and principal generalities. Since their interweaving is systematic, one may say a priori that no locus of the two discourses absolutely escapes it. For example, it suffices to accredit absolutely, here and there, the oppositions nature/convention, nature/arbitrary, animal/human, or the concepts of sign (signifier/signified), or of representation (representer/represented) for the totality of the discourse to be affected systematically. The effects of such an opposition – which we know goes back further than Plato – can occasion an infinite analysis from which no element of the text escapes.

(MP 151)

A contradiction must appear with regard to Rousseau's claim that language as what is purely social emerges from the purely natural. There must have been a moment where the natural forces became social language, but that point must be both social and natural. Since Rousseau is relying on there being an absolute opposition between the natural and social, the moment where both exist in the same place at the same time is an impossibility, a contradiction. From Rousseau's point of view, and from any metaphysical point of view, this is a trauma, an impossibility that must be so completely denied that is not even an issue in our conscious reflections on the topic.

Who will ever say if the lack within nature is *within* nature, if the catastrophe by which Nature *is separated from itself* is still natural? A natural catastrophe conforms to laws in order to overthrow the law. There is something catastrophic in the movement that brings about the emergence from the state of nature and in the awakening of the imagination which actualises the natural faculties and essentially actualises perfectibility.

(OG 258)

Not only does the issue appear at the moment where the natural must have become social, it is repeated everywhere in language as Rousseau resorts to the effect of natural forces to explain variations in languages, though language has been defined by Rousseau as the purely and absolutely non-natural.

Saussure's definitions rest on a metaphysical opposition between the natural and the social. They also rest on the superiority of system, or *langue*, over individual instances of language use, or *parole*. This is a clear recurrence of Platonist metaphysics. It places the one over the many, the essential unity of being over differences between beings. That extends into the static and a-temporal nature of language in Saussure that confirms the Platonist metaphysics, by placing what is unchangeable over time, or synchronic above changeability over time. Stasis and constancy of substance are raised above the diachronic aspects of movement and change over time. Time itself is denied as less real than the immutability of structure. These are all characteristics of Plato's forms. Saussure has another Platonist assumption, deep within his science, the assumption that the pure concept within the sign, what is signified, is essential in relation to the material signifier, the phonic or graphic force with which the concept is unified in the sign. The superiority of the concept is the superiority of the Platonic form over the diversity of appearances in the senses.

Since Derrida is often accused of linguistic idealism, it is very important to point out that the superiority of the concept is in Saussure, not in Derrida, and that Derrida criticizes Saussure, strongly on this very point. That is why Derrida is not a strange kind of idealist who believes that reality does not exist outside the concepts of language. Subjectivist and anti-realist philosophy would not in itself put Derrida beyond the limits of Analytic philosophy. George Berkeley, generally recognized as a precursor of Analytic empiricism, thought that the only reality was immaterial and consisted of the contents of ideas in someone's mind. Recent Analytic philosophers, such as Michael Dummett, have been happy to endorse versions of anti-realism, along with precursors of Analytic philosophy like Ernst Mach and all advocates of Phenomenalism, the claim that reality is no more than the phenomena which exist as the content of someone's mind.

The passages where Derrida finds the most positive aspects of Saussure are to do with difference and the materiality of the signifier. For Saussure, the system of language is not a form imposed on an already existing set of linguistic values, or meanings; it is the consequence of the differences between the signifiers. We can only give a sign a meaning, a linguistic value, through its differences from other signs. A word does not have a meaning through an isolated definition as a pure grasp of meaning: a definition must use other words. We can only define a word by using other words; and we can only separate words, or signs, from other words or signs, by reference to differences between words, not the essence within the word. 'Tree' means tree because it does not mean any kind of inanimate object, it does not mean any kind of animal object, it does not mean any kind of bush or vegetable, and so on. This is in line with Plato and Aristotle, but, for Derrida, their kind of argument already contains a disruption of metaphysical system that is very apparent in Saussure. In Saussure, meaning can only be determined by the differences between the material signifiers, so that we have what Derrida calls an economy, in which it is the exchange and equivalence between different linguistic values that determine meanings, not a structure that is intrinsically metaphysical. Saussure emphasizes the ideal crystalline structure of synchronic *langue*, but presents us with something else. That is an economy of exchange between linguistic values, in which no two values can be completely and perfectly exchanged with each other, including the same value at different times.[4] The economy is a material economy of forces for Derrida, not an ideal structure of words in their structural place organizing the world for us, which the critics who accuse Derrida of linguistic idealism are assuming. Derrida is not offering another version of metaphysical subjectivism, anti-realism or idealism here, any more than he is offering another version of epistemological scepticism or relativism at any point. He always denies the absolutes, but that is not the same thing as offering absolute subjectivism. Like the other anti-metaphysicians, Derrida is open to the charge of having a metaphysics, but it is a mixture of process metaphysics, materialism and empiricism. Process metaphysics puts becoming over being, change over constancy, the event over time above non-temporal structures and combines with a metaphysics of difference above identity.

The transmission of metaphysics through Rousseau is also an issue in the discussion of the anthropology of Lévi-Strauss in OG and 'Signature, sign and play in the discourse of the human sciences' (WD 10). Some of that will have to wait until Chapter 5 where we will deal with knowledge, including social science. The metaphysics emerges in the assumption that there can be such a thing as natural man. Particular metaphysical assumptions that go with this, and which are inherited from Rousseau, are that natural man is completely interior in consciousness, and therefore lacking in exteriority. The complete presence of interiority and the complete absence of exteriority appear in Lévi-Strauss as a complete lack of writing and history (OG II 1). The 'primitives' are the repetition of natural man in Rousseau who live completely in the present and are innocent of any attempt to present themselves to other humans, or of any conscious rules. Rousseau imagined 'primitive man' as solitary, so Lévi-Strauss at least has to deviate from that presumption. His fieldwork on stone-age peoples must deal with the reality of society at the earliest known stages of human development. The supposed interiority of primitive humans is not just a hypothesis of social thought in either Rousseau or Lévi-Strauss. The interiority and the immediacy of the present, with no intrusions, is a deeply metaphysical assumption.

The history of metaphysics, according to Derrida, is the history of what is absolutely present. These thoughts are partly derived from Heidegger, so it is important to distinguish what comes from Heidegger from what is Derridean. A standard criticism of Derrida is that he imitates Heidegger and does not add anything apart from Derridean style. This is simply wrong and it is clearly wrong. K? It is a misunderstanding that must be cleared out of the way before a proper assessment can be made of Derrida, negative or positive. Throughout a rich philosophical development, Heidegger was concerned with Being or Presence. These are both distinguished from beings or what is present. What is present in Heidegger is never Presence or Being itself. What is present is being where Being has withdrawn. A being (or entity) can only be such, as what has Being, but it can only be a being because it is not Being. Being is what is in a constant withdrawal from what it is. There is never a fully present in Heidegger (Heidegger 1972). For Heidegger, and Derrida would largely agree, the history of metaphysics is the history of some thing that is a substitute for Being, or Presence, and can be grasped only as present. Heidegger mainly concerns himself with the more rationalist aspects of this. That is his examples come from: Medieval Scholastic Philosophy: essence; Early Modern Rationalism: idea; German Idealism: spirit; and then his examples come from German Philosophy after Idealism: production in Marx and will to power in Nietzsche (Heidegger 1972). However, his argument applies to Empiricist positions in which logic and sensation are understood as being, as Presence that is present. In the classical British Empiricism of Locke, Berkeley and Hume, the sensation or impression is understood on the model of Descartes's Idea, which is purely rational. From Heidegger's point of view the Empiricists are below notice. Derrida is clearly in opposition to Heidegger on this issue. Derrida regards Deconstruction as the challenging of the transcendental by the empirical. He even refers to his position as 'radical empiricism', which may or may not be a deliberate reference to the American Pragmatist William James, but it is more likely that it is accidental. Pragmatists exclude all concepts that are not justified by use in action or experience. Derrida's self-description as 'radical empiricist' is potentially misleading, since Derrida's position is opposed to Empiricism in its most absolute forms where it rests on the assumption that what is given immediately in experience is the real or the true. The 'radical' in 'radical empiricism' may be a reference to that challenge to absolute empiricism. That would in fact be appropriate to the James reference, accidental or intentional. James, like the founder of Pragmatism Charles Peirce, was deeply affected by Hegel, and, though the radical empiricism looks opposed to any account of Hegel, there is emphasis derived from Hegel on context. For Hegel, any particular experience can only be grasped by giving it a name, that is necessarily universal; and then bringing it into the movements of consciousness, or science, taken as a whole. That line of argument appears in both Peirce and James, though with more reference to variable context and less to absolute system. Derrida shows little interest in, or knowledge of, Pragmatism or any other aspect of the history of Analytic philosophy. Nevertheless OG (OG I, 2) endorses Peirce's semiotic theory of the symbol as superior to Saussure (OG 48–50). Roughly speaking, it is possible to locate Derrida as a Hegelian empiricist in the manner of the Pragmatists, in which case he should certainly be compared with a number of prominent Analytic philosophers who have revised absolute empiricist philosophy in the light of Hegel. There is a notable centre of this tradition at the University of Pittsburgh, beginning with Wilfred Sellars, carried on currently by John McDowell, and Robert Brandom. This is not just a Pittsburgh phenomenon.

W.V.O. Quine, one of the great figures of Analytic philosophy, consciously followed the legacy of William James, and argued for a more holistic understanding of empiricism. Unfortunately, Quine completely blanked out the Hegelian heritage in James, and generally ignored the Continental European philosophers except to join ill-informed, and even malicious, attacks on any recognition of Derrida as a philosopher. Such is the cost of ignoring history. The Pragmatist heritage, amongst many other reasons, also suggests comparisons of Derrida's Deconstruction with the later work of Ludwig Wittgenstein who was deeply impressed by James.

Returning to Heidegger, what distinguishes Derrida from Heidegger is both that Heidegger dismissed Empiricism as just instrumentalist and non-philosophical; and that Heidegger refers to Being and Presence. These are never present, but they still appropriate, and give, beings. There is a sovereignty of Being and Presence in Heidegger, which Derrida does not endorse at all. Like Heidegger, Derrida thinks of Being or Presence as the unnameable and the ungraspable. However, the conclusions that Derrida draws are not those of Heidegger. There is no appropriation in Derrida. There is a constant withdrawal of Being, but this is as a desire not as a reality of any kind. Derrida suggests that Heidegger may be one side of Deconstruction, but only one side, in opposition to the affirmation of difference in Nietzsche. Heidegger, at most, represents one half of deconstruction. Even so, as with Nietzsche, the placing of Heidegger within Deconstruction is a change. Nietzsche is deprived of any tendencies to a metaphysics of will, and Heidegger is deprived of any tendency to a metaphysics of Being (OG 19–24; 'The ends of man' in MP).[5]

There is no Presence, or Being, in Derrida other than as the impossible and the contradictory. There is sometimes great closeness to the nostalgia for Being Derrida finds in Heidegger, but for Derrida there just is no Presence or Being, though we have an intrinsic tendency to search for such a thing, just as Kant thought that reason leads us to hope for contradictory notions of a metaphysical God. There is no more Being or Presence for Derrida than there is nature. Nature only exists as the opposite of the social, never as it is in itself, and the same applies to Being or Presence. They can only be the opposite of difference and absence.

Being and Nature are absent in nature and the notion of absence is important here. Metaphysics itself includes a tendency to assume what is present as completely present and exclude absence as illusion, difference and non-Being. However, for Derrida, Being itself can only be absent, and we are never confronted with Being itself. Absence is necessary for there to be difference. Returning to Saussure, we can only have an economy of linguistic values because no words have a completely present meaning. Meaning is always dependent on there being other different words, and there being difference from those words. Meaning is always contextual in various ways, and that includes the way in which language as a system can only exist as a system of differences. The meaning of a word depends on what it does not mean, because other words in the system have already excluded that meaning by possessing it.

HUSSERL AND THE METAPHYSICS OF PHENOMENOLOGY

As Derrida explains in '"Genesis and structure" and Phenomenology' (in WD) aspects of Structuralism in general are also embedded in a metaphysics that Derrida studied in Husserl, with great depth in the earlier part of his career.

> The first phase of phenomenology, in its style and its objects, is structuralist, because first and foremost it seeks to stay clear of psychologism and historicism. But it is not genetic interest *in general* which is disqualified, but only the genetic description which borrows its schemas from naturalism and causalism, and depends upon a science of 'facts' and therefore on an empiricism; and therefore concludes Husserl, depends upon a relativism incapable of insuring its own truth; therefore, on a scepticism.
>
> (WD 159)

His first book (IOG) was a long introduction to his translation of 'The origin of geometry' by Husserl, a short essay greatly exceeded in length by Derrida's introduction. The three books of

1967 in which Derrida emerged as a major figure include SP, which is a study of Husserl. WD, also from 1967, includes '"Genesis and structure" and Phenomenology' on Husserl (WD 4), which could serve as summary of IOG; and MP includes the essay on Husserl, 'Form and meaning: a note on the Phenomenology of language'. The last two essays are also included in the English edition of SP. Derrida liked the phrase 'genesis and structure' so much he also used it in OG for the title of a chapter on Rousseau, 'Genesis and structure of the *Essay on the Origin of Languages*' (OG II 3). Though that chapter rests on Derrida's arguments about genesis and structure in Phenomenology and its complicity with Structuralism, it is more concerned with Rousseau's views on ethics and sympathy.

Husserl's positions also have parallels with the Logical Positivists, in that he tries to exclude metaphysical questions, a process Husserl refers to as 'bracketing' or the phenomenological 'epoché'. As with the Logical Positivists there is a commitment to descriptions of experience, which precede any theoretical point of view. Like the Logical Positivists, Husserl looks for a formal approach in which there are pure forms, including logical judgements on one side, and empirical facts on the other side. There are equally significant differences from the Logical Positivists but it is these two independent approaches in early twentieth-century philosophy that do share some important presuppositions.

The Husserl of *Logical Investigations* (Husserl 2001) had a lot to say of interest to Analytic philosophers, including philosophers concerned with relatively technical questions such as mereology (the theory of parts and wholes) that takes much from sections of *Logical Investigations* on parts and wholes. *Logical Investigations* has been receiving increasing recognition as a classic of Analytic philosophy; significantly the latest English edition has a preface by the distinguished Analytic philosopher Michael Dummett. Husserl's text follows a dialogue with Gottlob Frege, a mathematician, logician and philosopher who is a foundational figure for Analytic philosophy. What Husserl might, or might not, have taken from Frege is a matter of discussion, but at this stage there are at least two issues on which there are striking parallels between Husserl and Frege: a rejection of psychologism (the explanation of any philosophical issue with reference to supposed truths of psychology, or the reduction of the contents of thought to the contents of subjective states of mind); and a related concern with language as signifying objects and as what has a general sense, which both operate in relation to, but independently of, subjective psychological associations. *Logical Investigations* is also an important classic for Continental European philosophy, a major moment in a Phenomenological tradition, which in varying ways was taken up, with reference to Husserl, by Heidegger, Jean-Paul Sartre, Maurice Merleau-Ponty and Emmanuel Lévinas as well as Derrida himself. Husserl strongly rejected what Heidegger did with his work as too subjective and historical instead of transcendental and formal. Nevertheless, Husserl himself tended to give more importance to the historical, the subjective and the intersubjective in the last phase of his work. It is that phase that Derrida picks up on in IOG. SP refers to Husserl in all his stages and tends to bring them together, so that tensions in Husserl's work are seen as operating throughout his career rather than as conflicts between different stages. Similarly Derrida's comments on Husserl are taken here as a whole, rather than with regard to possible changes in view on Husserl, none of which were significant enough for Derrida to mention himself.

The one really full and book-length attempt to rubbish Derrida as a bad philosopher, and bad reader of philosophy, comes from a rather traditional Husserl scholar, John Claude Evans (Evans 1991). It is important to realize that, despite the image that Derrida critics have tried to create of a charlatan whose claims and readings have all been decisively refuted, this is the one book-length scholarly attack on Derrida and that there is a greater body of work defending Derrida as a reader of Husserl, or referring to it as a respectable body of work, both in English- and French-speaking countries. Nevertheless, another misleading calumny of Derrida bashers is that only gullible Anglophones take Derrida seriously and that he is rubbished or ignored in France and the Francophone world. Evans's disagreement with Derrida is essentially that which could be found in any criticisms made by any philosopher, specialized in commentary on one philosopher, of a philosopher with a more general approach. Obvious examples, referring to work by well-known

Analytic philosophers, would include: the criticisms made by Leibniz specialists of Bertrand Russell's work on Leibniz, criticisms made by Kant specialists of P.F. Strawson's work on Kant, criticisms made by Wittgenstein specialists of Saul Kripke's work on Wittgenstein. Russell, Strawson and Kripke are three of the great Analytic philosophers, but their works of commentary on historical philosophers are not regarded as accurate by most of the specialized commentators in the area. Each example is a different story and this is not the place to go into the details. What can be said in general is that these studies continue to be read because although their commentary on individual points is always questionable, but original and creative ideas are brought to bear on classic texts, in a way that illuminates those texts; and provokes philosophical thought both in relation to those texts and in philosophy in general. The comparison of Derrida's reading of Husserl, and other philosophical classics, with the work of Russell, Strawson and Kripke, would in the first place show that Derrida is far more careful by a long way. With regard to Husserl, and in most other cases, Derrida is particularly careful to give long quotations, with the most important sentences given in the original language. In most cases, Derrida also pays a lot of attention to relevant commentaries, though in Husserl's case he concentrates on a direct response to the texts, without totally excluding commentaries. Russell, Strawson and Kripke mostly ignore other commentaries, but they also show much less concern with the detailed arguments at stake than Derrida does. Derrida's scholarship of Husserl was very thorough and very deep. He was studying philosophy at a time when knowledge of Husserl was considered central in Parisian philosophy, and he wrote a long master's thesis on Husserl. It is simply not plausible to claim that his scholarship of Husserl is lacking.

Evans tries to generally condemn Derrida for bad readings of Husserl, and most importantly claims that Derrida is falsely attributing ontological claims to Husserl's Phenomenology (Evans 1991: 19–20). Concentrating on the point about ontology, what Evans does is first to make the uncontroversial claim that Husserl said many things which suggest that he was trying to exclude ontological claims from Phenomenology; and what he then does is to claim that, if Derrida finds any ontological implications in what

Husserl says, then Derrida must have read Husserl badly, or even with the deliberate intention of imposing an unjustified reading of the text. It is hard to reach a definitive conclusion about these claims. Such claims are made by most commentators about other commentaries on 'their' philosopher; and particularly where the other commentator is not a complete specialist, and does not claim to be a complete follower of the philosopher concerned. If we are to take all such criticisms as valid, we will have to give up on critical creative commentary and restrict ourselves to reverent mediation on, and repetition of, the truths revealed by that great philosopher, and ignore the difficulties in deciding between the many interpretations always possible of a great philosophical work. Any commentary can always be found to have distorted the text it is commenting on, because it is not the complete repetition of the text. The most important specific problem with Evans's attack on Derrida is that he relies on the idea that there are no ontological claims in Husserl. That is what Husserl is claiming explicitly, but a text cannot be judged in every aspect by the more general claims made by its author. It certainly does not take any great interpretative trickery to notice that there are ontological aspects of Husserl's Phenomenology. *Logical Investigations* (Husserl 2001) contains comments on objects, parts and wholes, and abstractions that are unavoidably ontological. The clearest indication comes in I*deas Pertaining to a Pure Phenomenology and a Phenomenological Philosophy* (Husserl 1983 and 1990). Here Husserl openly claims to be a Platonist. That means Platonism in the sense of the status of abstract objects (universal types, universal qualities, ideas of objects). Platonism in ontology is generally recognized to mean a belief in the reality of abstract objects existing outside the mind and separately from physical objects. Husserl invokes Platonism to explain the status of the transcendental structure of consciousness (the general forms of our judgements), which he discusses continuously throughout his philosophical career. As he is anti-psychologistic, he wants to explain those structures as other than mental entities. The solution is to describe himself as a Platonist while holding to the Phenomenological claim that he is describing the contents of consciousness without reference to the ontological status of anything. The ambiguities here are clear enough and are reflected in the varying statements Husserl made about the status of Phenomenology throughout his career, as well as the varying statements made by Phenomenologists since Husserl. All that Derrida does is draw attention to the ambiguity, which is that Husserl claims he is concerned with the pure contents of consciousness independently of ontological considerations but that he takes pure forms in the pure ideas of the ideas of consciousness as the first principle of his philosophy. That looks remarkably like an ontological system. Derrida points out that this repeats an ambiguity of Kant. In Kant, there are pure ideas as categories of the understanding and the regulative ideals of reason. Kant puts these forward as formal claims rather than claims about reality in a move that sets the scene for both Logical Positivism and Phenomenology. The separation between formal ideas and objects, which provide the content for forms, is not easy to make in this case. If the categories necessary for there to be objects of experience, and the regulative ideals of reason, necessary for there to be understanding and experience, are not objects with reality claims then what are they? It is very difficult to avoid psychologism, turning these universal forms into subjective ideas or Platonism, which turns them into abstract objects, of greater substance and necessity than empirical objects. Derrida's analysis of Husserl as holding a Kantian transcendental view of pure ideas, and of holding a Platonist view of pure ideas underlying Kantian transcendentalism, which is in a constant tension with the empirical and historical or genetic concerns of Husserl, is consistent throughout the texts with which we are concerned, as can be seen by comparing the following: IOG II 45, 48 fn 41, VII 94, VIII 107, X 127, 142 fn 170, 144; SP 4 53, 7 101–2; WD 5 160, 166; MP 157–8, 172. Derrida was certainly not claiming that Husserl was just a Platonist-Kantian Idealist who thinks of ultimate reality as pure ideas; he did consistently argue that such a position exists irreducibly in Husserl in a tension with Husserl's concern for the historical and empirical in a way that is interestingly non-consistent, and, we shall see in the last chapter, that the tension anticipates Deconstruction.

The ontological status of pure categories is something Derrida deals with in 'The supplement of the copula: philosophy before linguistics' (in MP), in the context of the attempt of Émile Benveniste to turn the categories of Aristotle into the effects of linguistic categories. Derrida rejects this as formalism, which ignores the dependence of the criticism of Aristotle on the Kantian philosophical critique of Aristotelian categories, and which is purely empirical and descriptive. The same criticisms can be made of the linguistic approach as the Phenomenological approach, and Derrida makes this comparison with reference to Saussure and Husserl. All attempts to replace metaphysical ontological problems with formal problems that exclude ontological commitments are self-contradictory according to Derrida. This is because if we replace the ontological category by a formal category, linguistic or Phenomenological, then we have just created another ontological category. Husserl's Phenomenology rests on Kantian foundations (IOG 141), with reference to the most Platonist aspects of Kant (IOG 137), so that Phenomenology rests on Platonist metaphysics. Husserl himself claimed that there could be a Platonism without ontological commitments, an idea that Derrida finds contradictory. The pure form is an ontological entity, and is an example of metaphysics. It has the same status as a Platonist idea or form, that is the model for particular empirical contents of consciousness (IOG 144). For Plato, the empirical object is the secondary imitation of the form, or idea of the object, which unites many empirical objects. For Husserl, writing after Kant and in the light of Neo-Kantian formalism, the pure forms of consciousness are transcendental, that is beyond any particular object. Husserlian Phenomenology must always return to Platonism, even while claiming to be descriptive and non-metaphysical. The same must be true of any kind of anti-metaphysical formalism in philosophy, linguistics or any other discipline.

> One might think then that the *sense of Being* has been limited by the imposition of the *form* which, in its most overt value and since the origin of philosophy, seems to have assigned to Being, along with the authority of the *is*, the closure of presence, the form-of-presence, presence-in-form, form-presence. One might think, on the other hand, that formality – or formalization – is limited by the sense of Being which, in fact, throughout its entire history, has never been sep-

arated from its determination as presence, beneath the excellent
surveillance of the *is*: and that henceforth the thinking of form has the
power to extend itself beyond the thinking of Being. But that the two
limits thus denounced are *the same* may be what Husserl's enterprise
illustrates: phenomenology could push to its extreme limit the *formalist demand* and could criticise all previous formalism only on the
basis of a thinking of Being as *self-presence*, on the basis of a transcendental *experience* of pure consciousness.

(MP 172)

Derrida finds Husserl's Phenomenology to be both orientated
towards a transcendental metaphysics and a life philosophy (IOG
XI). The transcendental metaphysics is in the elaboration of the
transcendental forms of consciousness, which provide the basic
forms of judgement and intentions. In Phenomenology acts of consciousness are understood to be all directed towards an object,
which is 'intended' by consciousness and therefore all acts of consciousness can be defined as 'intentions'. In Husserl's
Phenomenology, on the model of Kant's theory of experience and
knowledge as judgement, there is also a strong tendency to understand those intentions as judgements about objects, though later
forms of Phenomenology tend to be less intellectualist. The life-
philosophy, metaphysics in the sense of a vitalistic life essence in
nature, emerges in the way that Husserl understands the transcendental structures to appear in the immediate experiences of every-
day life. All the contents of any instant of consciousness are
understood to be contents of the consciousness of a transcendental
ego, which must be the subject of the transcendental structures. If
there are transcendental ideas and transcendental structures for
intentionality, then whatever has those ideas and structures has
them as contents of consciousness, and the only consciousness that
can have such structures and ideas is a transcendental ego. That is a
self that exists as more than just a particular ego with particular
states of consciousness, but a pure form of the self that has pure
forms of consciousness. The transcendental purity itself becomes
part of a life-philosophy, in which every moment of consciousness
and all the contents of consciousness are filled with the transcendental consciousness that is in the life of the human self, and

defines the life of that self as the life of a human self. Derrida is making a general point here about metaphysics. If the Husserlian attempt to transcend metaphysics in Phenomenology is tied up with life-philosophy then this must be true of all metaphysical systems, including attempts since Kant to find a transcendental structure that precedes the particular contents of any metaphysical system. All metaphysics, as metaphysics, is caught up in the principles of consciousness as filling all of nature, giving both the individual human and nature a purpose. Metaphysics is always caught up in humanism, an issue to be discussed in Chapter 5.

> This situation of the Logos is profoundly analogous – and not by chance – to that of every ideality (such as our analysis of *language* has enabled us to specify this concept). Ideality is *at once* supratemporal and omnitemporal, and Husserl qualifies it sometimes in one fashion, sometimes in the other, according to whether or not he relates it to factual temporality. Only then can we say that pure sense, the ideality of ideality, which is *nothing other than* the appearing of being is at once supratemporal. Are not supratemporality and omnitemporality also the characteristics of *Time itself*? Are they not the characteristics of the Living Present, which is the absolute concrete form of phenomenological temporality and the primordial Absolute of all transcendental life?

> (IOG 148)

METAPHYSICS AND LANGUAGE

Right from IOG onwards, Derrida emphasises that the concepts of metaphysics require the concept of writing. Husserl distinguishes between the consciousness of a particular object and the consciousness of the general ideal object. The general ideal is separated from particular languages (IOG V) in some deeper sub-stratum of absolute objectivity. But it is still necessary to account for the essential fixity of the object independent of variations between languages, and within a language independent of different possible expressions. The ideality of the object itself relies on the object becoming part of language. The object of perception is changeable and contingent; it is the object as a meaning in language that has fixity and necessity. If language is necessary for there to be an ideal object, than ideality is caught up in the historical, cultural and intersubjective variations and ambiguities of language. Language as fixed and necessary means writing, since speech is tied to the moment of enunciation, the moment of consciousness. These aspects, according to Derrida, undermine the metaphysical-phenomenological starting point that is the contents of consciousness, understood as what is present now in someone's consciousness. These remarks do not only apply to Husserl. There is a whole philosophical tradition going back to Descartes, with which Husserl identifies as he shows when he gives one of his books the name *Cartesian Mediations*, in which philosophy tries to found itself on the self contemplating the contents of its own consciousness. That is not a feature of earlier philosophy, but for Derrida in the emphasis on the contents of consciousness Phenomenological philosophy itself rests on earlier traditions, which refer to the inside as pure and the outside as an impurity with regard to truth, ideas, the soul and so on.

> Is this to say that what opens the repetition to the infinite, or what is opened up when the movement of idealisation is assured, is a certain relation of an 'existent' to his death? And that the 'transcendental life' is the scene of this relationship? It is too soon to tell. First we must deal with the problem of language. No one will be surprised if we say that language is properly the medium for this play of presence and absence. Is there not within language – is it not language itself that might seem to unify *life* and *ideality*? But we ought to consider, on the one hand, that the element of signification – or the substance of expression – which best seems to preserve ideality and living presence in all its forms is living speech, the spirituality of the breath as *phōnē*; and, on the other hand, that phenomenology, the metaphysics of presence in the form of ideality, is also a philosophy of *life*.
>
> (SP 10)

The distinction between inside and outside (OG I, 2) is one way of setting up metaphysical oppositions, and a critique as deconstruction of metaphysical oppositions. Derrida defines metaphysics, and criticizes it, to a large degree on the basis that it is a reduction to oppositions. This kind of analysis can be seen in the opposition between the natural and the social in Rousseau and Saussure, as defined above. A list of the oppositions Derrida invokes clearly follows in the wake of Nietzsche. Nietzsche regarded the history of philosophy since Plato as largely a history of metaphysics derived from Plato's preference for a world of pure forms over the world of appearances. That is also a preference for life in another world to life in this world, so a condemnation of this life and this world. The denial of this life, this world and the appearances we perceive in it, is nihilism according to Nietzsche depriving this life of any value. Derrida does not really apply the Nietzschean condemnation of metaphysical nihilism; he refers more to an awareness of the inescapable contradiction between transcendental force and empirical force. The transcendental here refers to anything that is universal, abstract, conceptual or general in meaning, including the metaphysical. From that point of view, anything universal, abstract, conceptual or general is metaphysical, since it assumes something beyond the immediacy of material force. In that case, the metaphysical is in all use of language since every word, and every rule of grammar or linguistics, is an abstraction of some kind in relation to empirical reality. Derrida really assumes this, and rests his argument on what was already in Nietzsche. Nietzsche emphasizes that every word is an abstraction of the constant change and variety of sensation. Even in the simplest looking parts of language, such as the word 'leaf', there is an abstraction from the massive variety of leaves in nature. There is a different kind of leaf for every different kind of tree; and, even within one species, every particular leaf is different in some detail from every other leaf. Even if two leaves could be found that were identical in every single detail they would be in different places in time and space (though Leibniz famously claimed that where two objects are indiscernible in their inner qualities they must be an identical object; and no external relation such as place in time and space can distinguish between objects). Language and thought of any kind (presuming we can get behind symbolization in language, and other sign systems, to thought as something in itself) must be metaphysical; and the metaphysical cannot be eliminated by any particular philosophical argument, or even any list of philosophical arguments. This clearly distinguishes Nietzsche's way of being anti-metaphysical from Pragmatism or Logical Positivism; and Derrida follows Nietzsche in that respect. And although Derrida does not direct the same kind of absolute attack on metaphysics as nihilism, and something to be overcome in a rupture with thought, and even humanity as we have known it, he does give the priority to the empirical. The metaphysical, and the transcendental, always have a force that emerges from particular material forces in Derrida. That force acts on the empirical but only in a way that means that the transcendental, and the metaphysical, are contaminated with particular material force undermining any transcendental, or metaphysical, system.

It is not just in Nietzsche that we can see sources for Derrida's approach. Two other philosophers should be mentioned: one of whom is often associated with the background to Derrida's philosophy and one of whom is not often mentioned in connection with Derrida. The first is Hegel who is always mentioned in any history of philosophy from Kant to Derrida as someone Derrida finds important. Hegel is not important in the same way as Nietzsche and Heidegger, since Derrida does not take him as a precursor of Deconstruction, though he does take him as someone who has to be encountered. On the question of the relation between names and particular objects of experience, Hegel starts in a similar way to Nietzsche: the name is universal and therefore goes beyond any particular object named. He arrives at the opposite conclusion to Nietzsche though. For Hegel, if the name goes beyond the objects of experience, then the name is more real than particular experience. However, Hegel is not the opposite of Nietzsche in a way that would make him the repetition of Plato, even though both Plato and Hegel refer to 'dialectic' as the heart of philosophy. From a Hegelian point of view, Plato's dialectic is too simple and immediate. Hegel does not reduce the world to ideas, or forms; he sees the world as structured by the relation between particular existences in sensory reality and the complex rationality of reality as a whole, which rests on constant contradiction and becoming. The emphasis on becoming, and contradiction, brings Hegel close to Nietzsche, but for Hegel becoming and contradiction are always explained as

aspects of being as a whole, in its rational complexity, and purposive-
ness. For Nietzsche, reality is chaotic, and purposeless, so that there
is no intelligible rational reality as a whole. Hegel's exploration of
reason as constant negation of the particular by the negative, as
opposition of particular forces and contradiction within particular
propositions, because of the lack of reality of the particular compared
with reality as a whole, provides an inspiration to Derrida with
regard to constant negation, opposition and force, but not with
regard to an overall rational whole. Hegelian themes appear in
Derrida in such a way as to maximize the disruption of the rational-
istic system, in which reality is structured by laws of thought.

The other source of Derrida's anti-metaphysics, which has not so
far been much discussed, is G.W. Leibniz, mentioned above with
regard to his position on indiscernibles. Derrida never discusses
Leibniz in a systematic way, but he often appears as a point of reference. What draws Derrida to Leibniz is Leibniz's criticisms of
Descartes from the point of view of force. Descartes described reality in terms of geometry. For him, modern physics provided a way
of describing the movements of objects in geometrical relations,
external to the objects as things at some point in space. Leibniz
countered this with the necessity of force in physics. Physics does
not just rest on geometrically expressed movements and relations,
since movements are the result of force. Force is something that sci-
entists refer to in the laws governing the movement of objects, but
Leibniz went beyond that because he thought that 'force', as a concept used in physics, can only exist as a concept if it refers to force
as a metaphysical principle. The predominance of 'force' as a concept in physics, and which is calculated in its equations, shows that
it is basic to physics, and therefore more than any particular content of any particular observation, or set of observations. The
movement from physics to metaphysics through force is in some
respects the opposite of Derrida (or Nietzsche), but in some respects
he seems to anticipate the predominance of force in Derrida (and
Nietzsche). Derrida finds the Leibnizian example of the criticism of
Descartes, from the point of view of force, to be a useful precedent.
He criticizes the Structuralist analysis of literature in that way in
'Force and signification' (WD 1); it tries to reduce the literary text
to an abstract immaterial object defined by the pure forms of time,

theme, action and so on. Nothing, however, can eliminate force as a necessary in explaining the particularity of the contents of any literary object, or any object in any system, or in the rules of any system. Structuralism is in some respects a repetition of Cartesian metaphysics and Deconstruction is in some respects a repetition of Leibnizian force. Leibniz tends to be regarded as the paradigm of a pure metaphysical rationalist thinker, trying to define all experience as the product of rational laws of thought, which is perhaps why the use made by Derrida of Leibniz has not been acknowledged as it could have been. For Derrida, Leibniz often appears where it is the pure metaphysician who takes metaphysics to an extreme where the system is coming into overt contradiction with itself, as when Derrida refers briefly to Leibniz anticipating Husserl's ambiguities with regard to language (IOG VII, 100–10 fn 108; also SP 6, 81 fn 6) or to Leibniz on universal writing (OG 2, 1, 78–80).

The oppositions, which Nietzsche sees as definitive for metaphysics, are seen by Nietzsche as evidence of conflicting forces, which in itself undermines the view of thought and reason as more ideal and rationally real than the empirical and material world. His oppositions include: good and evil, real and apparent, true and false. These are picked up by Derrida, and conceived in terms of the inside and the outside. Metaphysics takes the inside as good, real and true; and takes the outside as evil, apparent and false. The inside and the outside also map onto being and non-being, presence and absence. In the discussion of language, metaphysics has taken speech as an inside that is good, real, true, present and has being; in opposition to writing which is taken as an outside that is evil, apparent, false, absent and has non-being.

Derrida makes a lot of the distinction between speech and writing in metaphysics, and writes of it as a constant in metaphysics. This looks strange to a lot of readers, because the issue has not been in the foreground in most philosophy, and a great deal of philosophy seems to emphasize rational, abstract thought and rules of reasoning, including the written symbolization of mathematics and logic over speech. There are maybe some infelicities of expression in Derrida on this question; sometimes he might seem to be claiming that all philosophy has contained a phonocentric theory, but the real question for him is that of 'logocentrism', which he specifically argues is dominant in all philosophers, including the rationalist ones such as Leibniz and Hegel, and is inescapable in philosophy. He also shows that the priority of speech over writing is an issue in the rationalist Plato, as well as in Rousseau and the empiricist Analytic philosopher J.L. Austin.

Derrida does show the intrinsic priority of speech over writing in the history of philosophy, and thought. The issue is not how many philosophers deliberately place speech above writing, and clearly highlight such a claim. The issue is whether philosophers have consistently assumed that meaning is to be found first, in both the temporal and logical senses, in speech and that writing is found to be secondary in both respects. To say that the claim is implicit is not to make an obscurantist argument. The claim and the argument are clear enough whatever the difficulties created on first reading by Derrida's style. In the *Phaedrus*, Plato through Socrates makes a clear argument that writing is inferior to speech because speech is the immediate expression of the speaker, and the speaker is there to clarify any uncertainties about meaning. In contrast, writing remains forever materially inscribed, and everyone will be able to come and read the words for a long time to come. Anyone reading the words, in the absence of the individual who inscribed them, is going to put any number of interpretations on them out of context and with no possibility of correction from the inscriber. Derrida combines this with the explicit phonocentrism of Rousseau and Saussure, who both presume that speaking is first in time, and in natural order, compared with writing. In a discussion of J.L. Austin, in 'Signature event context' (MP), Derrida notes that all the comments on language in its non-constative (non-descriptive) aspects refers to the speech act as the primary form of language. In his extensive discussions of Husserl, Derrida notes the primacy of inner speech for Husserl.

> Everything in my speech which is destined to manifest an experience to another must pass by the mediation of its physical side; this irreducible mediation involves every expression in an indicative function. Here we find the core of indication: indication takes place whenever the sense-giving act, the animating intention, the living spirituality of the meaning-intention is not fully present.
>
> (SP 38)

This is not an enormous sample from the history of philosophy, but it is indicative of assumption made throughout the history of philosophy. Language has always been taken as originating in the immediate expression of an intention in consciousness, which is first externalized as speech. Speech has been assumed to repeat the immediacy of inner intentions, or what Husserl refers to as inner speech. Writing has always been assumed to be a copy of speech that loses the immediacy of speech.

One of Derrida's best-known critics, John Searle, attacks this position in Derrida on the grounds that the history of philosophy has been full of the privileging of abstraction, metaphysical ideas, rationalist systems, and mathematical-logical notation that does not refer to speech (Searle 1977). Searle's criticisms are more of a polemical attack than a considered argument, and he set an unfortunate precedent for ill-thought-out polemics against Derrida by philosophers who should know better, and he does not make any honest attempt to reconstruct Derrida's argument. Searle even accuses Derrida of 'intellectual terrorism' (Searle 1987), if he defends himself against such representations, we might wonder who the 'terrorist' is here. Searle quotes Derrida's teacher from the ENS, Michel Foucault, on the 'intellectual terrorism' charge, from conversation. It has to be said here, that unlike Derrida, Foucault was prone to feuds. After writing a eulogistic preface for *Anti-Oedipus* (Gilles Deleuze and Félix Guattari 2004), he fell out with Deleuze; presumably this has something to do with the critical but respectful position Deleuze came to take on Foucault, culminating in a book Deleuze published on Foucault (Deleuze 1988), after Foucault's death. Foucault tried to reinterpret his praise for Deleuze (and Guattari) as criticism and denigrated Deleuze's work. Derrida wrote a long critical essay on Foucault's *Madness and Civilisation* (Foucault 2001a), 'Cogito and the history of madness' (WD 2). By most people's standards it is very respectful criticism, and a tribute to the importance of Foucault's work, which happens to express disagreement on some points around the discussion of Descartes. This may have been enough to leave Foucault with a lasting sense of grievance, particularly against the student who became too critical.

Searle's own attack on Derrida may have been intensified because the argument took place around the reading of Austin in

'Signature event context'. Searle had been Austin's doctoral student and clearly a fight over the right to interpret Searle's intellectual father figure is taking place here. Searle's initial attack on Derrida was harsh, and he only became harsher when Derrida suggested a lack of reading ethics on Searle's part. Since Searle judged Derrida on the basis of only one text and tries to present that text in the most uncharitable way possible, Derrida's charge really is not unreasonable.

On the charge of ignoring the importance of writing and abstract system in philosophy, Derrida explicitly acknowledges the analyses of the written in philosophy: that is the whole point of the title *Of Grammatology*. 'Grammatology' is the study of *'grammē'*, the written character. Derrida unearths a few examples where the study of language has been referred to in this way, and refers to the fascination of Leibniz and Hegel with rational systems. In Leibniz's case that included the urge for a universal language, which would be the product of written design rather than the development of speech; Hegel aimed for a philosophy of absolute science, logic, spirit or knowledge through the philosophical system. However, this is *not* the same as making writing a more immediate expression of intention than speech. Hegel is clearly advocating an absolute system on the basis of a spirit that is not accessed in the first place through writing, but through the immediate contents of inner consciousness. Leibniz's interest in the construction of a universal language has nothing to do with the origin of language in the immediate contents of consciousness, repeated in speech. Derrida does not ever say that all philosophy has been devoted to speech as superior to writing for doing philosophy, though Plato seems to be saying something like that in the *Phaedrus*. Derrida does not try to turn that particular claim of Plato, through Socrates, in one particular dialogue, into a general claim about the whole history of philosophy. The Plato of the *Phaedrus*'s suggestion that truth is best uncovered in speech is taken, by Derrida, as a symptom of the underlying claim that meaning is more stable and closer to inner intentions in speech than in writing. Searle simply attributes a claim to Derrida that Derrida never makes (the claim that philosophers value speech over writing as a way of communicating philosophical truths) and attacks Derrida on that basis, also accusing Derrida of intellectual terrorism with no sense of irony.

The more general claim that Derrida makes is that philosophy, or metaphysical philosophy, has been the history of logocentrism. Logocentrism is Derrida's neologism and refers to what is centred on '*logos*', an argument developed particularly in the early sections of OG. The Ancient Greek word '*logos*' can be translated in various ways that include: language, discourse, knowledge, the word. What Derrida means, in particular, is an approach at the heart of metaphysics according to which truth, knowledge or being are present at some particular moment. This is a variation on Heidegger's claim that metaphysics is a history of the reduction of Being or Presence to particular experiences, or a particular abstract idea of reason. Heidegger calls this 'Onto-Theology' by which he means the reduction of Being (or God) to some concept of discourse, which is necessarily metaphysical. For Heidegger, no one idea or being can capture Being in itself, and it is something that can only be approached in its withdrawal, or difference, from particular beings or ideas (Heidegger 1972). In Derrida's understanding of logocentrism, Heidegger is still logocentrist, because Being or Presence, or the difference between being and Being, is the place where there is truth. There just is no place of truth according to Derrida. This kind of claim is the kind of thing that gets Derrida accused of irrationalism and lacking in serious philosophical arguments. It is important to realize that there is a strong inclination to scepticism about truth existing as substantial thing within Analytic philosophy. This is known as a 'deflationary' approach to truth. Deflationary approaches vary, but include the following: Redundancy theory of truth, according to which 'true' is an unnecessary word and nothing is added by 'true' to saying something is the case; truth as a predicate, according to which all propositions are true or false, but that is just to use a predicate for which there are rules of usage but no definition; truth as an undefined primitive word, so to say that a proposition is true is no more than to state the claim made in the proposition.

That Derrida says that there is no substantive definition of truth, and that there is no place in which truth reveals itself, does not put him outside the mainstream of Analytic philosophy and even connects with what a lot of Analytic philosophers say about truth, as may be observed in the work of Richard Rorty (Rorty 1991b), who moved from Analytic philosophy into a deep concern with Derrida and his predecessors (Rorty 1980).

Logocentrism in Derrida refers to the philosophical tendency to find truth in the presentation of Being, Spirit, Consciousness, History across a philosophical system or any idea, mode of experience, emphasized in a philosophical system. Plato is logocentric because his dialogues claim to reveal truth with reference to dialectical speech; Descartes is logocentric because he claims to reveal truth in the clear and distinct ideas of our consciousness; Hegel is logocentric because he claims to reveal truth in absolute spirit. A more empirical philosopher like Austin is still logocentric, because the truth of language appears in the immediate situation of the utterance of particular statements. The challenge to the philosophical transcendental, from the empirical, in Derrida requires abandoning the idea that the meaning of a statement can be placed beyond doubt in any situation.

Derrida's position on metaphysics is clearly not of holding a position in metaphysics. Like Wittgenstein, he aims to get outside metaphysics. And, just like Wittgenstein, Derrida sees not just philosophical systems as full of metaphysics, but our usages of language itself as prone to metaphysics. For both, writing outside metaphysics is a contradictory, but necessary, way of doing philosophy that will leave us with a style constantly struggling with the tendency of words to become abstract concepts and therefore metaphysical. What distinguishes Derrida is the view that metaphysical, or transcendental, forces are perpetually present. We cannot regard them as negatives; they are necessary for there to be language, communication, concepts and philosophy. There is no kind of pure empirical, or logical, method that removes the metaphysical. In that case we will just end up with formalism, the belief in pure forms of knowledge, language, logic or consciousness in which the forms have a metaphysical structure.

3

LANGUAGE

SENSE AND MEANING

NAMES

The phrase 'sense and meaning' indicates that this chapter is concerned with Derrida's contribution to what is usually classified as philosophy of language, and overlaps with philosophy of logic. What 'sense and meaning' partly refers to is a distinction established by Gottlob Frege in the 1890s, in the famous paper 'On sense and meaning', between the general sense of names and the objects that they pick out, or mean. Frege calls this the problem of '*Sinn*' and '*Bedeutung*', which would normally be translated as sense and meaning, but since Frege uses '*Bedeutung*' in a way that emphasizes a referring function of picking out some object for the name, the essay is often known as 'On sense and reference' and the question has generally become known as a question of sense and reference. Derrida does not contribute directly to this issue and does not make any reference to the literature since Frege, which takes in Bertrand Russell, Wittgenstein, P. F. Strawson, Saul Kripke and many others, but Derrida must be discussed in this context. Where Derrida comes closest to this tradition is through his concern with Edmund Husserl. In *Logical Investigations* (Husserl 2001), Husserl has much to say about indication, expression, objective correlates, meaning content, subjective and objective meaning. He does not concern himself with some of the core Analytic questions that have come out of the sense and reference issue, within language and logic.

1 What is the relation of the sense of a name to the object picked out by the name?
2 How do these aspects of naming operate in the context of a sentence?
3 How do we pick out and identify objects through language?
4 How far can we analyse sentences as concerned with reference to, and identification, of objects?

However, in his Phenomenological analysis of the contents, and structures, of *consciousness* and judgement as a function of consciousness, Husserl does address the status of the name, the conditions for meaning, indication of objects and other issues relevant to post-Fregean questions of philosophy of language, which will emerge later in this chapter.

What Derrida is sometimes concerned with is the question of the proper name. A relevant extract from OG will help establish Derrida's position and provide an opportunity to clarify his way of arguing.

> [T]he name, especially the so-called proper name, is always caught in a chain or a system of differences. It becomes an appellation only to the extent that it may inscribe itself within a figuration. Whether it be linked by its origin to the representation of things in space or whether it remains caught in a system of phonic differences or social classifications apparently released from ordinary space, the proper-ness of the name does not escape spacing. Metaphor shapes and undermines the proper name. The proper meaning does not exist, its 'appearance' is a necessary function – and must be analysed as such – in the system of differences and metaphors.
>
> (OG 89)

This passage appears in the context of a discussion about why writing cannot be a pure copy of speech, meaning that there can be no phonocentric writing, and adding to Derrida's claim that speech should not be considered as primary in language. Any kind of written symbolism must go beyond the moment of speech in its scope, and since speech itself lacks the pure immediacy assumed by phonocentrism it cannot provide a model for writing of immediacy. Some of the reasons for this will emerge in this chapter. The proper name can never stand out as an absolutely distinct part of language. The proper name can never be completely proper since it is part of language and is therefore marked by difference, representation, classification and spacing. The strangest looking expression here is spacing, so we will begin with that. 'Spacing' in Derrida refers to the way that any kind of sign must appear in a unity of time and space. That unity is not unique to the sign; we must refer to spacing in discussion of consciousness. There is no pure moment isolated from the movement of time. Any perception must be in the flux of time, where one moment is constantly becoming the next moment. There is no perception that does not take time; the most minute duration in time is still a duration in which time moves. Not only must the perception exist in time, it must exist in spatial representations. The perception is somewhere in the space of our perceptions, therefore it cannot be identified in isolation from its spatial relations with the whole spatial field. The axes of time and space cannot be separated from each other. Perception of spatial relations takes time, and the perception of something over time grasps something that exists within space and within spatial relations. The ways in which we define the meanings of signs, including words, must be understood in the same way. We cannot allow the kind of absolute distinction Saussure made between the diachronic (changes over time) and the synchronic (the non-temporal structure of the system). Words only have existence in 'spacing'; they do not exist as pure isolated items of meaning in a table of signs. The kind of linguistic system Saussure describes must itself be in constant change over time. Looking at the tabulation of signs necessarily involves the kind of minimum duration of consciousness over time, just described. The difference between signs, which Saussure emphasizes as the basis of definition, itself subordinates the individual sign to the movement of spacing that inevitably conditions the differences between signs.

The proper name does not exist outside spacing, difference, system and classification. The proper name should not be taken as an example of an indivisible immediate unity between sign and bearer. The proper name is not intrinsically and necessarily tied to the bearer as its meaning. The proper name is where the bearer is absent as absent from the word sign that exists in the spacing and difference that conditions all signs. The proper name is no less open to vagueness, ambiguity and contextuality than the rest of language. It even provides the strongest examples of vagueness, ambiguity and contextuality. It is what must be understood as what is uniquely tied to a unique object, but it must be a common name with the features of any name, so it is naming at its most ambiguous point. It defines ambiguity because it is the point where ambiguity and determinacy coincide. The suggestion that the conditions for the possibility of proper names are also the conditions for their impossibility is typical of Derrida's deconstructive strategies. He always aims to show that the conditions of possibility are necessarily the conditions of impossibility. Questions of subjectivity and consciousness also arise here, as the proper name is embedded in the sense of self of the bearer of the proper name. That particular issue will be addressed in the next chapter.

The issue of naming particularly demands some context in Analytic philosophy. Despite his general lack of engagement with the Analytic, on the question of names Derrida accidentally, or by design, gets into the same territory. The most likely reason is the brief but significant comments by Husserl in *Logical Investigations*: 'Investigation I. Expression and meaning'. It will be very helpful to situate Derrida's discussion with regard to some particularly influential positions on the proper name in Analytic philosophy.

Gottlob Frege. The proper name in ordinary language refers to an object uniquely, but does so through a sense that is indefinite since a large variety of defining qualities can be mentioned in association with any proper name in order to fix its reference. In logically reformed language such ambiguity should be replaced by definite limited qualities. In a sentence the name loses its reference, as the sentence as a whole has reference, which is its truth or falsity.

Bertrand Russell. Proper names in ordinary language only denote something (refer to something) in the context of a sentence. Ideally we eliminate names through replacing them with a logical variable (a symbol used in logic that we can say does or does not exist, in a universal or singular way) and a description that is attached to the variable. Russell did not apply this to proper names, though W.V.O. Quine tried to do so and suggested a way of turning any proper name into a description. According to Russell, there are 'logically proper names', but they are not names in the normal sense. They are demonstratives, such as 'that', 'this' and 'I', which name some immediate content of my perceptions.

Ludwig Wittgenstein. A proper name, or any name, has a reference fixed by an indefinite list of descriptions. That is, for any name there are a number of possible descriptions of an object that we can attach to the name. If all the descriptions apply to one and the same object, then the name clearly names that object. If no descriptions apply to one and the same object, then the name clearly does not name that object. If some descriptions apply to the same object, then the name may or may not be the name of that object, and there is no point at which we can say that the name does name that object.

Saul Kripke. Any name is a rigid designator for an object that it does not describe. It is connected to that object by a causal chain of usage going back to the moment of naming, referred to by Kripke as initial baptism. The rigid designator names the same object in all possible universes.

The discussion of names since Frege has revolved around issues of: description, reference, their place in a sentence, and definiteness versus vagueness. We can summarize the above position on the basis of those considerations. Frege: proper names are disguised descriptions that can only be vaguely determined, and they fix reference. In logical language proper names are disguised descriptions of a definite sort. Russell: names are disguised descriptions within a sentence that are definitely determined and fix reference; however logically proper names have no description and refer outside sentences, they are vague in the sense that the same word can refer to anything according to context, and definite in the sense that there is no ambiguity about what their reference is. Wittgenstein: names are disguised descriptions vaguely determined inside or outside a sentence, but context always affects their sense and reference; logically proper names and logical language are marginal in relation to how language as a whole works. Kripke: all names refer with no descriptive content inside and outside sentences, in logical and ordinary languages.

Derrida's position combines the anti-descriptive theory of names in Kripke with the highly contextual theory of naming in Wittgenstein, with which we can group the more contextual aspects of Russell and Frege. For Derrida, the name can never be isolated from context, in a sentence, and all other forms of context, linguistic and extra-linguistic. These claims are true of all names, and all parts of language. However, the proper name both belongs to language as a whole and does not. The point of a proper name being proper is that it designates something rigidly without regard to description (to put it in Kripke's terms); there really are such things as proper names and they refer without regard to description. My name does not include any description of me, and while various descriptions would help members of the language community fix the reference of my name, the person who has such and such qualities, they are not the equivalent of my name. From a Derridean point of view, Russell's logically proper names are an unnecessary logical-metaphysical assumption, for very much the same reasons that Wittgenstein said so. Names are something to be used in language, so we are not looking for perfect reference but for the level of determinacy of reference that will fix reference well enough when we are using language. The claim that logically proper names can pick anything out rests on what Wittgenstein calls the 'private language argument';[1] Derrida also has things to say about 'private language' arguments, but with reference to Husserl. The private language argument will be discussed later in the chapter. There is something interesting about Russell's logically proper names from a Derridean point of view, which is that they are an example of a kind of radical contextuality. There just is no limit to what 'I', 'that' and 'this' could refer to, given the appropriate context; and there just is nothing to be said about their reference outside a context. Derrida thinks of language in that way, as what works through total contextuality in every aspect.

However, language cannot just work through contextuality without the proper aspect, the aspect of what gives language a relation to things, including any individual user of language. We cannot have language without proper names. There certainly is no language without names, and the nature of naming is that is can be used to name something. The act of naming, or of using a name, is always proper, it is always the suggestion that the name belongs to a single, particular thing, or kind, bearing in mind that all kinds belong to the general kind of thing since all kinds are things of some kind. Any individuated thing is a unique thing, and any individuated kind is a unique kind, so any name is proper in the sense of naming a unique thing; the proper name in the normal sense is however improper in that it could always be used improperly and there is never a guarantee that the same proper name has not been applied to different things. A proper name, or any name, is always proper in one aspect of its usage, but always improper in other aspects. The contextual nature of language itself undermines the possibility that a name can have a unique reference, because its reference always exists in a context and therefore must vary with context.

FICTIONS, CONTEXT AND CONTRADICTIONS

One aspect of context that is fundamental for Derrida is the possibility that any name, or any sentence, or any item of language might be fictional.

> [I]f it is admitted that, as we have tried to show, every sign whatever is of an originally repetitive structure, the general distinction between the fictitious and effective use of the sign is threatened. *The sign is originally wrought by fiction.* From this point on, whether with respect to indicative communication or expression, there is no sure criterion by which to distinguish an outward language from an inward language or, in the hypothesis of an inward language, an effective language from a fictitious language.
>
> (SP 56)

The idea is developed in the one essay by Derrida that considers an Analytic philosopher, the discussion of J.L. Austin in 'Signature event context' (in MP).

> [I]s not what Austin excludes an anomalous, exceptional, 'non-seri-
> ous', that is, *citation* (on the stage, in a poem, or in a soliloquy), the
> determined modification of a general citationality – or rather a gen-
> eral iterability – without which there would not even be a 'successful'
> performative? Such that – a paradoxical but inevitable consequence –
> a successful performative is necessarily an 'impure' performative.
>
> (MP 325)

The passage from Derrida above sets up the issue of fictionality, with some other important issues that will be clarified here before expanding on fictionality.

The most mysterious looking word above is 'iterability', which means repeatability, and through its Sanskrit root 'iter' refers to otherness. Derrida use iteration, and iterability, in order to high-light the linguistic, and ontological, necessity of repetition. The possibility of meaning in language rests on the possibility of repe-tition, since a word only has a meaning if it can be used with the same meaning more than once. Wittgenstein has similar argu-ments in *Philosophical Investigations* (Wittgenstein 2001). The semantics, the meaningful aspect, of language rests on a rule of iterability. The rules of language are its syntactic, formal aspect. For Derrida, the occurrence of iteration in language is where semantics and syntax are inseparable and the same is true of his account of contradiction, as we shall see. Repetition also arises in ontology because, when we are talking about objects in the world, we are talking about repetition of single objects over time, neces-sary for them to maintain their identity; and we are talking about repetition within general types of objects so that a type is not just one object but a series of objects that repeat each other.[2] The per-ception of language and ontology as intertwined in this way is very indicative of Derrida's views of language, metaphysics and knowledge.

Another word in need of explanation, in the passage above, is 'performative', a term used by Austin and strongly associated with him. In *How to Do Things with Words* (Austin 1975), Austin develops a contrast between two kinds of sentence in language: constative and performative. Constative sentences are descriptive. Performative sentences bring things about, are actions in the world. Austin's examples of performative sentences include promising, betting, naming a ship and the words used in a marriage ceremony. In all these cases we change something in the world by using words in a way that changes the human world. That is, the world as it exists in social and linguistic forms. Austin regards the performative as tied in with the social contract that establishes all our social, legal and political institutions, including language itself. After developing the account of the performative in *How to Do Things with Words,* Austin then replaces the performative/constative distinction with another way of analysing language. He suggests that we can look at all sentences as locutions that have illocutionary force of meaning and perlocutionary force in the world. All sentences are perlocutionary in some way, with the possible exception of very pure abstract and theoretical sentences. The distinction between constative and performative sentences is replaced by the distinction between different aspects within the same sentence. The move from external distinctions between two types of sentence and internal distinctions within a sentence is very interesting for Derrida. In Derrida's approach, there are always these kinds of movement between internal and external distinctions, since we can never adequately define the distinction between the internal and the external. The distinction between the internal and the external refers to the metaphysical distinction between the inside and the outside. Austin's account also appeals to Derrida because the notion of the performative ties the world and language together, as inseparable, again a rather Wittgensteinian attitude.

Austin's approach to the performative, and the perlocutionary, refers the meaning of sentences to context in a very strong way. There is no separation between inner meaning and external context with regard to the performative or the perlocutionary. The words of a wedding ceremony mean nothing outside a properly conducted ceremony; a bet means nothing without the social institution of making a bet. The meaning for the performative/perlocutionary is the effect in the external world. The contextuality follows a tendency in Analytic philosophy. In Frege and Russell the sense of words is affected by the context of the sentence. In Wittgenstein, language as a whole is a necessary context. In reaction to Russell, Strawson suggests that language must be studied from the point of view of general use and particular utterances, as well as logical analysis of isolated sentences. Wittgenstein's holism has earlier roots in American Pragmatism, which itself drew on the Idealist holism of G.W.F. Hegel. For Hegel, any individual proposition, or judgement, must be placed within a universal context for that category of judgement, or proposition, that itself depends on the possibility of an absolute knowledge or science that is the most complete holistic knowledge or science. In the Pragmatists and Wittgenstein, there is more emphasis on the varying external factors and parts of language that give words and sentences context, but there is a lot of argument in common. A more technical-logical argument for linguistic holism comes from the formal semantics of Alfred Tarski, for whom semantic terms must be defined to apply to every occurrence of that term in a language. On the face of it, the mode of argument is far from Hegel or Derrida, but like them Tarski emphasizes the importance of contradiction. In particular the possibility of the Liar Paradox, as discussed in the last chapter, is a strong reason for adopting a holistic theory that will limit the kind of sentences for which truth can be, or should be, defined. In Hegel and Derrida, the possibility of contradiction requires us to recognize that sentences do not have meaning in isolation, but must be interpreted within a context that enables us to identify the contradiction in the sentence, and place it in context. In Hegel, the placing in context makes our understanding of the meaning to become more universal, and closer to the absolute; in Derrida, the placing in context is to become aware of language as a network of incomplete and contradictory fragments, where full meaning is just the product of context at one moment. After Wittgenstein, holism appears in a highly influential form in the work of Quine where Pragmatic holism, without any acknowledgement of Hegel, is unified with Tarski's formalist variation. For Quine, sentences are just never completely determinate except at two extremes: pure logic and those sentences that directly report stimulation situations (moments of sensation).

The interest in contextuality in philosophy of language since Frege has included an interest in how to define expressions and sentences in fiction. The topic is marginal at first but has come

closer and closer to the centre of analysis. For Frege, fictional
names and sentences must be regarded as having sense without
reference. That leaves aside two questions: what it is to be true
within a fiction; what of the possibility that sentences, which are
not obviously fictions, may be fictions? Fictions appear in
Strawson's metaphysical work *Individuals* (Strawson 1990),[3] with
regard to the role of stories in identification. Identifying objects
within our metaphysical framework of time and space is to create a
story, and that relies on smaller stories about the identification of
objects in the time–space framework. The basic framework of our
metaphysics, for Strawson, includes the claim that our knowledge
of the world derives from objects with which we are directly
acquainted. However, most of what we can say about objects
depends on the stories of other people as Strawson acknowledges.
What Strawson does not acknowledge is the implication that our
framework, and our ability to pick out objects with sentences and
referring expressions, rests on the stories of others. Stories are not
necessarily fictions, but they could be; anyway the use of the word
story does introduce a fictional structure to reality. Reality is
implicitly becoming a fiction we create for ourselves. That is true
of reality as a whole, and our identification of objects that rests on
the stories we are told, and if we consider previous states of ourselves as other selves, though Strawson does not, no identifying
situation escapes the situation of being a story we receive from
another person, which could be fictions. That is extrapolating a
long way from what Strawson says himself, but that cannot just be
an interpretation of Strawson twisted by an excessive diet of
Derrida. These issues have been raised by those directly in
Strawson's line of philosophical tradition, perhaps most significantly Gareth Evans in *The Varieties of Reference* (Evans 1982).
The most obvious difference between Evans and Derrida is that for
Evans evidently the question of reference is at the centre, and it is
not even mentioned by Derrida. That may be a lack in Derrida, but
it would be wrong to say that Derrida is just an out of control
sceptic who does not care about truth and reality. Since he does not
raise the question of reference, he is not troubled by failure to
determine reference and is not pushed towards scepticism. The
Derridean approach does not preclude interests in reference, but it

does preclude the confusion of questions of meaning in language with questions of knowledge and overcoming scepticism. The emphasis on reference turns the questions of meaning into questions of how language connects with what is out there and therefore of how we know what is out there, and how we know that language is connecting with it. The growth of Analytic holism is very largely concerned with acknowledging the impossibility of defining language by trying to tie any words, expressions or sentences item by item with items in reality out there. On the issues of meaning, Evans's exploration of all the interruptions to the referential function of language converges with a Derridean approach as does some work which claims that we cannot be sure about the meaning of what we think or say. Hilary Putnam's 'The meaning of "meaning"'(Putnam 1975) is a notable example.[4]

The Evans approach to fiction is not the same as Derrida but there is enough in common to show that Derrida is not outside the limits of reason as defined by Analytic philosophy, even if his style and references look strange by Analytic standards. The importance of the fiction in the Austinian performative for Derrida is that, as the citation above suggests, the performative might always be a fiction. Austin emphasizes that a fully functioning performative must be sincere. We cannot talk about a successful performance unless the speaker means what he or she says. The performative will be shown to be unsuccessful if the speaker does not behave according to the contract implicit in the performative, after the event of the performative. Austin introduced two difficulties for the understanding of the performative, or the perlocutionary, here. One is that we need to be able to grasp someone's state of mind in evaluating the success of a performative; the other is that we need to be able to see into the future in evaluating the success of a performative.

> I ask the following question: is this general possibility necessarily that of a failure or a trap into which language might *fall*, or in which language might lose itself, as if in an abyss situated outside or in front of it? What about *parasitism*? In other words, does the generality of the risk admitted by Austin *surround* language like a kind of *ditch*, a place of external perdition into which locution might never venture, that it

might avoid by remaining at home, in itself, sheltered by its essence or *telos*? Or indeed is this risk, on the contrary, its internal and positive condition of possibility? this outside its inside? the very force and law of its emergence? In this last case, what would an 'ordinary' language defined by the very law of language signify? Is it that in excluding the general theory of this structural parasitism, Austin who nevertheless pretends to describe the facts and events of ordinary language, makes us accept as ordinary a teleological and ethical determination (the univocality of the statement – which he recognises elsewhere remains a philosophical 'ideal', – the self-presence of a total context, the transparency of intentions, the presence of meaning for the absolutely singular oneness of a speech act, etc)? For finally, is not what Austin excludes as anomalous, exceptional, 'non-serious', that is, *citation* (on the stage, in a poem, or in a soliloquy), the determined modification of a general citationality – or rather, a general, iterability – without which there would not even be a 'successful' performative? Such that – a paradoxical, but inevitable consequence – a successful performative is necessarily an 'impure' performative, to use the word that Austin will employ later on when he recognises that there is no 'pure' performative.

(MP 325)

Derrida points out that we have no way of being sure that a sentence is uttered sincerely, and he emphasizes the fictional aspect of this. There is no way in which we can be sure that the sentence is not a moment of dramatic performance or literary recitation. All of language is iterable, which means that any sentence can always be cited in the context of a fictional literary work. There is no determinate limit between the fictional and the 'serious', because there can always be citation and the sentence could always be a citation. For practical purposes, we are reasonably confident most of the time about what is fictional and what is literal, about what is citation and what is non-citation. Derrida's point is that from the perspective of logical, or absolute, certainty, we can never be sure about this. It is always possible that language is being used in a secondary way, like a parasite feeding off its host, where we can see the parasite as para-citation, the way in which language could always be a citation from some other place. If citation is always

possible there is no clear distinction between the proper and cita-
tional, or parasitic, use of language. The fictional-literary situation
is particularly easy to notice on the face of it, but the parasitical
possibility can be there in more subtle ways. How do we know if
words are uttered seriously or as a joke, not just as an obvious
attempt to provoke laughter, but with some quiet irony? Again
these concerns have some precedent in Wittgenstein. Wittgenstein
suggests that words, and sentences, do not have meaning outside
the context of language games. Any sentence belongs to more than
one possible language game and therefore contains different possible meanings, which are going to contradict each other. As part of
different language games, the sentence can be said to exist in distinct versions, which are different in their application rather than
contradicting each other in meaning (Wittgenstein 2001). From a
deconstructive point of view, if we are going to regard the sentence
as maintaining any kind of continuous identity across different
usages, and if we do not, then it is just not the same sentence, then
we must accept the inevitability of contradiction with regard to the
meaning of the sentence.

Derrida's reading of Austin was the stimulus for John Searle's
assault on him (Searle 1977), in which Searle claimed that Derrida's
reading of Austin was completely mistaken; and in a potentially
contradictory way both claimed that Derrida was too confusing to
understand and that his arguments were wrong. Despite Searle's
claims to have proved Derrida wrong, and the repetition of that
claim by some, all with the aim of asserting that Derrida was not up
to proper Analytic standards of argument, various philosophers
well qualified in Analytic philosophy have defended Derrida.[5]
Searle had written his doctorate at Oxford under the supervision of
Austin and Strawson. Searle seems inclined to regard Austin's
legacy as his possession and that it is a legacy to be understood in a
very commonsensical way, avoiding the ways in which Austin, like
Wittgenstein, separated himself from philosophical theory and
pushed at the limits of the expressible. Austin made comments on
questioning the division between truth and falsity, for example,
which sound a lot more like Derrida than Searle. A more appreciative attitude to Derrida's reading of Austin can be found in Stanley
Cavell, who has devoted a lot of work to the understanding of

Austin, in relation to the late Wittgenstein, and can be considered at least as reliable and well informed a commentator as Searle. Cavell clearly belongs to the Analytic tradition, even if like Austin and Wittgenstein he was pushing at its limits.[6] The main problem with Cavell's reading of Derrida reading Austin is that Cavell rather puzzlingly claims that Derrida is not concerned with the ethical dimension of the presence, or absence, of the other in communication (Cavell 1995). Not only are such concerns present in Derrida, they are central to what he is doing, as will be explained in Chapter 6. A better grasp of this is shown by Simon Glendinning in *On Being with Others* (Glendinning 1998), whose position is essentially derived from Cavell and so acts as a corrective to Cavell's misapprehensions of Derrida on ethics, within Cavell's reading, rather than as an alternative.

The impossibility of determining the performative, or any sentence, as serious or non-serious, original or parasitic, is also a question of contradiction. There is no way of determining the status in one way or the other, in which case we are faced both with indeterminacy and contradiction. There is indeterminacy because the sentence is never clearly on one side of any definition through opposition; there is contradiction because if it is equally true of a sentence that it is serious, or original, and that it is not serious or original, then we are holding contrary positions about the sentence simultaneously. Deconstruction in large part means facing the contradiction rather than trying to eliminate it. All concepts are contradictory for Derrida. If sentences in language are indeterminate, and therefore contradictory, then the concept of the sentence is contradictory, since the sentence must both be what conveys meaning and what cannot convey meaning. The sentence cannot be isolated as a meaning unit from its context, so that is does not exist in a stable self-identical way, as the same sentence may have different meanings in different contexts. The sentence must both be what it is and not what it is. The same applies to all aspects of meaning. The contradiction is sharper in the Derridean account than in the Wittgensteinian account, where contradiction emerges implicitly from the variable context of sentences. There is no escape from contradiction in Derrida through looking at the different possible meanings as different usages in different clearly individuated language games, which is one way of reading Wittgenstein in order to attempt the elimination of contradiction. The idea of distinct language games does not exist in Derrida, and even in Wittgenstein they overlap so that the possibility of contradiction cannot be ignored.

All sentences are necessarily contradictory in Derrida's account, because they both mean and do not mean according to a distinct meaning content within the sentence that shapes it. Discussion of this can be found in 'The double session' (in D), with regard to Stéphane Mallarmé, a nineteenth-century French poet, influential in French and world literature. Derrida is commenting on a short prose extract, and he brings out the theme of contradiction in language, as appearing at the limit of language, in a way that is emphasized in poetry and the more poetic kind of prose writing. This particularly applies to literature of a Symbolist kind and in literature since. Symbolist literature emphasizes the word itself as an entity, and the pure form of literature as autonomous; such ideas are particularly relevant to Mallarmé both with regard to his poetic practice, and to his thoughts about language and poetry. What Derrida highlights in 'The double session' is that in the case of Mallarmé the possible contradictions of meaning inherent in language, and played upon by poetry, are exposed by moments in the poetic work where there is a sense of being at the limit of language and where there is an eruption of pure physicality, of the non-verbal through death, orgasm and the sneeze. In particular, Derrida deals with the 'hymen' in Mallarmé, as Mallarmé himself plays upon the meanings of hymen as the membrane that remains intact in a virginal woman and in relation to marriage, a ceremony that traditionally legitimates sexual acts and the penetration of the hymen (though of course the link between marriage and the end of female virginity is not so prevalent in modern cultures). This kind of approach in Derrida represents, for Derrida's critics, the epitome of Derrida's charlatanism as he replaces argument with verbal play. However, there is nothing unique to Derrida about concern with trying to write at the limits of language. Frege suggested that, when we think about the basic concepts, we are left with no possibility of explanation and justification of what we are claiming, so that we just have to accept that sometimes we are at a limit where we cannot justify our analysis through more analysis. These brief considerations in Frege go much further in Wittgenstein, as can be seen in both his main books, *Tractatus Logico-Philosophicus* (Wittgenstein 1961) and the *Philosophical Investigations* (Wittgenstein 2001). Another criticism of Derrida from various directions is that he is a linguistic idealist. This claim itself rests on confusion between discussion of language and discussion of epistemology, which will be discussed fully in Chapter 5. It is a confusion deeply rooted in the tendency of philosophy since Descartes to treat the danger of complete scepticism about reality, and the struggle to overcome such a danger, as the primary question of philosophy. The emphasis on the body at the necessary limit of language, as language must be defined by what limits it, suggests the limitations of the 'linguistic idealist' interpretation of Derrida. The problems with the idealist claims about Derrida can also be seen if we consider the emphasis on language as emerging from material psychic forces rather than immaterial mental space, as discussed in 'Différance' (MP D) and 'Freud and the scene of writing' (WD 7).

The contradictions of meaning, and sentences, are also explored by Derrida with regard to the model of a communication between the sender of a message and its receiver. Such a model may have many pragmatic advantages for examining empirical linguistic situations. However, it cannot be taken as beyond contradiction, or as a basic philosophical principle. The communication of a message means that something has left the consciousness of the sender, so that it is not an internal part of the consciousness of that person. Even in consciousness, the message does not originate as the clear intention of a clear consciousness. Consciousness itself is opaque because our internal self-introspecting (when we are looking into our own minds) is delayed by time, and therefore we never grasp exactly what it is we are trying to grasp. The message sent by a sender just could never have been the pure copy of a pure intention of a perfectly transparent consciousness. The sending of the message multiplies interruptions to the message, which were there before the message was sent. During the communication, the message can be delayed, lost and diverted in many ways. The sender could die, leaving us without the opportunity to ask what exactly was meant by the message. However quickly the message arrives, there is a temporal gap between the act of sending and the act of receiving. The context must be different in arriving at a view of the meaning for the sender and the receiver. These considerations apply just as much to speech as to writing. Even in the situation of immediately hearing what someone has said, the issues of context and temporal delay are still there. Asking what the sender means, is rather less helpful than Plato had assumed in the *Phaedrus* since consciousness is not the sort of thing that is completely transparent to itself, so no one can say for certainty what the words they have uttered mean. This sort of thing in Derrida is taken as bizarrely sceptical by his critics, but it is not a scepticism about the reality of consciousness, meaning and language. It is an argument for saying that meaning in language depends on the possibility of contradiction, which is what the Liar Paradox and related issues have suggested to many philosophers.

METAPHORICAL AND PRIVATE LANGUAGE

Derrida's position on language is also characterized by a commitment to the metaphoricity of language, including in the most metaphysical texts that may appear to offer a literal theory of truth and reality beyond any figure of speech. However, we should beware of presuming that Derrida is trying to turn all of philosophy into a playful metaphor, even if he is playful with metaphors himself on many occasions. The major discussion of this issue is in 'White mythology' (in MP).[7] Here Derrida concentrates on Aristotle's views of the metaphorical and the proper in language. Aristotle assumes an opposition between language used to say directly what reality is, in its literal use; and to compare something with something in the metaphorical use of language. Derrida's claim is that Aristotle cannot exclude metaphor from the text of his philosophy, and it cannot generally be excluded from philosophy. The assumption exists that metaphor only exists in the philosophical text as dead metaphor, the metaphor that just says something through a very familiar phrase, which directs us towards the proper object of the words rather than to any metaphorical illumination of the words and their usage. Looking at Aristotle, Derrida asks what in Aristotle escapes metaphor. For Aristotle, the answer should be knowledge and knowledge as clarification. Derrida points out that if knowledge is so intertwined with the idea of clarification, then our idea of knowledge rests on metaphor of light. Aristotle works with a structure in which metaphor is a secondary form of language compared with the proper use of words, properly defined through naming with a single meaning. Metaphor is viewed as the transportation of words so that they are used in a secondary way, instead of their primary way with reference to what they name. Metaphor derives from nature, from the nature of objects, and is a secondary effect of nature transferring natural qualities between objects for the sake of comparison and linguistic effect.

For Derrida this is another example of the contradictions that constitute our use of concepts. The application of a word to something in naming is, itself, something that requires catachresis, the turning of a word. What makes a word proper to the object of naming? There is already an act of turning within language; the word is considered to name in its essence that with which it is not essentially linked.

> If every metaphor is an elliptical comparison or analogy, in this case we are dealing with a metaphor par excellence, a metaphorical redoubling, an ellipsis of ellipsis. But the missing term calls for a noun which names something properly. The present terms (the sun, the rays, the act of sowing, the seed) are not in themselves, according to Aristotle, tropes. Here, the metaphor consists in a substitution of proper names having a fixed meaning and referent, especially when we are dealing with the sun whose referent has the originality of always being original, unique and irreplaceable, at least in the representation we give of it. There is only one sun in this system. The proper name, here, is the nonmetaphorical prime mover of metaphor, the father of all figures. Everything turns around it, everything turns toward it. And yet, in one sentence, in a parenthesis that is immediately closed, Aristotle invokes the case of a *lexis* that would be metaphorical in all its aspects.

> (MP 243)

The word itself is divisible in various ways according to sounds and letters, and lacks any natural existence as a unified thing. It is what can always be diverted or divided in its proper usage. The assumption of a name as proper use of language itself assumes something natural to language. But language is what cannot be regarded as natural as it is a human convention. The name itself is regarded as the natural core of language by Aristotle, because it directly designates an object, picking out its natural qualities. However, a name can only be a name because of its definition, which ties it to the object, according to naming theories of language. However, the definition requires reference to language as a whole, and therefore contradicts the assumption that language can be derived from a purely natural pre-linguistic and pre-metaphorical relation of names to objects. The most determinedly non-descriptive theory of naming is still going to have to deal with what ties a name to an object and that will always bring in language as whole, in its metaphorical aspect. Derrida connects the discussion of the irreducibility of metaphor with *The Poetics*, where Aristotle is concerned with the nature of imitation. Imitation appears in Aristotle as both a natural mimicry, a natural resemblance, and as a relation of analogy which does not reduplicate what is imitated. That contradictory and undecidable structure conditions the word as name, as what is repeating, or imitating, what it names. The name is always an analogy of something, since it is not identical with what it names. Naming requires us to see a word as something, and to see something as that word. Metaphor, and the analogical structure underlying it, cannot be eliminated from language and provide the necessary context for naming.

Derrida focuses on the example of the sun in Aristotle. The sun is the easiest thing to recognize and name. It is the natural source of the visibility in which we can perceive our world; it appears in Plato as the symbol of what illuminates all the forms. The relation between sun and word looks like the model for naming as a clear relation, which can be the basis of language and metaphysics. However, Aristotle notes that the sun is what is not completely visible since it is out of our sight at night. Therefore we do not know the sun for a large part of the time, and our naming of it is the naming of something to which we have a relation of considerable uncertainty. The logical, epistemological, metaphysical and psychological certainty provided by naming is now challenged at its centre. The name itself is the transportation of a word to refer to some object that is uncertain, hidden and unknowable for us. We cannot know what qualities are tied up with the name and therefore the name lacks the dialectical definition necessary for it to have a role in Aristotle's metaphysics. The need for dialectic itself might be considered to contaminate any claim to metaphysical certainty, since this can only be accepted after contextualization through dialectical differentiation. These comments on Aristotle are traced back to Plato by Derrida. They are rooted in Plato's concerns with myth, rhetoric and art as what conceal truth but are necessary to truth, so that Aristotle both depends on Platonic distinctions and condemns poetic metaphor within Plato's Theory of Forms.

The concern with the problems of grounding the meaning of names also takes another direction in Derrida, which comes from his interest in Husserl, connects again with Wittgenstein, and will lead us into the chapter on consciousness. The search for absolute grounds to meaning in philosophy is explored by Derrida in relation to Husserl's interest in interior monologue, solitary mental life, and pre-expressive intentions. The topic comes up particularly in SP on 'Meaning as soliloquy' (SP 2) and reappears more briefly, with regard to the discussion of Austin, in 'Signature event context' (in MP):

> Let us imagine a writing with a code idiomatic enough to have been founded and known, as a secret cipher, only by two 'subjects'. Can it still be said that upon the death of the addressee, that is of two partners, the mark left by one of them is still a writing? Yes, to the extent to which, governed by a code, even if unknown and non-linguistic, it is constituted, in its identity as a mark, by its iterability in the absence of whoever, and therefore ultimately in the absence of every empirically determinable 'subject'. This implies that there is no code – an organon of iterability – that is structurally secret. The possibility of repeating, and therefore of identifying, marks is implied in every code, making of it a communicable, transmittable, decipherable grid that is iterable for a third party, and thus for any possible user in general. All

writing, therefore, in order to be what it is, must be able to function in the radical absence of every empirically determined addressee in general. And this absence is not a continuous modification of presence; it is a break in presence, 'death', or the possibility of the 'death' of the addressee, inscribed in the structure of the mark.

(MP 315–16)

The example above is writing rather than speech, or internal monologue, but for Derrida what must apply to the structural necessities of writing must apply to all language, and all consciousness. There is no consciousness before writing for Derrida, in the sense that the structural necessities of writing (repeatability, repetition of an absent origin, contextuality and indeterminacy of meaning) are all in consciousness. It is a necessary strategy to define consciousness in terms of writing rather than the other way round. Not only does that apply to the contents of consciousness, it applies to the forces from which consciousness emerges, or which constitute consciousness in that they are psychic forces. They can be better understood on the model of the inscription of repeatable marks in writing rather than with reference to pure consciousness abstracted from materiality.

Derrida is largely concerned with Husserl's Phenomenology on this, but in the discussion of Austin he needs to show that there is no way of grounding language on an absolutely private inner intentionality. If there is language, it is communication between two people. If one dies then in principle someone else can always grasp what the linguistic codes mean. If the codes are completely opaque, there could not have been any communication in the first place, not even of one consciousness with itself. The argument on consciousness is really to be found earlier in the essays on Husserl. For Austin, it is necessary to emphasize that the codes must be public, and learnable by anyone, in principle with regard to his appeal to sincerity as the ground of the performative. Derrida aims to show that inner sincerity cannot explain anything, since we are talking about publicly communicable codes here. The end point for Derrida is to argue that it is the proper name of the speaker, as signature, which is the only ground for the performative. The performative depends on my enunciation of my sincerity, which is the equivalent of signing the performative as my own.

The discussion of Husserl engages with a notion of inner intentionality that connects with a lot of other things in philosophy since Descartes. Husserl must refer to an intentionality that precedes expression, because for him the intention, as pure intention, is something in consciousness concerned with itself. The expressiveness of language must be preceded by intentionality, or, as Husserl also thinks of it, the intentionality must lie in a deeper stratum than the indicativeness and expressivity of signs. If that is the case, then language as spoken, or written, as communication between subjects, must be preceded by the inner monologue of intentions, private mental life. The communicative language is seen as a copy of the monologue of pure intentionality. This kind of argument is rooted in a philosophical tradition that sees words as signs that are the copies of inner ideas, a tradition that includes Descartes, Locke, Berkeley and Hume. From Derrida's point of view, Austin's belief in the foundational role of sincerity is still caught in that tradition. These criticisms of words as representations of inner ideas are not at all unique to Derrida, and bring up issues that will be discussed in the next chapter. It is necessary to note here that Derrida's criticisms of an absolutely inner language parallel Wittgenstein's celebrated 'private language argument'.[8] The target of Wittgenstein's argument is not as explicit as the target of Derrida's argument, but he is presumably concerned in general with the Cartesian emphasis on the primacy of inner representation, as followed by Locke, Berkeley and Hume, and then by Russell in the doctrine of 'logically proper names' and the Logical Positivist version of Phenomenalism. Phenomenalism originates in Berkeley's suggestion in the eighteenth century that all we can say exists, is the phenomena that make up the perceptions (which Berkeley referred to as ideas) of our consciousness. In the early twentieth century it was suggested that all we can perceive are 'qualia', 'sensibilia' or 'sense data' in our sensory consciousness, and that objects can only be inferred from them so that they can only be said to exist in a secondary way. Wittgenstein appears to have this in his sights when he referred to a private language, which is unique to me. He only mentions such an idea in order to oppose it, as a way of exposing the false assumptions of Phenomenalism, or anything else in philosophy that might take language as representations of inner states of consciousness. Wittgenstein's riposte is that I can describe, or represent inner states, in a language that is unique to one person. We can all make up words for ourselves; the point is that our private words would tell us nothing about inner states than what the normal words do. The private words must belong to the same linguistic structure of the normal words, in that to be words it must be the case that they can be used and repeated in language games, which have some public observable purpose.

The argument in Derrida and Wittgenstein is certainly not identical. Wittgenstein definitely does not have anything to say about death, an important issue for Derrida that will be discussed in later chapters. Wittgenstein's argument is mostly directed against extreme philosophical Empiricism rather than against Idealism, and not at all against Husserl's tendencies towards a Platonist belief in abstractions as real things. For Husserl, the structures of consciousness are Platonist ideas, rather than empirical facts. Derrida's 'private language argument' is that the Husserlian argument is contradictory, or leads to contradictions, although Husserl is trying to eliminate contradictions in a philosophy of pure description without theoretical assumptions. The contradictions are that Husserl has to assume an ideal autonomous consciousness on one side, as the subject of pure expressiveness, but must assume something other as a contamination of the purity of consciousness. The existence of language, and we cannot talk about consciousness without talking about language, is a contamination of such an assumed transcendental consciousness. Derrida's suggestion that language cannot be eliminated from any discussion of consciousness should not be confused with any claim that thought only exists as something linguistic. What Derrida claims is neutral on this point; the important issue is the space of writing, which exists as an economy of forces, differentiated and differentiating from each other through the structure of repetition. Some of Derrida's formulations may appear to advocate a kind of linguistic sovereignty, or idealism, but careful reading does not support such an interpretation. Language, including its aspects of sense and meaning, must be grasped from the point of view of the material economy of forces. Husserl recognizes repetition, but as the infinite repetition of pure forms and ideas that transcendentalize beyond the empirical, or any material economy. The impurities that language introduces into transcendental consciousness are: the intersubjective, the body and the empirical. There can be no language without communication with others, so language cannot be a pure soliloquy in essence; it must include the possibility of the other with whom consciousness communicates. The content of the inner soliloquy must be signs and they must refer to an empirical material world outside consciousness, and as such they must refer to the body.

4

CONSCIOUSNESS

INTENTIONALITY AND PERCEPTION

THE MENTAL AND THE MATERIAL

Discussions of sense and meaning in the last chapter have often brought us into issues of consciousness: the 'private language argument', or what Derrida refers to as arguments based on soliloquy, inner monologue, or pre-expressive intentionality, brings us to the centre of such issues. Much of the last chapter was explained with reference to Wittgenstein. Though the relevant text of Wittgenstein for discussions of consciousness is still *Philosophical Investigations* (Wittgenstein 2001), there is less to be gained for the purposes of clarifying Derrida by bringing in Wittgenstein. Wittgenstein's positions on the mind and consciousness are very orientated towards externally observable behaviour, in a way that is not to be found in Derrida. Both try to eliminate mental contents as things that are at the origin of language and actions: a view of the mind as a set of mechanical causes outside the material world. This is a common theme in twentieth-century philosophy in many schools. For Derrida, the most relevant comparison is Maurice Merleau-Ponty, even though Derrida has little to say about his predecessor in French philosophy at the stage of his work with which we are concerned in the present book.

Derrida's position on mind and consciousness belongs to the Phenomenological tradition since Husserl and the most useful context for placing Derrida on these topics is Merleau-Ponty's reaction to the Phenomenological tradition. On the explicit level, Derrida largely prefers to discuss psychoanalysis rather than Phenomenology. SP addresses Husserl, as do essays from WD and MP. However, after IOG it is psychoanalysis that has come to the fore. After MP and D, there is little direct discussion of Husserl, and certainly not of Phenomenological work on the status of consciousness. Later discussions of consciousness largely occur through discussions of Freud, and other psychoanalytic theorists such as Jacques Lacan, Nicholas Abraham and Maria Torok. There is certainly no engagement with philosophy of mind in the Analytic mode. However, one of the major figures in philosophy of mind, Stephen Stich, makes a particularly ambiguous tribute by naming one of his books *Deconstructing the Mind* (Stich 1996). On this occasion it is worth quoting the way Stich situates himself with regard to Deconstruction in the first chapter. He does not make it clear who he means, or what texts he is referring to, so we cannot be sure if he has read Derrida at all. He both attacks 'Deconstruction' in the usual blustering tone of those who are totally hostile, but he nevertheless finds something of value in there, though he claims it is not an original thought

> For some years now, deconstructionism has been a pretentious and obfuscatory blight on the intellectual landscape. But buried in the heaps of badly written blather produced by people who call themselves 'deconstructionists', there is at least one idea – not original with them – that is worth noting. This is the thesis that in many domains both intellectual activity and everyday practice presuppose a significant body of largely tacit theory. Since the tacit theories are typically all but invisible, it is easy to proceed without examining them critically. Yet once these tacit theories are subject to scrutiny, they are often seen to be very tenuous indeed; there is nothing obvious or inevitable about them.
>
> (Stich 1996: 9)

Stich's comments do accurately refer to at least one aspect of Derrida's 'deconstructionism'. That is the uncovering of tacit theories, which Derrida regards as metaphysical, and the attempt to see

what the relevant domain of knowledge looks like once we eliminate theories that have been assumed without justification. Stich is
specifically concerned here, as he is throughout most of his work,
with 'Eliminativism' in psychology and the philosophy of mind.
Eliminativism refers to the claim that standard common-sense
psychological, or 'folk psychological', terms such as 'intention',
'belief', 'will' can be eliminated as causal factors in human action
and replaced by a pure materialist language of what is happening
in the brain. In *Deconstructing the Mind*, he is more cautious
about a complete Eliminativist programme than in his earlier
work.

Stich is following a hard-science naturalist programme in philosophy, according to which philosophical problems can be
approached by considering them as questions in the natural world,
using the methods and results of the natural, or hard, sciences.
This is not the place to consider the various forms of this programme, and their claims, but in order to situate Derrida we need
to note the enormous influence of this approach in Analytic philosophy, particularly since the late 1960s. Naturalist work in philosophy of mind does not appear to have much in common with
Derrida, who is largely concerned with classics of philosophy,
along with texts of equal stature in the humanities and social sciences. In some respects Derrida must be taken as in opposition to
Naturalism since his criticisms of Positivism in all its forms, but
particularly Structuralism, should apply to the Naturalist programme in philosophy, which in some ways carries on the posi-
tivistic reduction of philosophy to science. Perhaps the clearest
example is his criticisms of Benveniste's attempts to subordinate
philosophy to linguistics, in 'The supplement of copula' (in MP).

However, attempts to divide philosophy neatly into schools, and
a set of disagreements between them, are intrinsically misleading.
Derrida's references to Freud place him with Naturalism, even if
most Analytic Naturalism is more concerned with brain sciences
and experimental psychology. Some Analytic philosophers dismiss
any claims of scientific objectivity for Freud, or just ignore him,
but the same could be said of the attitude of some figures in
Continental European philosophy to Freud; and since
Wittgenstein, at least, there has been Analytic and Naturalist

interest in Freudian analysis. Wittgenstein's own place with regard to Naturalism is ambiguous since he is a target of criticism in Naturalist philosophy, which to some degree displaced Wittgenstein from the centre of current Analytic philosophy to the history of Analytic philosophy, but he can also be read in a Naturalist way. Naturalism is such a broad term that it can encompass a very wide range of philosophers and positions. So, for example, Nietzsche has been taken up by some as a Naturalist, even though he is often read as a philosopher of subjective aestheticism.

There are extreme variations of opinion about the status of psychoanalysis in all philosophical traditions. We will not attempt to arrive at a conclusion about the status of psychoanalysis, or Derrida's status as a commentator on psychoanalysis. The discussion will be confined to what Derrida's discussion of psychoanalysis says about the mind and consciousness, as far as possible focusing on what belongs to any discussion of the mind, and not just to a discussion of psychoanalysis.

What Derrida has to say about Freud, particularly in 'Freud and the scene of writing' (WD 7), brings his views of writing into the study of the mind. What he emphasizes is the status of writing as repetition with no origin present. It is particularly in the discussions of the mind in Phenomenology and in psychoanalysis that Derrida puts this in the context of 'trace' and 'deferral'. In the context of psychoanalysis, he also brings in the 'nachträglich'. This is a word Freud uses for the way that the unconscious mind, particularly as it may be accessed in dreams, always shows itself as an after work of the unconscious thought. The primary elements of the unconscious mind never show themselves; they are never present in their original form. We are always looking at an after work, the effects of the thought or the event in our memory, after the event. We always have a memory of the event, not the event itself, or even the original form of the memory. In its general usage, 'nachträglich' can be translated as additional or supplementary, something Derrida emphasizes. The whole Freudian model of the after work in the mind can be conceived as 'writing' in Derrida's sense of those necessary aspects of language in which intention and meaning are always a repetition of an absent original intention or meaning.

The conscious text is thus not a transcription, because there is no text *present elsewhere* as an unconscious one to be transposed or transported. For the value of presence can also dangerously affect the concept of the unconscious. There is then no unconscious truth to be rediscovered by virtue of having been written elsewhere. There is no text written and present elsewhere which would then be subjected, without being changed in the process, to an operation and a temporalisation (the latter belonging to consciousness if we follow Freud literally) which would be external to it, floating on its surface. There is no present text in general, and there is not even a past present text, a text which is past as having been present. The text is not conceivable in an originary or modified form of presence. The unconscious text is already a wave of pure traces, differences in which meaning and force are united – a text nowhere present, consisting of archives which are *always already* transcriptions. Originary prints. Everything begins reproduction. Always already: repositories of a meaning which was never present, whose signified presence is always reconstituted by deferral, *nachträglich*, belatedly, *supplementarily*: for the *nachträglich* also means *supplementary*. The call of the supplement is primary, here, and it hollows out that which will be reconstituted by deferral as the present.

(WD 211)

Writing appears above as 'text', which is another way of referring to what Derrida is emphasizing in 'writing'. Given the lack of literal writing in the unconscious, the 'text' as a means of communication becomes the convenient reference. On this basis he mixes references to writing and printing, both of which are characterized as copies of unseen originals so that there is no presence of the truth of what is in the unconscious. We cannot grasp the content of the unconscious by thinking in terms of truth, because there is no end to the series of repetitions that make up the unconscious, which is more like a kind of pure space or energy than a thing, in the more common-sense understanding of 'thing'. However, the Freudian unconscious is not just a convenient ready-made example of Deconstruction or writing. Derrida just as much emphasizes the metaphysics of Freud's model. There is always a lurking sense in Freud of the presence of truth in the unconscious, even if his discussion of the unconscious provides the tools to overcome that.

The passage cited above does not just emphasize the 'deconstructive' aspects of Freud; it refers to the way that Freud assumes that temporalization belongs to the conscious mind. For Derrida, it is certainly the case that the Freudian unconscious might provide an example of how to get beyond a view of time as a linear sequence of moments, in which each moment is immediately present at that moment and is therefore an instance of present. That should lead us to conceive of time in the sense of after work, in which there is no moment that was just immediately there; every moment is already an effect of itself, existing in relation to past and future, which prevents the moment from ever achieving presence as an isolated moment in the present. The view of time Derrida brings in here is a very clear example of his relation with Heidegger. Heidegger develops such views in *Being and Time* (Heidegger 1962) and then modifies them, in a way summed up by 'Time and being' (in Heidegger 1972) to avoid the priority of time over space and the future over the other aspects of time, which Heidegger tends to assume in *Being and Time*.

However, other aspects of Derrida's discussion of the Freudian unconscious clearly refer to Nietzsche, as can be seen in the reference to the unity of force and meaning. Derrida draws attention to the way that the Freudian unconscious rests on a language of psychic forces with neurological origins, which recalls Nietzsche's fragmentation of the mind into physical and psychological forces, which are all physical in the end.[1] This should remind us of the eliminative materialism mentioned earlier in this chapter with reference to Stich, though Stich does not connect his work with Nietzsche. We see that there might be more that associates Derrida with some work in Analytic or Naturalistic philosophy than is often assumed. Where Derrida refers to force above, he is maybe thinking in part of the force of the transcendental in meaning on the empirical, but he cannot be separating this from the location of force and meaning in the psychic forces of the unconscious. The force of the transcendental, in Derrida, always marks the presence of the empirical in the abstract and the transcendental.

Freud emphasises this: psychic writing does not lend itself to translation because it is a single energetic system (however differentiated it may be), and because it covers the entirety of the psychical apparatus. Despite the difference of agencies, psychical writing in general is not a displacement of meanings within the limpidity of an immobile, pre-given space and the blank neutral of discourse. A discourse which might be coded without ceasing to be diaphanous. Here energy cannot be reduced; it does not limit meaning but rather produces it. The distinction between force and meaning is derivative in relation to an archi-trace; it belongs to the metaphysics of consciousness and of presence, or rather of presence in the word, in the hallucination of a language determined on the basis of the word or of verbal representation.

(WD 213)

What Derrida emphasizes above, in Freud, is the materialist elements of 'energetic system' and 'apparatus'. The distinction between force and meaning is read as secondary to archi-trace. In itself that seems to leave it open whether empirical material force or transcendental abstract meaning is primary. However, the passage as a whole gives the primary role to force, since it is energy that produces meaning; and in the sentence where the distinction between force and meaning is mentioned in the first part, the second part suggests that the distinction itself is metaphysical. Metaphysics includes consciousness, which Derrida explains through Presence. Consciousness undeniably exists, but, like the Materialist Eliminativists, Derrida presumes that we cannot explain consciousness through what is present in conscious thoughts. Some of the reasons Derrida offers are distinct from Materialist Eliminativism, which itself sometimes include positions that develop Merleau-Ponty's version of Phenomenology. What Derrida has in common with the Naturalist philosophy of mind in recent Analytic philosophy is that the contents of consciousness are treated as emergent from material properties, or, as Analytic philosophers often say, supervene on material properties. Words like 'emergent' or 'supervenes' tend to indicate a difficult philosophical jump. That jump covers a wide range of possible interpretations of what is going on in the emergence and supervenience; and in how far emergence or supervenience means the reduction of what emerges, or supervenes, to whatever it is that it emerges from, or supervenes on. In this case, we can at least say

that for Derrida that where there is any meaning present in consciousness, there is force in the energy, or apparatus, known as the
mind. In this case, mind, or consciousness, is a way of describing
material events. There is a capacity for self-introspection and self-
consciousness that distinguishes conscious matter from unconscious matter. For the most extreme Materialist Eliminativists, this
is not important, since if we can define the physical processes there
is nothing to add unless we confuse ourselves by inventing mental
entities, other than physical entities. It certainly looks like Derrida
should be grouped with the more moderate Eliminativists, since he
certainly has a lot to say about what is going on in consciousness
and implicitly accepts that mental and physical events are identical,
but are described in different ways.

SELF-CONSCIOUSNESS

> [P]henomenology seems to us tormented, if not contested from
> within, by its own descriptions of the movement of temporalization
> and of the constitution of intersubjectivity. At the heart of what ties
> together these two decisive moments of description we recognise an
> irreducible nonpresence as having a constituting value and with it a
> nonlife, a nonpresence or nonself-belonging of the living present, an
> ineradicable nonprimordiality. The names which it assumes only ren-
> der more palpable the resistance to the form of presence. Briefly, it is
> a question of (1) the necessary transition from retention to *re-presen-
> tation* (*Vergegenwärtigung*) in the constitution of the presence of a
> temporal object (*Gegenstand*) whose identity may be repeated; and
> (2) the necessary transition by way of *appresentation* in relation to the
> *alter ego*, that is, in relation to what also makes possible an ideal
> objectivity in general; for intersubjectivity is the condition for objectiv-
> ity, which is absolute only in the case of ideal objects.
>
> (SP 6–7)

Comments on Derrida's materialism are reinforced by his comments on language, in the passage above, where he refers to the
view of language as metaphysical if it is conceived as determined
by the word or verbal representation. This is partly a discussion of

ways of reading Freud, in which Derrida puts material forces mentioned by Freud above those places where Freud might be interpreted as giving psychic sovereignty to linguistic symbolism and the words present in our consciousness (and may well be an implicit criticism of Jacques Lacan).[2] These remarks certainly contradict the widespread assumption that Derrida is a linguistic idealist; and establish a general position where language is an inescapable moment in discussing consciousness, just as it is in any sphere of the human knowledge, but it is never sovereign as an abstraction from material forces. They also put into doubt another reading of Derrida in which he has largely taken over unacknowledged terms used by Jean-Paul Sartre in *Being and Nothingness* (Sartre 2003).[3] No doubt Derrida can be accused of not acknowledging Sartre enough as an influence, and the same goes only more so for Merleau-Ponty to whom he is closer, but this is a secondary issue at most. What is important is Derrida's relation with Sartre's account of the non-transparent aspects of consciousness. For our purposes, Sartre emphasizes two important things: 'bad faith' in which we deny our essential freedom by adopting an identity; that identity comes from taking ourselves as 'in-itself', a fixed entity, rather than as 'for-itself, consciousness with an infinity of possible changeable content'. 'Bad faith', the infinity of the for-itself and our tendency to reduce the for-itself to the in-itself all constitute opaque aspects of consciousness that anticipate the criticisms of any transparent consciousness in Derrida or anywhere else. These criticisms are usually referred to as Anti-Representationalism within Analytic philosophy, and sometimes draw on Continental European philosophy, including Sartre and Merleau-Ponty. However, the most notable example of this convergence occurs in Hubert Dreyfus's use of Heidegger's *Being and Time*.[4] Nevertheless Sartre's account really rests on the assumption that there is a transparent consciousness where intentions or meanings are completely present. Sartre's discussions of the opacities of consciousness are strongly moralistic in tone, and reflect an underlying assumption that we essentially have a transparent consciousness that exists as our moral ideal, and which we are distracted from by choices that are bad choices morally without the courage to face the pure transcendental emptiness of consciousness itself, which is where our freedom lies. These arguments have precedents in Fichte, Hegel and Kierkegaard, and are subject to criticism by Merleau-Ponty (Merleau-Ponty 1962).

Merleau-Ponty, like Sartre, made his philosophical name with a long treatise on Phenomenology. In Sartre's case it is *Being and Nothingness: A Phenomenological Ontology* (Sartre 2003) and in Merleau-Ponty's case it is *The Phenomenology of Perception* (Merleau-Ponty 1962). Merleau-Ponty has a strong argument for the deep intrinsic opacity of consciousness, which distinguishes him from the opposition between in-itself and for-itself assumed by Sartre. There are many appreciative mentions of Sartre in *Phenomenology of Perception*, with regard to the Phenomenological analyses of *Being and Nothingness* and the earlier *Sketch for a Theory of the Emotions* (Sartre 2001), but there is a constant shift away from any view in which there is a transparent consciousness waiting for us when we get past 'bad faith'. These arguments also distinguish Merleau-Ponty from the intellectualist and transcendental aspects of Husserl's Phenomenology, in which Merleau-Ponty anticipates Derrida and that puts Derrida in a full Phenomenological context. In part Merleau-Ponty draws on Husserl to oppose Sartre, because Husserl's emphasis on the sedimentation of consciousness, on the layers of consciousness, undermines the idea of a consciousness that can be grasped in its entirety with no opaque parts. What unifies Husserl and Sartre, from Merleau-Ponty's point of view, is the tendency to assume that consciousness is transcendental and can be treated as an intellectual construct. Merleau-Ponty remains within the Phenomenological view according to which any 'intention' of consciousness transcends the objects of consciousness, but nevertheless consciousness for Merleau-Ponty is continuous with the body and the world. The contents of consciousness, even if abstracted from the world and the body, are opaque. Consciousness is structured as a relation between figure, background and horizon. What this means is that whatever we are focusing on in the foreground of our consciousness can only be there in a relation with the background of consciousness and the periphery where perceptions are coming into, and going out of, consciousness. In *Phenomenology of Perception*, Merleau-Ponty partly explains this with recourse to

Gestalt psychology, observations of perceptual and mental dys-functions, and occasionally the physical functioning of the brain. In his last book, *The Visible and the Invisible* (Merleau-Ponty 1968), the references to scientific psychology are absent and there is a more purely philosophical concern with the contradictions that arise when trying to focus on the perceptions of consciousness, contradictions in that there is an origin, but it is never completely available to us. In relation to Sartre, there is a constant criticism of the metaphysically absolute distinction between in-itself and for-itself, even though Sartre himself sometimes used examples from scientific psychology himself, which is overtly directed at Hegel, but is definitely a covert criticism of Sartre. There is no absolute opposition between opaque material finitude and infinite transpar-ent consciousness; consciousness is opaque in relation to itself, and even where we put the body aside as in the later Merleau-Ponty it must return in the opacity at the origin and limit of perceptions, which Merleau-Ponty labels 'flesh' in *The Visible and the Invisible*.

Derrida's own work on the phenomenology of consciousness, particularly in SP, clearly has relations with Merleau-Ponty's posi-tion. However, he explores claims that can be found in Merleau-Ponty in his own terms. In particular, the claims that consciousness is not transparent to itself; and that it cannot be abstracted from relations with the body or the outside (defined both as physical environment and intersubjective communication with other con-scious beings). Much of what Derrida has to say on these topics builds on Hegel and Heidegger, brings in Freud, and, for Phenomenological advances on Husserl, mostly refers to Emmanuel Lévinas, though in SP Lévinas is only invoked indirectly. Lévinas is best known as a moral and religious philosopher, but his work is concerned with Phenomenology as a whole, including the status of metaphysics, language and consciousness. His influence on ideas of ethics and religion mean that we will focus more on Lévinas in Chapter 6, but his work is important for grasping Derrida's early Phenomenological essays. The most important text from that point of view is *Totality and Infinity* (Lévinas 1999). There is another text that is usually taken to form the centre of Lévinas's work, along with *Totality and Infinity*, *Otherwise than Being* (Lévinas 1998);

however, it appeared after the texts by Derrida we are considering, and is marked by a reaction to those texts, particularly 'Violence and metaphysics', a long essay on Lévinas in WD. The earlier phase of Lévinas's work is highly relevant to SP, as Lévinas argues for the impossibility of the self grasping its own consciousness as an absolute. The self can never be absolute because it always exists in relation to its outside, which always transcends it, in a way that Lévinas refers to as God and as the face of the Other, with whom we are always in an ethical relation.

Derrida had strong differences with Lévinas, which will be mentioned in later chapters; however, the points in Lévinas concerned with otherness are very pertinent for Derrida's approach to consciousness. There is no possibility of a self-enclosed sovereign consciousness that is transparent to itself abstracted from any externalities. In Derrida, the points are made through a close discussion of Husserl, which is where Lévinas started his own academic work, where Derrida follows the deconstructive procedure of arguing for unavoidable contradictions in Husserl's Phenomenology. Husserl refers to an ego that is transcendent in relation to the outside world and any empirical content of consciousness. As we have seen in the last chapter, this meant for Husserl that, preceding all communication and language, there is an inner monologue. According to Derrida, if we are going to do more in the discussion of consciousness than create abstract transcendental schemata, we must acknowledge that the pure soliloquy is impossible. There is no consciousness that does not include the outside within itself, because of the nature of communication and language. This can be shown to be the case in any analysis of consciousness, however much we try to isolate it from any outside. All the perceptions of consciousness are conditioned by time and death.

> If the experience of my disappearance in general must somehow be experienced in order for a relationship with presence in general to be instituted, we can no longer say that the experience of the possibility of my absolute disappearance (my death) affects me, occurs to an *I am*, and modifies a subject. The *I am*, being experienced only as an *I am present*, itself presupposes the relationship with presence in general, with being as presence. The appearing of the *I* to itself in the *I*

am is thus originally a relation with its own possible disappearance. Therefore, *I am* originally means *I am mortal*. *I am immortal* is an impossible proposition. We can even go further: as a linguistic statement 'I am that who am' is the admission of a mortal.

(SP 54 [Slightly modified translation. BS])

It is with regard to these points that Hegel and Heidegger make the most obvious appearance in Derrida's arguments about consciousness. The position on death can be traced back to the place of death in Hegel's *Phenomenology of Spirit* (Hegel 1977). For Hegel, death appears in a general way in his dialectic and in a particular moment. Hegel's dialectic depends on the negation of any particular judgement, in order to arrive at a more universal judgement. Negation cannot just be a logical act for Hegel; dialectic is not about formal logic, which is just a moment in the dialectic. Negation is the negation of the contents of consciousness, as in Hegel's Idealism, as in the other German Idealists, Kant, Fichte and Schelling, a judgement is always an act of consciousness because an idea is always an idea in consciousness, never something abstracted from consciousness. The negation of the particular in the dialectic is the negation of the contents of a state of consciousness. The negation can only take hold if consciousness is negated, which means the consciousness having awareness of the possibility of its negation. If consciousness is aware of its possible negation, it is aware of its own possible death, that is death as necessary for there to be consciousness.

Derrida does not follow the Idealist programme, so the contents of judgement are never restricted to the contents of consciousness as the judgement is something that exceeds any particular state of consciousness in its scope and can be made by any number of different consciousnesses. The possibility of its repetition and multiple use means that it cannot be reduced to the contents of any particular intention. The judgement as an act of consciousness is never a purely conscious event in the sphere of conscious ideals and thought. The judgement as a particular meaningful event is the product of force, energy and material apparatus. There is no possible elimination of the particularity of force except in a Platonist metaphysics, which completely excludes consciousness from judgement. Husserl has to bring in Platonist metaphysics to explain the transcendental structures of the ego, which creates an uneliminable tension with the Phenomenological description of the contents of consciousness. At the origins of logically orientated Analytic philosophy, Gottlob Frege resorted to Platonist metaphysics in order to establish the independence of logically formed propositions from particular states of mind. Ever since, Analytic philosophers have distinguished between the proposition as a pure abstract meaning and the empirical sentence.

Derrida approaches death in Hegel from a position that is distinct from Hegel's Idealism. What Derrida emphasizes in the role of death is that the subject of consciousness necessarily might die before grasping the contents of any state of consciousness.

> To think of presence as the universal form of transcendental life is to open myself to the knowledge that in my absence, beyond my empirical existence, before my birth and after my death, *the present is*. I can empty all empirical content, imagine an absolute overthrow of the *content* of every possible experience, a radical transformation of the world. I have a strange and unique certitude that this universal form of presence, since it contains no determined being, will not be affected by it. The relationship with *my death* (my disappearance in general) thus lurks in this determination of being as presence, ideality, the absolute possibility of repetition. The possibility of the sign is this relationship with death. The determination and elimination of the sign in metaphysics is the dissimulation of this relationship with death, which yet produced signification.
>
> (SP 54)

That place of death disrupts the certainty of intersubjective communication, as was discussed in the last chapter, but its effect is internal to the conscious subject as well. There is a monologue of consciousness, so Husserl was not wrong to suggest there is such a thing, but there is no instantaneous grasp by the subject of the contents of monologue. The moment of origin is always distinct from the moment of comprehending reception, and that always allows for the possibility of the death of the subject who will never grasp that moment of the monologue though it took place within the subject. The monologue is always a dialogue, and as such it is always an intersubjective communication. This again has some roots in Hegel, for whom self-consciousness is always divided between its itself as consciousness and its otherness as consciousness aware of contents that come from outside itself. Such a distinction is always a distinction between the inner contents of consciousness and the existence of an outside of consciousness that is received into the contents of consciousness.

Death also appears in Heidegger, in a particularly famous section from *Being and Time* (Heidegger 1962) on Being-towards-death. In Heidegger's argument, death is the impossibility as the end of possibilities, which is the possibility most authentic for *Dasein*, the kind of being that humans have. It is authentic for *Dasein* because it is non-relational, that is death is unique to an individual and cannot be communicated. Death is not just the biological death of the body; it is the possibility that we always have of death and that we may die at any moment. Death is more than the end that comes to entities: it is an end already within *Dasein* because it is a condition of *Dasein* to have a possibility unique to itself, which exceeds the grasp of any other *Dasein*. It is an end of which *Dasein* is always aware, when it is directed to what it is, and away from external distractions. These comments are important for Derrida, but, as with Hegel, in a transformed context. Derrida does not refer to *Dasein* or authenticity; his reasons for doing so are particularly explained in 'The ends of man' (in MP), and will be discussed in Chapter 6. What can be said here is that Derrida finds these terms to be a form of metaphysics, in which the human is entirely directed to a metaphysical goal of a human essence. Death is a major preoccupation for Derrida, though not in the sense that he is obviously morbid. Death is to do with the lack of essence within consciousness, the way in which there is constant change of content, which following Nietzsche and Freud can be regarded as emergent from the forces from which consciousness itself emerges. The awareness of otherness, the outside and the limits of consciousness, always confronts us with a limitation, which is the death of consciousness as absolute or sovereign.

The appearance of death in consciousness, and other aspects of Derrida's philosophy, also refers to the work of Maurice Blanchot. Blanchot's work includes literary creation, literary criticism and philosophy. As with Lévinas, there was a mutual influence that was important for both sides. Blanchot also had an important impact on Lévinas and Foucault. Derrida's explicit discussions of Blanchot largely belong to a later stage of his career than is covered by the present book. What can be said here is that Blanchot dwelled on the limits of experience, particularly literature as a place of the limits of experience.[5] For Blanchot, literature is not so much an expression of subjective inner consciousness as an expression of the limits of consciousness, which Blanchot referred to as death, night, the neutral and so on. If literature is really literary then it is where the self is dying, as it becomes a literary work where the self is absent from its creation, and where the experience of the loss of self, of death, in various forms is marked. Consciousness is conditioned by death and time according to Derrida, with the account of time strongly oriented towards that of Heidegger. Heidegger's position in *Being and Time*, as the title suggests, is to make time primary in grasping Being. Being is grasped from the point of view of *Dasein*, which is the kind of being that humans have, and *Dasein* is a being that is concerned with the question of Being. As such, *Dasein* experiences itself as ahead of itself, as what has potentiality, as what goes outside of itself in its Being-in-the-world. Death is fundamental in establishing the way in which *Dasein* is directed ahead of itself, so that it experiences itself as Being-in-time and experiences temporality as the horizon of Being. Therefore, the interpretation of Being must be a temporal interpretation. At this point, for Heidegger, a non-metaphysical way of thinking depends on a grasp of time and a temporal grasp of Being. Time itself must be grasped in a non-metaphysical way, and that means avoiding the interpretation in which time is a series of now-points. Instead time must be seen as a fusion of past, present and future, orientated towards the future. There is change in Heidegger's position so that later works put much less emphasis on time and give a different account of time, particularly in 'Time and being' (in Heidegger 1972), where the threefold of time is unified in a four play with space, which is itself defined with reference to appropriation, defined in turn with reference to Presence or Being.

Again, for Derrida, there is an important attempt to overcome metaphysics here along with a continuing adherence to a metaphysics of the essence of humanity in Being or Presence. For his account of consciousness, largely staged as a reading of Husserl rather than as a direct philosophical argument about the mind, Heidegger's account of time is clearly significant. Consciousness is in part opaque because of time; the instant in which I need to grasp the contents of consciousness distances me from that content, which always evades our grasp in this way.

> As soon as we admit this continuity of the now and the not-now, perception and non-perception, in the zone of primordiality common to primordial impression and primordial retention, we admit the other into the self-identity of the *Augenblick* [the instant/blink of the eye. BS]; nonpresence and nonevidence are admitted into the blink of the instant. There is a duration to the blink, and it closes the eye. This alterity is in fact the condition for presence, presentation, and thus for *Vorstellung* [presentation in the sense of an idea. BS]. The difference between retention and reproduction, between primary and secondary memory, is not the radical difference Husserl wanted between perception and nonperception. Whatever the phenomenological difference between these two modifications may be, and despite the immense problems it poses and the necessity of taking them into account, it only serves to separate two ways of relating them to the irreducible nonpresence of another now. Once again, this relation to nonpresence neither befalls, surrounds, nor conceals the presence of the primordial impression; rather it makes possible its ever renewed upsurge and virginity. However, it radically destroys any possibility of a simple self-identity. And this holds in depth for the constituting flux itself.
>
> (SP 65–6)

The moments of time cannot be grasped because they only exist in a shifting fusion of past, present and future. In this case, there is possibility of the presence of any content of consciousness in 'the blink of an eye' (SP 5). The momentary content of consciousness is always conditioned by temporality and is never a self-contained point in time, defined as a series of points. There is no suggestion of the priority of the future in Derrida, putting him closer to the later Heidegger than the earlier Heidegger on that point. The impossibility of the pure presence of a living present is defined with regard to the impossibility of eliminating memory from Husserlian Phenomenology, though Husserl would like to elimi-

nate memory from the pure description of the contents of consciousness. Since no moment is present to us in a self-contained
way, there is always retention in experience. In every moment of
experience, however fleeting it may appear, there is the retention
of something from the past, in order for there to be an experience.
Experience cannot be defined in a momentary way as it always
includes memory in some minimal form as retention.

> Husserl specifies . . . that my transcendental ego is radically different
> from my natural and human ego; and yet it is distinguished by noth-
> ing, nothing that can be determined in the natural sense of distinc-
> tion. The (transcendental) ego is not an other. It is certainly not the
> formal or metaphysical phantom of the empirical ego. Indeed this
> leads us to take the ego – as absolute spectator of its own psychic
> self – to be but a theoretical image and metaphor. We would also
> expose the analogical character of language which must sometimes
> be used to announce the transcendental reduction as well as to
> describe that unusual 'object', the psychic self as it confronts the
> absolute transcendental self. In fact no language can cope with the
> operation by which the transcendental ego constitutes and opposes
> itself to its worldly self, its soul, reflecting itself.
>
> (SP 11–12)

The problems of any attempt to define consciousness as transparent, and as containing at any moment a purely present immediate
experience, also apply to self-awareness. There is no possibility of
grasping my inner self as a whole. At this point language has a
particularly important role to play in Derrida's argument. The
need for consciousness to represent its moments, to itself, means
that it is always already caught up in language. Language becomes
even more notable when we are concerned with the relation of the
self, to itself. The self relates to itself, by naming itself. That kind
of naming is both the most proper and unique kind of naming,
because it is the name the self gives to itself within its own consciousness and is therefore fixed in the least ambiguous way possible; and it is the most universal and general kind of name. It is the
most general and universal kind of name because it is the self that
knows itself as 'I'. 'I' has a purely contextual meaning: that is there

is no content to 'I' and there is no description attached to it other than the particular self given to us in a particular context. These qualities of 'I' are generally referred to by labelling it a shifter, a demonstrative or an indexical. These labels are used because 'I' shifts in meaning according to context, has its meaning in the particular thing it demonstrates in a particular context, and exists only as an index of the thing that is the 'I' in a particular context. The 'I' is the most proper and improper of names, the unique name and the universal name. As was argued in the last chapter, for Derrida the proper is the opposite of what it is claimed to be. The proper must be metaphorical, the improper use of a name since no name can be used in a strictly and absolutely proper sense. The 'I' must be understood on that model; it is the improper proper name, so it is attached by metaphor. There is no description or content that can tie the 'I' to the self of the speaker. No name is further removed from what it names, because it is the most universal name. Only a metaphorical relation can attach the name of the speaking subject to the subject, the most pure metaphor in which the universal sign is turned away from its universal place to the most particular place, which is metaphor for Derrida. And it can only be applied within consciousness as conditioned by time and death. It is always the name that must be improper because the state of consciousness referred to in the 'I' has disappeared by the time the 'I' names it as a moment in the experience of 'I'. 'I' can only apply across moments, and therefore can only apply to the moment, on the condition of a retention across moments that contaminates the purity of the moment, which is the moment where 'I' is present at this moment. There can only be an 'I' as a name that 'I' gives to itself, and in the moment of that naming 'I' could die, so that the name is never the name of anything. For Derrida, the possibility of non-arrival of name, of a message of any kind, as described in 'Signature event context' (in MP), shows that its arrival is non-necessary and cannot be taken as part of the name or message, therefore the sending of the name or message rests on the possibility of its non-arrival. It is only possible through the contradiction between a sending premised on the arrival of what is sent, and the non-arrival of what is sent.

5

KNOWLEDGE
ORIGIN AND STRUCTURE

OBJECTS OF KNOWLEDGE

Derrida deals with knowledge largely with reference to the history of science, the philosophy of social science and the nature of consciousness, which has already been discussed in the last chapter. Epistemology is the branch of philosophy devoted to knowledge. The philosophy of science and the philosophy of social science can be considered as branches of epistemology, though generally the word 'epistemology' is reserved for the more general problems of knowledge, while the philosophy of science and the philosophy of social science are demarcated as branches dealing with more specific issues. Epistemology as a general branch tends to converge with philosophy of mind, since the question of the mind's relation with the outside world has often been taken as the essential problem of epistemology.

Derrida does not provide a position on what the best theory of knowledge or philosophy of science is. He has very little at all to say about the physical sciences, and, apart from his early discussion of geometry with regard to Husserl, it is mostly social and linguistic science that concerns him. This is particularly the case for OG, which largely deals with these areas. Derrida is more concerned with the presence of metaphysical assumptions in discussions of knowledge, along with the philosophical pre-conditions of there being knowledge of any kind. This is more an exploration of the ambiguities of reason than a contribution to the theory of knowledge. What Derrida finds in philosophical discussion of knowledge, particularly with regard to Husserl's Phenomenology, is that it requires notions of 'origin' and 'structure', which are both opposed to, and dependent on, each other, placing knowledge in a position of perpetual equivocation.

> But while completely justifying the priority of his reflections on logic, Husserl also specifies in *Formal and Transcendental Logic* that this is only one path among others: '*Other paths* are possible for sense-investigations with a radical aim; and this present work attempts to open up, at least in the main sections, one suggested by the histori-cally given relation of the idea of genuine science to logic as its antecedent norm.' Also, by a *spiralling movement*, which is the major find of our text, a bold clearing is brought about within the regional limits of the investigations and transgresses them toward a new form of radicality. Concerning the intentional history of a particular eidetic science in general, a sense-condition investigation of its conditions of possibility will reveal to us exemplarily the conditions and sense then of the historicity of science in general, then of universal historicity – the last horizon for all sense and Objectivity in general. Consequently, the architectonic relations evoked a moment ago are complicated, if not inverted. This would demonstrate, if it were still necessary, at what point the juridical order of implications is not so linear and how difficult it is to recognize the starting point.
>
> (IOG 33–4)

As we have mentioned a few times before, Derrida's philosophy is rather burdened with the image of extreme scepticism, despite Derrida's resistance to such a label. The sceptical label is applied to Derrida on the assumption that he is engaged in the rather unsub-tle business of undermining all knowledge claims for the sake of scepticism as an end in itself. All this is part of the negative stereo-type of Derrida as an unserious writer who tries to undermine any positive claims in philosophy. Though Derrida does not establish a theory of knowledge, he does establish claims about what condi-tions any particular theory of knowledge, in the sense both of what is necessary in order for there to be any possible theory of knowledge; and the effects on all theories of knowledge. In that way Derrida contributes to the theory of knowledge by establishing the following conditions for it: an equivocal distinction between origin and structure; an equivocal distinction between the contents of experience and the contents of abstract thought including general laws; an equivocal distinction between origin as historical beginning and origin as first principles; an equivocal distinction between the structural qualities of knowledge and the purpose of knowledge. In the case of social science, there is also an equivocal distinction between the natural and the social. Derrida's first notable publication was a contribution to theory of knowledge. This did not take the form of a work on knowledge, but instead appears in the long introduction Derrida wrote to Husserl's short essay, 'The origin of geometry' (IOG). Derrida does not offer a theory of knowledge but explores the implications of Husserl's texts and what that might show us going beyond the more obvious claims made by Husserl.

In 'The origin of geometry', Husserl is concerned with the relation between the origin of geometry in ideal structures of thought and the origin of geometry as its genesis at a moment of time in history. The relation between genesis and structure in Husserl is the theme of another essay by Derrida. The origin of geometrical knowledge has historical and ideal aspects, which cannot easily be combined. There must be a moment at which any geometrical theorem appears; there may be difficulties in defining such a moment but that is not the issue here. There is definitely a historical event, or process, of some kind in which the knowledge claims of geometry appear. However, the objects of geometrical knowledge never appear anywhere in time and space. We do not encounter geometrical objects as we investigate the world, since the geometrical objects do not exist outside the rules and principles of geometry. There are many objects we may describe as circular or triangular, but the geometrical circle of triangle is a perfect shape. Its lines have no width and its points occupy no space at all. These objects cannot exist except as ideal objects. Ideal objects have no particular origin at a particular moment in space. Their origin is a logical relation of dependence on the principles necessary to describe such objects and use them in geometry.

In a non-descriptive pure science, the mode of sedimentation is such that no signification ceases to circulate at any moment and can always be reconceived and reawakened in its circulation. If it was necessary then to distinguish between natural reality and spiritual culture, we must now discriminate, in order to understand pure culture and traditionality in general, between empirical culture and that of truth. In other words, between de facto historical culture, on the one hand, in which sense-sedimentation does not exclude the fact that validity (which is rooted in a language, terrain, epoch, and so forth) can become dated, and on the other hand, the culture of truth, whose ideality is absolutely normative. No doubt, the latter would be *in fact* impossible without the former. But on the other hand, the culture of truth is the highest and most irreducible possibility of empirical culture, on the other hand, the culture of truth is itself only the possibility of a *reduction* of empirical culture and is manifested to itself only through such a reduction, a reduction which has become possible by an irruption of the infinite as a revolution within empirical culture.

(IOG 59)

Husserl's priority is the ideal objects of geometry. That follows from Husserl's Platonist inclinations, according to which objects exist primarily as ideal objects of consciousness. Consciousness itself exists primarily as ideal structures with ideal objects of pure intentionality abstracted from any empirical content of consciousness. That is why geometry is of interest to Husserl; it seems like the model for all science since it has the qualities of pure Phenomenology. Geometry is concerned with objects of consciousness, which are ideal and lacking in empirical content. For Husserl, geometry is more interesting than the other parts of mathematics since it is geometry that is concerned with objects, which can be objects of perception. The geometrical object itself is never perceived, only represented in the diagrams that assist geometrical demonstration. Nevertheless, we can represent geometrical objects as empirical objects of perception, and that is generally what is going on in geometrical demonstrations. This gives geometry a quality lacking in the rest of mathematics. The ideal object that never appears empirically but can be represented empirically could be a description of how Husserl thinks of pure Phenomenological objects. The essential object of knowledge for Husserl is the ideal object of pure consciousness, and the nearest we can get to that in a specific science may be geometry. Phenomenology is not set up to be concerned with specific sciences, but with the basis of all sciences. Particular sciences can only refer to regions of Phenomenology, not to the objects of Phenomenology as pure Phenomenology. Despite this, there are evident qualities of geometry that attract Husserl as the model of science as conceived in Phenomenology.

There is precedent for this going back to Plato. A famous passage in the *Meno* shows Socrates arguing that knowledge is a form of memory by getting an uneducated slave boy to follow a geometrical demonstration. Socrates argues that if the slave boy followed the demonstration with no previous knowledge of geometry, then the knowledge was already in him, and must have been there since birth. This applies to all the knowledge that everyone has. Since we cannot recognize something without previous knowledge of it, and we cannot have knowledge of things unless we recognize them, we must have knowledge from recognition rooted in memories that precede our conscious learning processes. Another precedent can be found in Kant, where geometry is derived from the absolute forms of our institution of the space of the outside world. Before Kant, Descartes, Spinoza and Pascal all suggested in various ways that geometry is a paradigm of knowledge, though in the case of Pascal it is also a paradigm of the contradictions inherent in any attempt to find foundations for knowledge.[1] According to Pascal, first principles in geometry cannot be justified. They cannot be justified by geometry since we have to assume these principles in order to have a science of geometry. They cannot be justified by any other source since geometry is the most pure of sciences, not resting on other knowledge or principles. The first principles of geometry can only be known as 'self-evident', that is ideas that we recognize as true at the moment in which we grasp them. Self-evidence is its own justification, since if we try to find a justification two things can happen. First, we may get into a circle as self-evident first principles can only be justified by a return to themselves in their self-evident first principles status. Second, we may get into an abyss, or infinite regress, in which justifications require justifications, which require justifications and so on in a logically infinite series. This is a response to clear and simple ideas in Descartes, according to which knowledge comes from those ideas in our minds that are most perfectly clear and simple. Nothing is obscure in them; to grasp them or to be acquainted with them is to know them perfectly; and they cannot be broken down into more basic ideas. Pascal's discussion of geometry, and of clear and simple ideas, with reference to Descartes, anticipates Derrida's discussion of Husserl on geometry.

Both Pascal and Derrida are concerned with the paradoxes at the origin of knowledge, at the origin of what appears to be the most definite form of knowledge. Unlike Pascal, though, Derrida is concerned with the historical nature of geometry. The science must have a history, a necessity that is in tension with the claims of science to be concerned with abstract truths beyond empirical circumstances in history. Both the ideal nature of geometry and its historical nature infect geometry with a human perspective. The ideal exists as an ideal of human consciousness and the history is the history of human consciousness. This does in general repeat Pascal's concern with the futility and inapplicability of pure Rationalism in philosophy and in geometry. The empirical is no alternative for Pascal, since the empirical is what belongs to experience and experience is subject to a large variety of illusions and deceptions. Pascal is not just a sceptic though; he argues that we can find grounds for knowledge in 'reasons of the heart', which are less subjective than the phrase suggests. Given that there is no justification of a purely rational or purely empirical kind for knowledge and science, we must refer back to the inner inclinations towards certain principles that do provide a successful basis for science, if not knowledge at its most absolute. The emphasis on 'reasons of the heart' is not present in Derrida, but this sense of knowledge as emerging from paradox is. That is paradox in the sense of paradoxes of reason and the sense of a paradoxical relation between the transcendental (reason) and the empirical. From that point of view, knowledge can only emerge in an arbitrary moment of force, when an idea is adopted without complete justification in order to provide a beginning for knowledge and science.

THEORIES OF KNOWLEDGE AND THE
EPISTEMOLOGICAL BREAK

In terms of the standard discussion of epistemological theories, Derrida (like Pascal) is a critic of 'Foundationalism'. 'Foundationalism' refers to a widespread distinction between Foundationalism and Coherentism in the theory of knowledge. A Foundationalist position is one in which knowledge is derived from absolute foundations in contents of consciousness that cannot be doubted; a Coherentist position is one in which knowledge is derived from ideas in consciousness that cohere with each other. In each case, the definition may be expressed in a more social and intersubjective way. Derrida does not explicitly take up either of these positions, or alternatives such as Pragmatism, which suggests that knowledge is where we have ideas, which can produce desired results in practice. Derrida's comments on Husserl could be applied to all these positions. Foundationalism, Coherentism and Pragmatism are all caught in an equivocation between pure ideas in knowledge and the empirical conditions in which these ideas arise.

The precedents for Derrida's epistemological reflections can be found in Heidegger and in a French approach to epistemology, which can be found in Gaston Bachelard, Georges Canguilhelm, Louis Althusser and Michel Foucault. All four, like Derrida, spent all or part of their career in Paris at the Sorbonne and the connected *École normale supérieure*. They are all connected by the concept of 'epistemological break' (referred to as 'epistemological breach' in the English edition of OG). The phrase was made well known by Louis Althusser, who had been Bachelard's doctoral student, at a time when Althusser was a major influence in the study of Marx and Marxist philosophy.[2] Althusser was a teacher of both Foucault and Derrida, though neither was a clear Marxist at the time of their major publications. Althusser famously suggested an epistemological break between an early humanist-idealist Marx and a later materialist-scientific Marx. This was part of a view of science as a series of continents established by the break with pre-scientific concepts, so establishing the correct object for scientific concepts. It was Bachelard who coined the phrase 'epistemological break' in his discussion of science since Einstein, which he suggested broke with the old distinction between the materialist and the idealist, since contemporary physics refers to the point of view of the observer ('Idealism') in its description of physical objects ('Materialism') and is less mechanically deterministic than previous science. He later went on to discuss the Phenomenology of objects in a particularly subjective and aesthetic way, which tries to exclude any transcendental or metaphysical ideas, or any claim to have pure ideas independent of subjective experience. Derrida refers to this aspect of Bachelard in IOG, briefly to the 'epistemological breach' in 'Of grammatology as a positive science' (OG I 3), and to the 'epistemological break' in 'The linguistic circle of Geneva' (in MP). The 'epistemological break' was taken up by Canguilhelm with reference to work in the history of biology and medicine, where he explored the status of the object of science, which he took as the concepts created by scientific reason rather than empirical objects themselves, and which can never be known independently of the concepts we use in our scientific systems. Like Bachelard, he emphasized changes in the concepts of science, and the general shifts in scientific outlook, which make change in concepts necessary. This line of thought bears comparison with the extremely influential work of the American historian and philosopher of science, Thomas Kuhn. In *The Structure of Scientific Revolutions* (Kuhn 1996), he claimed that science shifts between systems over time and that their assumptions are so distinct that their concepts cannot be compared, that is they are 'incommensurable' as there is no neutral way of testing them. Any test belongs to a system and its theoretical assumptions, which also incorporate social pressures within the scientific community and society as a whole. Foucault wrote an introduction to the most famous of Canguilhelm's books, *The Normal and the Pathological* (Canguilhelm 1991). Foucault took up the changeable opposition of the normal and the pathological, investigated by Canguilhelm, in *The Birth of the Clinic* (Foucault 2003) and *Madness and Civilisation* (Foucault 2001a). On a more general level, he took up the 'epistemological break' in *Archaeology of Knowledge* (Foucault 2002) in the discussion of changes in that archaeology. Like Althusser's work on Marx, this more parallels Derrida's early work on Husserl than anticipates it, but presumably Derrida's view of

Husserl was conditioned by Althusser and Foucault's lecture hall and seminar room expositions of the 'epistemological break'.

The reference in OG (OG 80–1) is a fleeting one in the context of a movement away from the prejudice in linguistics that Chinese characters are a form of hieroglyphics. A more substantial use appears in 'The linguistic circle of Geneva' (in MP), a text so closely related to OG it can serve as a partial summary of the book.

> On the condition and in the sense of a systematic formulation, one that defines the project of a theoretical science of language, in its method, its object, and its rigorously proper field. This might be accomplished by means of a gesture that for convenience's sake could be called an 'epistemological break', there being no assurance that the stated intention to 'break' has such an effect, nor that the so-called break is ever a – unique – datum in a work or an author. This first condition and first sense should always be implied by what we will entitle the *opening of the field*, it being understood that such an opening also amounts to a *delimitation* of the field.
>
> (MP 140)

Derrida continues the use of the 'epistemological break' a few pages later in the essay:

> [L]et us note that the so-called 'epistemological break' paradoxically corresponds to a kind of break in the field of natural causality. If 'speech', 'the first social institution, owes its form to natural causes alone', then the latter, themselves acting as a force of break with nature, *naturally* inaugurate an order radically *heterogeneous* to the natural order.
>
> (MP 143)

What Derrida brings to the understanding of the 'epistemological break' is that the institution of a field of science is always an epistemological break, which seems consistent with earlier usage. The interesting addition comes when Derrida points to the paradox underlying the notion of an epistemological break, in the context of language. Language is what defines the separation of the social from the natural, but, as was pointed out in Chapter 3, this establishes the paradox that a force which must have been natural in the first instance turns against nature in order to institute a break with nature, within nature. Derrida has little else to say explicitly about the epistemological break, but if the paradox of origin and structure in the Phenomenological account of geometry is repeated in every development of geometry, then the same must apply to the epistemological break. The break must be a paradoxical moment in which force is directed against transcendental claims, within those transcendental claims in order to establish new claims. One response to this might be to do more on the 'external' history of geometry, and other sciences, looking at their historical conditions rather than their 'internal' origin in concepts or ideas. However, this would leave the paradox of structure and origin in place. The 'epistemological break', like the relation of structure with origin, must be understood as an expression of unavoidable paradox, which will always be repeated however much work is done on the details of the history of science.

This paradox is concerned with circularity, which is half the point of the title 'The linguistic circle of Geneva', since it argues that the attempt to describe the origin of language will never avoid the circularity in which language, like all social institutions, only has an origin in its own concepts.

> [T]he circle in which tradition (or transmission) and language, thought and language, society and language, each precede the other, postulate and produce each other reciprocally. But these apparent, and apparently avowed, confusions have a reverse side for which in a way they pay the price. The circle, as a vicious circle, a logical circle, by the same token constitutes rigorously limited, closed, and original autonomy of a field. If there is no entry into the circle, if it is closed, if one is always already set down within it, if it has always already begun to carry us along in its movement, no matter where it entered, it is because the circle forms a perfectly underivable figure and does so by means of a continuous causality, something other than itself.
>
> (MP 145)

The possibility of circularity in the justification of knowledge is a constant concern for epistemologists. For the German tradition after Kant, circularity has often been taken as something inevitable in a non-threatening way. This position is established by Hegel in the Preface to the *Phenomenology of Spirit* and by Fichte in the early sections of the *Science of Knowledge* (Fichte 1982). Heidegger's version of this in the light of Husserl, and Hermeneutic discussions of interpretation, can be found in section 32 of *Being and Time* (Heidegger 1962). There, Heidegger discusses 'Understanding and interpretation' emphasizing the mutual inter-dependence between seeing that something is something and seeing that something as something. Heidegger concedes that this leads to circular reasoning but denies that the circle is vicious. The problem of circularity can be taken back at least as far as Plato in the *Meno* and the *Theaetetus*, which are both concerned in different ways with the difficulty of establishing knowledge of something, unless we already have knowledge of that thing. Anticipating the decon-structive position, Kierkegaard emphasizes these problems of the *Meno* in *Concluding Unscientific Postscript* (Kierkegaard 1992a).

INTERNAL AND EXTERNAL KNOWLEDGE

Derrida's account of knowledge and science in Husserl is concerned with the ideal structures of Husserl's thought and their relations with empirical historical conditions, in a deep constant equivoca-tion that belongs to the architectonic of Husserl's Phenomenology. In referring to an architectonic, Derrida also casts doubt on this model of knowledge, which appears in Foucault's earlier work, by pointing out the instability of any structure to which we might try to reduce knowledge. The model of the architectonic goes back to Kant and is therefore associated with his claims that there is a transcendental structure of reason preceding any particular knowl-edge or science. Derrida casts doubt on this rationalism, just as much as the kind of 'Foundationalist' reduction of knowledge to the purely empirical parts of consciousness, favoured by Empiricist philosophers. The Foucauldian model is always supposed to be more historicized than the Kantian model, but, from the Derridean point of view, it is inevitably caught up in an equivocation between empirical facts and pure structures.

The position is established in the discussion of Husserl, when Derrida refers to the difficulty Husserl has in reconciling his commitment to pure structures of transcendental consciousness with the empirical origins of knowledge. Here, two fundamental terms throughout Derrida's philosophy come into play in the early discussion of Husserl: double reduction and iterability. Husserl's Phenomenology relies on both in an unconscious way. Husserl consistently refers to a Phenomenological reduction in which there is a pure description of the contents of consciousness with no metaphysical or theoretical assumptions. The pure description requires two reductive moves of Husserl: the reduction of phenomena to pure ideas; the reduction of phenomena to the original empirical ideas in which they appear. These two reductions are not obviously consistent, and for Derrida they are an expression of the inevitable contradictions that arise in all attempts at pure philosophical foundations.

The other requirement for Phenomenology, which Derrida suggests undermines Phenomenology, is iterability. Iterability refers to repetition, but with an additional suggestion of otherness, as Derrida explains in 'Signature event context' (in MP). Iterability arises in Phenomenology because the pure idea is the copy of a finite idea. The existence of the pure idea is premised on the infinite repeatability of the finite idea, since the pure idea is an idea with infinite scope, which can contain an infinite number of identical finite ideas. The pure idea requires the iterability of the finite idea. The iterability of the finite idea undermines the consistent sense of an idea that is finite. If the idea is infinitely repeatable then it is already the pure idea with an infinite scope within its range. There is no idea that is not already the pure Phenomenological idea, leaving the empirical world obliterated. That paradox of iterability is itself contained within the question of the double reduction, since that rests on the unavoidable equivocation between the finite and infinite idea. Phenomenology must refer to the origin of ideas, including the ideas of science and knowledge in two senses: the necessary infinity of ideas; the necessarily finite nature of the first idea that is repeated as, or by, pure ideas.

Husserl's discussion of the history of geometry provides specific examples of these paradoxes, which have particular significance because of the status of geometry discussed above. Husserl must both emphasize the infinite scope of the pure ideas of geometry, as the origin of geometry, where it has its first principles; and the finite ideas that must have been the historical beginning of geometry. Someone, or maybe many people, must have had the principles of geometry as finite ideas in intuition, with regard to specific examples, before they were established as pure principles that are infinite in scope. However, since these ideas were the principles of geometry, there is an irreducible equivocation about whether geometry begins with pure ideas or with finite ideas. The problem is repeated at every stage of geometry. The appearance of new principles raises the same issue of whether they originate in pure or finite ideas.

Those are the genetic questions of geometry, but the structure is necessarily contradictory in its relation to the genesis of geometry. The very co-existence of the origin and the structure creates problems with regard to the consistency of the two. As pure science, as science of a particularly pure kind, geometry should transcend historical conditions as impurities in relation to structure. However, historical conditioning cannot be eliminated. Geometry has a history, in which there is a sedimentation of layers from the earlier history of the science. The science of geometry develops over time, so that the earlier developments are layers beneath the later developments. Geometry has emerged through building one layer of knowledge on top of another, and that conditions the appearance of the science at any one time. The infinite ideas of geometry belong to pure consciousness, but must have emerged in an intersubjective way, because ideas exist in the context of communicability in language. Chapter 3 has already referred to Derrida's criticisms of the idea of a pure soliloquy or a purely secret code, which parallel Wittgenstein's criticisms of a philosophically private language. The ideas of geometry can only exist as intersubjective ideas, and therefore cannot be pure ideas of transcendental consciousness. The issues of communicability also bring us to other issues of language. Geometrical science rests on linguistic expression, since it must be a part of language. Geometry, a science presented through symbols and written calculations, requires a written language, but from Husserl's point of view it must refer to pure ideas of inner consciousness. In that case geometry is again constituted by the equivocation of a double origin. Geometry must both originate in its permanent externally written form and the internal representations of consciousness. Within Husserlian Phenomenology, it must be the origin in inner consciousness which is primary, but that is destructive for geometrical science, for all science and for knowledge in general. Since knowledge exists as something that can be grasped outside the unique inner space of a single consciousness, it cannot essentially be something that exists as the pure ideas of one consciousness. That one consciousness itself is equivocal between consciousness in general, shared by many different minds, and the particular individual consciousness of one empirical mind. The purity of consciousness is itself equivocal between the oneness of all thought; and the manifold of different centres of consciousness. Once we discuss a particular consciousness in terms of its transcendental structure, then we have absorbed that consciousness into general consciousness. Once we refer to particular objects of general consciousness, we are back with the external empirical origins of the contents of mind.

Here Derrida raises issues familiar from debates about Internalism and Externalism in recent Analytic philosophy of mind, language and knowledge.[3] That is questions of whether the contents of the mind are explained by what goes on inside or by the causal effects of external facts on the mind. This is not an argument Derrida ever engaged with, and of which he had probably read little, if anything. Nevertheless a position on Internalism and Externalism does emerge in Derrida's thought, since he suggests a constant equivocation between them in questions of knowledge. There is a middle point in Derrida, but not in the sense of the place where moderate Internalism and moderate Externalism meet and merge with each other. It is more the place where the opposites come together because they require each other. There are no internal ideas without external facts as their source; and no external facts without the ideas that make sense of them. That relation is partly acknowledged in Husserl's discussion of sense and materiality, as in the distinction between expression and signification, discussed in Chapter 3 above. The Internalist–Externalist debate, and

Derrida's solution, look familiar from the point of view of Kant's philosophy. Kant distinguished between two philosophical tendencies, preceding his own work: empirical sceptical and metaphysical dogmatist. This equates with the distinction established since Kant between: Rationalism in Descartes, Spinoza and Leibniz; and Empiricism in Locke, Berkeley and Hume. The distinction emerges in Kant's philosophy in the opposition between concepts and intuitions in experience, and the opposition between their corresponding faculties of understanding and imagination in the mind. Kant's aim is to mediate between the two tendencies and their corresponding elements in experience and in the mind. The line of dogmatic metaphysics – rationalism – concepts – the understanding anticipates Internalism, while the line of sceptical empiricism – intuitions – the imagination anticipates Externalism. Internalism is where the mind constructs knowledge from its inner ideas, while Externalism is where the mind constructs knowledge from the contents of our experience of the external world. Kant mediates between the two extremes, but from the point of view of Internalism as he wishes to keep the possibility of transcendental entities, which he refers to as things-in-themselves, including a soul unaffected by empirical causality. Though Derrida suggests the indissoluble unity of the internal and the external, he does so from the point of view of Externalism, since he emphasizes that Deconstruction belongs to a philosophical tradition of challenging the transcendental from the point of view of the empirical. For example, he indicates sympathy with Nietzsche, and a liaison between Nietzsche and 'English thought', which must refer to the British Empiricists (MP 322). He suggests the role of Empiricist liberation from metaphysics in Nietzsche at greater length in 'The written being/the being written' (OG I 1).

> Radicalising the concepts of *interpretation, perspective, evaluation, difference*, and all the 'empiricist' or nonphilosophical motifs that have constantly tormented philosophy throughout the history of the West, and besides, have had nothing but the inevitable weakness of being produced in the field of philosophy. Nietzsche, far from remaining *simply* (with Hegel and as Heidegger wished) *within* metaphysics, contributed a great deal to the liberation of the signifier from its

dependence or derivation with respect to the logos and the related concept of truth or the primary signified, in whatever sense that is understood.

(OG 19)

Derrida places Hegel and Heidegger on the 'Internalist' side in opposition to Nietzsche's greater 'Externalism'. Derrida's reading of Husserl implicitly places him with Hegel and Heidegger in an exposé of the underlying Rationalism and Platonist metaphysics in Husserl's focus on pure ideas; and argues for the impossibility of eliminating the empirical. By situating these arguments with regard to Kant, we aim to show that Derrida's positions are comparable with what is going on in Analytic philosophy. Kant tends to provide a convenient way of finding common ground between Continental European philosophy and Analytic philosophy, since both can be shown to draw on positions and questions established by Kant. Despite Derrida's apparent distance from Analytic philosophy, it must be acknowledged that at least one major figure in recent Analytic epistemology, John McDowell, refers approvingly to Richard Rorty's book *Philosophy and the Mirror of Nature* (Rorty 1980), which is partly Derridean in inspiration.[4]

The emphasis of pure ideas in Husserl itself leads to the kind of metaphysical humanism discussed below in Chapter 6. There is a teleology inherent in the reduction to pure Ideas, which comes into conflict with the requirement of purity of structure for geometrical science, and which creates another level of equivocation in defining knowledge. The pure Ideas that Husserl seeks for in geometry, and in all science, must exist within consciousness and that can only mean within human consciousness. In that case, the structure of science must be guided by Ideas that exist as pure Ideas within consciousness. Empirical ideas outside the pure inwardness of consciousness are not sufficient as elements of science. For Husserl, this can only come from the capacity of the mind to create infinite ideas, which are pure ideas transcending empirical facts. That mind is a human mind, and as transcendental mind is the mind of humanity as transcendental humanity. In that case, Ideas are not just an element in the existing structure of science, they are the transcendental goal of science. Since the transcendental goal is contained in the mind of humanity, science unfolds in the historical progress of humanity. There is a *telos,* or goal of science, which is its completion as pure ideas and that is dependent on the development of humanity in a progress over history. Husserl's transcendentalism leads straight to a form of historicism, in which science exists as the result of the unfolding of an ideal history. The search for pure science has resulted in a Humanist teleology; and in an equivocation between science as pure structure and science as orientated by an external goal of the completion of humanity's discovery of itself in transcendental ideas.

KNOWLEDGE WITHOUT A CENTRE

Derrida's other contributions to the theory of knowledge are largely concerned with issues that arise from Lévi-Strauss's anthropology. The issue for the discussion of Lévi-Strauss in 'Structure, sign and play' is the difficulties in establishing a complete description of myths. When Lévi-Strauss tries to produce a totality of myths he is faced with the inevitability of a totality without a centre. That problem is significantly disruptive for metaphysical conceptions of knowledge:

> And again on the basis of what we call the centre (and which, because it can be either inside or outside, can also indifferently be called the origin or end, *archē* or *telos*), repetitions, substitutions, transformations, and permutations are always *taken* from a history of meaning — that is, in a word, a history, whose origin may always be reawakened or whose end may always be anticipated in the form of presence. This is why one perhaps could say that the movement of any archaeology, like that of any eschatology, is an accomplice of this reduction of the structurality of structure and always attempts to conceive of structure on the basis of a full presence which is beyond play.
>
> (WD 279)

This particularly enigmatic example of Derrida's style needs some explanation that will further the exposition of his epistemological contribution. Any totality has a centre, otherwise it will not be a totality, but a system of some other kind. The centre can be inside the totality, or outside it, as origin and first principle, end and goal. The notions of archaeology, or structure, in any system, rest on the assumption that the system has an origin and a goal. The origin and goal orientate the structure, and the archaeology, otherwise there is no possibility of structurality. Structurality requires a centre that constitutes the system from the point of view of its origin and goal. However, the origin and the goal are in a paradoxical situation. The centre must be part of, and separate from, the system. The centre cannot be a centre unless it is distinguished from the centre, in which case there must be equivocation about whether the centre is part of the system it orientates. This means that the centre can only be completely present in the system in a limit situation, which Derrida describes as eschatological, and as a full presence beyond play. Eschatology is the end of time, history and days. It refers to a religious conception of the end in which there is a rupture with previous temporal experience. That sense of eschatology is closely related with full presence. Within religious conceptions, the eschatological occurs when God, God's law and God's word become fully present on earth. That is why there is an end of previous time and experience, because time and experience rest on the absence of the presence of pure Being. If everything in Being was fully present to consciousness, consciousness would not experience the differentiation of Being in time, and would not experience any differentiation, so that experience itself would have come to an end. This is an impossible situation, though for Derrida it is a constant orientation of consciousness and thought, since they are trying to abolish the difference between themselves and their objects in the very acts of consciousness and thought. These essential conditions of consciousness and thought condition any system of knowledge.

Lévi-Strauss's anthropological theory has to deal with the problems of totality, as they arise in two ways. First, Lévi-Strauss recognizes that the nature/culture distinction cannot be justified, though he defends it as a useful instrument of analysis. No consistent distinction can be made between the natural and cultural, but we should continue to make an operational distinction between the natural and cultural as a useful way of organizing the results of anthropological investigation. The loss of an absolute distinction between nature and culture undermines the idea of a centre to a system of anthropological knowledge that exists as a totality. The other loss of totality with a centre arises when Lévi-Strauss tries to deal with the classification of myth. He finds it hard to distinguish between the theory of myth and the myths themselves. What is the theory of myth other than a structure that unifies all myths by serving as the master structure and key? The theory of myths is the myth of all myths. The distinction between the object of knowledge and the concepts, or theories, contained within knowledge is now undermined. Lévi-Strauss suggested a distinction between the engineer and the *bricoleur* in social science. The engineer has a system based on principles in which all empirical evidence can be placed; the *bricoleur* puts together a *bricolage*, a patchwork, of evidence. Lévi-Struss suggests that the anthropologist has to serve as a *bricoleur*, but the result of the dominance of *bricolage* must mean that the engineer is a kind of *bricoleur*, and no clear distinction can be made between *bricoleur* and engineer. The possibility of a social science system as a totality with a centre is now strongly undermined, as again the distance between the object of knowledge, the system of knowledge itself, collapses. The *bricoleur* must be another myth maker, putting myths together as does the teller of myths.

The system that has no centre, which must be all systems for Derrida, has a movable focus understood through language and the inter-substitution of signs, in their repetition and displacement. Metaphysically oriented notions of totality can only be a special case of this. Metaphysics itself lends itself to substitution and repetition, as various names can serve for the centre of a totality: essence, form, substance, energy and so on. Once the metaphysical nature of an archaeology, or structure, of knowledge is exposed, then we have to consider the play of the signifier in the system. This is the kind of expression that gets Derrida labelled as an extreme sceptic, with little thought behind the scepticism. However, Derrida is definitely not saying that questions of knowledge are just questions of playing with words. What he is emphasizing is that a system can only have a movable focus where there is always a possibility of a renaming as replacement, or displacement, of a previous name. The system is always constituted by the possibility of substitution in its focus, and the urge to return to the focus as centre of a totality. The nature/culture distinction in Rousseau and in Lévi-Strauss is an example of the focus taken as a centre considered with nostalgia. Everything in the system can be seen as derived from nature, copying nature, and returning to nature. However, the return can never be made because the system is always separated from nature by repeatability and substitutability. The system relies on signs, and the place of signs in language. Linguistic signs can always be replaced by other signs, and they are never identical with what they signify. The signifier (material sign) is never identical with the signified (the concept) and the sign is never the same as its referent.

For readers of Wittgenstein's *Philosophical Investigations* (Wittgenstein 2001), some of this may seem familiar. Wittgenstein suggests that language as a whole consist of a series of overlapping language games, which can use the same word in different ways according to the contexts to which the language games apply. According to Wittgenstein, there is no essence to language: it is merely the indefinitely extendable series of different language games. In Wittgenstein the empirical aspects of language appear to triumph over any abstract transcendental purpose. However, the difference between Derrida and Wittgenstein on this point is that for Derrida there is no escape from knowledge as a totality with an archaeology or structure. If there is a system of knowledge, then the tendency to establish a centre of a totality will persist. The possibility of establishing a system depends on the possibility of searching for the presence of a centre. The presence of the centre would obliterate knowledge as unnecessary in our pure, direct and uninterrupted intuitive grasp of the centre. There is always tension, paradox and contradiction in Derrida's account of knowledge as with everything else. Knowledge is a paradox because to claim knowledge is to claim to have a system that is totality with a centre, but in such circumstances the need for knowledge, and its very possibility, is obliterated. Knowledge is knowledge of an object distinct from the knowing subject, which brings about unavoidable paradoxes of knowledge as what is the impossible knowledge of the unknown, or the redundant knowledge of what is already known.

The paradoxes of knowledge achieve other forms with regard to the decisionistic nature of knowledge and the equivocation of philosophical discourse. The discussion of Foucault in 'Cogito and the history of madness' (WD 2) brings in the divide within knowledge, *logos* and language with regard to madness and reason. The possibility of a total deception of the mind in madness, which Descartes links with our total deception by a demon, is a permanent possibility. There is a constant decision to be made between reason and madness. The 'demon' must be understood as within consciousness, or in the less subjective attributes of the system of knowledge, in its language. There can always be deception within the language of knowledge since language can always deceive. Language is never completely transparent, so that we know what the meaning or reference of a word is with certainty. This concealing nature of language could always lead to a collapse of reason as we always have reason to say we know nothing. The distinction between reason and madness is intrinsically ungrounded. There is no basis for the distinction other than a decision that one thing belongs to madness and another belongs to reason. The decision itself is a deranged moment lacking in a rational basis. Derrida accuses Foucault of following Descartes in assuming the possibility of reason simply repressing madness. There is just no system for saying what is mad and what is reason; there can only be a system of knowledge because the decision has already been made.

In 'Plato's pharmacy' (in D), Derrida suggests that we examine the distinction between philosophical knowledge and Sophistic deception in Plato's *Phaedrus*. The *Phaedrus* contains an attack on writing and memorizing texts, as the contamination of the mind in its pure thought. We can only have real knowledge on the basis of a dialogue in which the hearer can grasp thought immediately through spoken words, and the speaker knows that the spoken words have expressed inner meanings. Writing and the memorization of texts is a *'pharmakon'*, that is a poison. However, *'pharmakon'* also means medicine in Ancient Greek and Plato also uses the word in that way. His language is equivocal, and alludes to a deeper equivocation. What Plato condemns as poison is really a condition of his theory of forms, which he claims is the highest reality in an intelligible world that is the model for the world of appearances. Plato condemns writing as external to the self, but the same could be said of the ideas or forms, which Plato suggests are the only content of real knowledge. Knowledge is knowledge of forms, and knowledge of them comes from the way ideas are present in memory from birth. One reason that Plato condemns writing is that it relies on an external memory, rather than what is in our mind, and on the inner memory that does not depend on external aids. By this argument the ideas, or forms, are present in our memory, but not in an immediately present way, only buried deep in what is given to us from outside. Plato's language suggests that Socrates is a '*pharmakon*' in a therapeutic medical way, but also associates him with magic and poison. Magic is strongly condemned by Plato and his suggested punishment is remarkably close to Socrates' execution by the Athenians by means of a compulsory suicide.

> What can be said about this *analogy* that ceaselessly refers the socratic *pharmakon* to the sophistic *pharmakon* and, proportioning them to each other, makes us go back indefinitely from one to the other? How can they be distinguished? Irony does not consist in the dissolution of a sophistic charm or in the dismantling of an occult substance through analysis and questioning. It does not consist in undoing the charlatanesque confidence of a *pharmakeus* from the vantage point of some obstinate instance of transparent reason or innocent *logos*. Socratic irony precipitates out one *pharmakon* by bringing it in contact with another *pharmakon*. Or rather, it reverses the *pharmakon*'s powers and turns its surface over – thus taking effect, being recorded and dated, in the act of *classing the pharmakon*, through the fact that the *pharmakon* properly consists in a certain inconsistency, a certain impropriety, this non-identity-with-itself always allowing it to be turned against itself.
>
> (D 119)

What troubles Plato is that he assumes that knowledge must be internal, so that any external source of knowledge is not only epistemically dubious but is also morally condemned. However, he cannot resist acknowledging the external sources of knowledge. His struggle to hold the line and the contradictions he gets into reflect the arbitrariness in the nature of the decision that distinguishes reason from madness; and all the equivocations of origin and structure.

6

VALUES

ETHICS, SOVEREIGNTY, HUMANISM AND RELIGION

ETHICS AND LÉVINAS

Derrida has more to say directly about the issues in this chapter, later in his career. The texts we are concerned with are concerned with philosophical method and reflection on what philosophy is along with the basic questions of knowledge, language and metaphysics. Nevertheless, a lot comes up with regard to ethics and the other value-orientated questions referred to in the title of this chapter. Derrida's concern with sovereignty is at this stage not so much with questions of law, the state and politics as with the concept of sovereignty itself. That is the concept of sovereignty as a concept of ownership, possession and mastery, which raises issues of self-ownership, possession and mastery in ways that impinge on personal identity. He is concerned with humanism as it applies to questions of man as an ideal, and the social world of man as distinguished from the natural animal world. In both cases, he is concerned with the metaphysical implications of defining humanity and man. Religion enters into Derrida's philosophy in important ways, though he himself does not appear to have believed in God, or to have followed any religion. Nevertheless, for Derrida, the questions of God can never be avoided. Where the question of the absolute arises, where metaphysics becomes possible, God inevitably arises as a name for a space in our world, which might or might not refer to a God who exists.

Derrida's positions on ethics must be situated with regard to a dialogue with Emmanuel Lévinas, a friend of Derrida, who developed a position in which ethics is the first philosophy. Though, like Derrida, Lévinas is rooted in Phenomenology, and associated European philosophical traditions, and his writing style is far removed from that normal in Analytic philosophy, one of the most influential Analytic philosophers, Hilary Putnam, has taken up Lévinas's ethics in *Ethics without Ontology* (Putnam 2004). The title of Putnam's book refers to one of the main themes in Lévinas, the suggestion that ethics should replace ontology as first philosophy. Lévinas describes the European philosophical tradition since the Ancient Greeks as one that puts ontology at the foundations of philosophy. This has anti-ethical consequences for Lévinas. Ontology, which Lévinas distinguishes from metaphysics, is a philosophy of Being that reduces all things to the oneness of Being. That essentially requires a reduction of the other to the same, which is the reduction of I to other. For Lévinas, the questions of ontology arise within the concerns of Phenomenology: the essential content and structure of experience. This can clearly be traced back to Descartes's concentration on the contents of consciousness as the starting point of philosophy. The Phenomenological and Cartesian traditions are not bad traditions for Lévinas, though sometimes he makes remarks which suggest he thinks that these traditions, along with the whole of the European philosophical tradition, should be supplanted by Judaic ethics. Like Derrida, Lévinas began his philosophical research as a Husserl scholar and was deeply under the influence of Heidegger. Unlike Derrida, the relation with Heidegger was partly based on personal contact during research with Heidegger in the 1930s. Lévinas's main philosophical works take a very condemnatory view of Heidegger as a philosopher of power, and this must be under the influence of Heidegger's adherence to Nazism. The condemnation of Heidegger as a philosopher of the state disguised as Being, and the implicit condemnation of his philosophy as a Nazi philosophy, is extended to Hegel and Husserl (though Husserl was of Jewish origin), and to the whole of the European philosophical tradition. The condemnation is highly ambiguous since Lévinas's work is deeply embedded in the legacy of the three great H's (Hegel, Husserl, Heidegger) of

German philosophy, along with the interpretation of texts of Plato and Descartes.

These are not specifically ethical concerns in Lévinas, but they are unavoidable in explaining his ethics, as is acknowledged by Derrida's lengthy response to Lévinas in 'Violence and meta-physics' (WD 4), which largely deals with *Totality and Infinity*. Lévinas took Derrida's criticisms seriously and responded to them without referring directly to Derrida in *Otherwise than Being*. Their relationship was an exemplary mixture of friendship and philosophical dialogue, in which they were often opposed but never in a destructive or uncivilized way. This culminated in Derrida's oration at Lévinas's funeral (Derrida 1996). The relationship included a shared interest in Judaism, though for Lévinas this meant a religious and political orientation. That is Lévinas was a practising religious Jew, giving Talmudic classes for children; and he was a Zionist who identified strongly with the state of Israel. For Derrida, the Judaic heritage was of great value, but he saw it as cultural, intellectual and aesthetic heritage. He was not a religious Jew and did not belong to any synagogue. While he visited Israel on a few occasions, he did not identify with the Israeli state or adopt Zionist principles (according to which Jews can only survive as a people in their own nation). Furthermore, unlike Lévinas, he was very sympathetic to the Palestinian point of view in the Arab–Israeli conflict, though at all times he supported peaceful dialogue between the sides and opposed terror. His upbringing as a French Jew, living in the Arab majority French colony of Algeria, was a point of reference for him in these questions.

Having situated the dialogue between Derrida and Lévinas, it is possible to look at the more specifically ethical questions. Lévinas sought a philosophy that would take ethics as the first philosophy. This would be metaphysical but not ontological. The metaphysics appears in the transcendence of the same (the self, consciousness, the I) by the other. From the Phenomenological point of view that means that I cannot describe the contents of my inner experience without referring to exteriority: what comes from outside myself and cannot be reduced to the product of my own inner intentions. Lévinas described that partly with reference to Plato's view of the Good in the *Republic* and partly with regard to Descartes's proof of the existence of God in the *Meditations on the First Philosophy*. These arguments are complex and important, but we will have to restrict ourselves to a brief indication of what Lévinas takes from them. In Book VI of the *Republic*, Plato argues that there are permanent forms of the changeable things we perceive through the senses. The highest form is the form of Good and that this precedes all the other forms, illuminating them as the sun illuminates the world. The Good precedes all forms and is more than a form. In the 'Third Meditation', Descartes argues that God must exist because the idea of perfect being must originate in a perfect being, which can only be God, and not in any imperfect beings such as the individual thinking human.

God and the Good precede any being, or even Being as discussed by the Ancient Greeks or Heidegger. There is no Being as such, without the transcendence that is always the transcendence of the same by the other. This cannot be an abstract philosophical relation for Lévinas, otherwise we will be caught up again in the ontology that he describes as neutral, where Being subordinates everything to its sameness. The Phenomenology of our experience, and any intellectual construction of reality, always leads us towards exteriority and alterity, where there is more than myself. According to Lévinas, there is a relation of absolute non-violence, which can be described as a relation with a particular face. The other exists as a face, to which I feel obliged and which I must put above myself. I cannot kill the other; even a physical murder of another person still leaves me constituted in my interior self in a relation with the other. There is never a same, which exists in an isolated, self-contained way, given by its interiority. As the same, I cannot be the same without the other, and the face of the other. As I only exist, I can only be the same; in a relation with what transcends me, in which I am always less than the other. Ethics arises because I can only be violent to the other at the risk of destroying my own ego. There can only be ethics where there is non-violence, which is only the case where the other is sovereign. For Lévinas the European philosophical tradition is embedded in violence, even where it tries to relate to the other. Despite the weight Lévinas gives to the passages in Plato and Descartes discussed above, he sees all the European, or Greek-German, attempts at accounting for the other as failures. He mentions the I–Thou relation in Martin Buber, and the criticisms of abstract universal ethics in Søren Kierkegaard as examples of such failures. Buber gives too much priority to the 'I' to be truly ethical, according to Lévinas's argument; and Kierkegaard only replaces an alienated abstract ethics of universal rules with the priority of subjectivity.

The Greek tradition is opposed by Lévinas to a Jewish tradition in which ethics is primary. Lévinas regards the Jewish tradition as one that subordinates the same to the other as widow, orphan and stranger. It is concerned with the fragility of the other who needs the same; the ego as same must respond since it only exists in relation with the other. There is law in the Jewish tradition, but it is based on the absoluteness of the priority of the face of the other, as the concrete existence of the ethical relation. God exists in an ethical way in Judaism, so that ethics does not spring from absolute obedience to God, but emerges in the priority of the other, which allows us to even argue with God about what might be necessary for there to be an ethical relation. From that view of Judaism, Lévinas suggests that philosophy has been an act of ontological violence from the side of the Greek tradition directed against the Jewish tradition.

Derrida attributes great importance to these arguments in Lévinas, but finds them marked by metaphysics in the sense of absolute oppositions. Lévinas rests on oppositions between same and other, interiority and exteriority, Greek and Jew.

> Thus Lévinas exhorts us to a second parricide. The Greek father who still holds us under his sway must be killed; and this is what a Greek – Plato – could never resolve to do, deferring the act into a hallucinatory murder. A hallucination within the hallucination that is already speech. But will a non-Greek ever succeed in doing what a Greek in this case could not do, except by disguising himself as a Greek, by *speaking* Greek, by feigning to speak Greek in order to get near the king? And since it is a question of killing a speech, will we ever know who is the last victim of this stratagem? Can one feign speaking a language? The Eleatic stranger and disciple of Parmenides had to give language its due for having vanquished him: shaping non-Being according to Being, he to 'say farewell to an unnameable opposite

of Being' and had to confine non-Being to its relativity to Being, that
is to the movement of alterity.

(WD 89)

For Derrida, the metaphysical tradition has always included a moral
view of Good and Evil as absolute opposites, which belongs to a
series of oppositions. These are the oppositions of truth and falsity,
being and seeming, the inside and the outside, the natural and the
social. In this case, an ethics derived from the opposition between
Good and Evil is part of metaphysics. Lévinas complicates this in
that like Derrida he seeks a critical viewpoint on the philosophical
tradition, but unlike Derrida he assumes a 'metaphysical' point of
view. Within that metaphysical position, Lévinas argues for the transcendence of interiority by exteriority, as a basis for ethics, and philosophy in general that Lévinas derives from ethics. The opposition
between the inside and the outside is reversed in Lévinas. The reversal is not enough in itself to go beyond the metaphysical tradition,
according to Derrida, since the point is to avoid the hierarchy rather
than invert it. Nevertheless, for Derrida inverting the hierarchy can
be the first stage of deconstructive strategy since it shakes the hold
of metaphysical assumptions and can lead us to find ways that resist
the formation of these hierarchies. The Lévinasian reversal is
embedded in a general attempt to dissolve the priority of the same,
the dissolve of any attempt to reduce phenomena to the expression
of a single neutral Being, separate from all phenomenal forces.

The ethics that emerges in Lévinas seems distinct from the normal ethical theories, and that is deliberate. There is an attempt to
precede particular theories, which follows from the transcendental
claims of Phenomenology, and before that Kant. Kant suggested
that metaphysical theories should be preceded by a search for the
conditions necessary for us to have knowledge and experience of
anything. Husserl suggested that, in Phenomenology, metaphysical theories should be preceded by a search for pure phenomena of
consciousness, and the transcendental structures of consciousness
within which we can define pure phenomena. These transcendental
positions have a bearing on Deconstruction, as will be discussed in
the last chapter. Lévinas does not contribute in any obvious way to
the familiar positions in ethical theory. There is no statement of

whether ethics refers to the consequences of actions (consequentialism/utilitarianism) or the intrinsic value of principles (intrinsicalism/deontology); the cultivation of natural human dispositions (virtue theory); or the grasp of pure ethical values outside the natural world (intuitionism). There are, however, transcendental principles that emerge in Lévinas. These are of non-violence towards the other and the absolute claim of the other on the self. There is a suspicion of any claim of subjectivity, though subjectivity itself is described in a Phenomenology that emphasizes ways in which subjectivity exists as constituted by obligations towards the other, or towards alterity.

Derrida engages with this rather than rejecting it. He regards Lévinas in a similar way to Nietzsche and Heidegger, as a figure who tries to stand apart from the philosophical tradition while still operating within metaphysics. The philosophical tradition was always like that in the first place; there could never be any philosophy without incorporation of the non-philosophical in conflict with the transcendental claims of philosophy. Nietzsche, Heidegger and Lévinas make that constant deconstructive element of philosophy more explicit. That engagement with Lévinas, particularly with *Totality and Infinity*, is certainly very critical. Derrida rejects the notion of a divide between Greek and Jewish traditions. He argues that they contain each other, since the ethical aspects Lévinas attributes to the Jewish tradition are in 'Greek' philosophy. Lévinas's own elevation of the Jewish tradition over the Greek tradition is, itself, a violence on the Greek tradition, and is therefore not ethical by Lévinas's own standards. This is a general problem in Lévinas's position that appears in his specific arguments and examples. Derrida claims that the reading of Kierkegaard (WD 110–11) in Lévinas is itself a violence imposition, which obscures the importance of otherness in Kierkegaard's subjectivity. The relation between the self and its other is not an isolation of the self from its other, but rather changes the self that is shown to be impossible outside that relation, which exists within subjectivity. Similar comments are made by Derrida with regard to Lévinas's reading of the German H's.

Derrida's view on ethics is that it cannot be defined by what is other than violence. That requires a passivity in the face of the other, which undermines any ethical notion of a self with responsibilities and obligations. There can be no relation that does not include violence since where there is a relation it changes something in both the elements that are related. All changes and modification, and therefore all relations, are violence of some kind. The existence of a force is the existence of violence. Lévinas himself criticizes ontological 'neutrality', but that can only be the criticism of Being in general, which denies all change and difference, and therefore denies forces of change and differentiation. Lévinas's search for a philosophy of peace can only be violence against violence.

> *We do not say pure non-violence.* Like pure violence, pure non-violence is a contradictory concept. [WD 146] Now, there is no phrase which is indeterminate, that is which does not pass through the violence of the concept. Violence appears with *articulation.* And the latter is opened only by (the at first preconceptual) circulation of Being. The very elocution of non-violent metaphysics is its first disavowal. Doubtless Lévinas would not deny that every historical language carries within it an irreducible conceptual moment, and therefore a certain violence. From his point of view, the origin and possibility of the concept are simply not the thought of Being, but the gift of the world to the other as totally-other. In its original possibility as *offer,* in its still silent intention, language is non-violent (but can it be language, in this pure intention?). It becomes violent only in its history, in what we have called the phrase, which obliges it to *articulate itself* in a conceptual syntax opening the circulation of the same, permitting itself to be governed both by 'ontology' and by what remains, for Lévinas, the concept of concepts: Being. Now, for Lévinas, the concept of Being would be only an abstract means produced for the gift of the world to the other who is *above Being.* Hence, only in its silent origin, before Being, would language be non-violent. But why history? Why does the phrase impose itself? Because if one does not uproot the silent origin from itself violently, if one decides not to speak, then the worst violence will silently cohabit the *idea* of peace? Peace is made only in a *certain silence,* which is determined and protected by the violence of speech. Since speech says nothing other than the horizon of this silent peace by which it has itself summoned and that is its mission to protect and to prepare, speech *indefinitely* remains silent. One never escapes the *economy of war.*
>
> (WD 147–8)

The restraint of the forces of change and differentiation can only occur as a violence on them. This is an aspect of Derrida's claims about transcendental and metaphysical questions. In the context of Lévinas, we can see how that relates with ethical issues.

The discussion of Lévinas is related with the discussion of nature, with regard to Rousseau and Lévi-Strauss. Derrida finds Lévi-Strauss to be assuming a natural non-violence in 'primitive' peoples, in that they commit no violence on nature in the immediacy of their lives, which are totally in the present. That is regarded by Derrida as a version of Rousseau's view in which natural man lives without violence towards fellow humans, or nature, in a natural sympathy for other humans. For Lévi-Strauss and Rousseau, language is a violence on nature, on the immediacy of consciousness, which is repeated by the violence of writing on the naturalness of speech.

> If one moves along the course of the supplementary series, he sees that imagination belongs to the same chain of significations as the anticipation of death. A proposition that one may define or make indefinite thus: *the* image is *a* death or (*the*) death is *an* image. Imagination is the power that allows life to affect itself with its own re-presentation. The image cannot represent and add the representer to the represented, except in so far as the presence of the re-presented is already folded back upon itself in the world, in so far as life refers to itself as to its own lack, to its own wish for a supplement. The presence of the represented is constituted with the help of the addition to itself of that nothing which is the image, announcement of its dispossession within its own representer and within its death. The property of the subject is merely the movement of that representative expropriation. In that sense imagination, like death, is *representative and supplementary*.
>
> (OG 184)

The ethical position which follows from Derrida's account of these issues of language, society and metaphysics is that ethics cannot be a pure ethics. There is no pure good, or pure evil. This does not mean that Derrida is a moral relativist, any more than he is an epistemological relativist. There are things that are to be morally condemned according to Derrida, with a universal sanction, not just as the expression of a personal opinion, or a specific cultural value. It does mean that even the most clearly 'good' position is violent. Opposing 'bad' things is violent, and is a violence we have to accept, but that violence undermines any notion of moral purity or absolute good. Derrida's ethics largely appears in opposition to ethical absolutes in Lévinas and Rousseau, in a manner that aims to show the contradictions within the conceptions of good in their ethics. The emphasis on describing and fully articulating the contradictions is where Derrida's own ethics emerges. As usual in any aspect of Derrida's philosophy, it can be difficult to work out where the text, which is the object of commentary, ends and where Derrida's own position begins.

What emerges in the discussion of Lévinas also refers back to the discussion of Husserl in SP. The self is never completely present to itself. Since consciousness is never able to grasp itself fully, in its constant movement, the self is other to itself. The self is already engaged in a relation with itself, which has ethical dimensions. Responsibility for myself is not just responsibility for myself: it is responsibility for the otherness in myself. This draws on Lévinas's conception of the same as transcended by the other, and the associated discussion of my way of dwelling and perceiving. The implication that Derrida finds in Lévinas's philosophy is that the same is never the same as itself. The transcendence of the same by the other, in Lévinas, still leaves the same as the same. For Derrida, the structure of the relation of the same with the other, as infinity, God, the Good, or alterity in Lévinas is an interior relation rather than an external relation between objects. It is not just an interior relation, since it questions the opposition of the outside and the inside. The inside of consciousness must be structured by a relation with what transcends consciousness.[1]

SOVEREIGNTY

For Derrida, consciousness must have the external within itself because that is what memory is. In his discussions of Husserl and Plato, he emphasizes that the use of language of any kind refers to a memory of the meaning of words. The flow of language itself depends on a flow of consciousness in which elements are retained, so that their existence is prolonged over time. This gives us the origin of the fear of evil inside ourselves. Descartes's suggestion that our thoughts might be given to us by a demon, which Derrida discusses in 'Cogito and the history of madness' (WD 2), is evidence of this. We cannot be sure that our thoughts come from within consciousness, so that is a place of exteriority, of a potentially evil incursion. This is what is at stake in Derrida's account of memory and the *pharmakon* in Plato ('Plato's pharmacy' in D). Memory is both medicinal and potentially poisonous, which are both meanings of *pharmakon*, because it can assist us, but it is an invasion of the purity of the psyche. The word 'psyche' is used deliberately here, because it is an Ancient Greek word in origin, and there are no direct equivalents in Ancient Greek in Plato, or anywhere else, for words like consciousness and mind. The emphasis on Good as the form of forms, before Being in Plato, might be considered to contradict the emphasis on the pure interiority of the psyche in Plato, and Derrida suggests such a thing about Plato. The outside cannot be eliminated from any account of the psyche.

Lévinas reverses the aspect of Plato, which emphasizes the purity of the interior because he takes exteriority as the positive ethical value. The problem for Derrida is that there is still an ethical absolute, an ethical purity, assumed here. Similar problems arise with regard to nature. The issue of the natural as good versus the invented thing as contamination is an issue in Plato's condemnation of writing, which he assumes to be less natural than speech. The issue continues with particular emphasis in Rousseau's account of the natural and the social. What Derrida is arguing is that there can be no good or bad, good or evil, in nature, since these terms clearly assume the social community along with history, writing, politics and all the other impurities that destroy the natural. The good is retrospectively projected as pure good into nature. Rousseau cannot separate unethical violence from nature though. His *Essay on the Origin of Language* refers to language as the point at which the social separates from the natural. What Derrida points out is that, the force, which the social imposes on nature, as it obliterates the natural can only come from nature itself. It can only be natural forces that provide the force against nature. The natural only exists in opposition to the social, and therefore only exists as part of the social, or certainly as what cannot eliminate the social from itself. Social evil must be present in natural good. Derrida's discussion of these features of Rousseau on language also refers to the well-known ambiguities of Rousseau's account of the natural and the social with regard to the social and the political. Rousseau finds that society is where man, who is naturally free, is in chains, but also that our freedom comes from the laws of the social body, and that freedom only comes from such laws. Derrida does not address this directly, but the relation is very clear and must be taken as part of what Derrida was doing in the discussion of Rousseau. Ferdinand de Saussure is also taken up in Derrida's discussion of metaphysics in linguistics. One paper refers to 'The linguistic circle of Geneva' (in MP), meaning Rousseau and Saussure, invoking not only their common home city but also what Derrida sees as the continuity, and repetition, of thought about language from Rousseau to Saussure. He points to the ethically laden contrast between nature and society in Saussure, including an emphasis on the naturalness of speech compared with writing, in which writing appears as a deviation from nature particularly if it influences the development of spoken language. The reading of Saussure tends to bring moments in which Saussure echoes Rousseau's political and social thought, though this is not what Derrida emphasizes. It is nevertheless of importance that Saussure refers to the loss of the natural in the social institution of language with a tone of regret, and a suggestion that social humanity is alienated from itself.

What Rousseau partly deals with in his social and political thought is the question of sovereignty. The question is what gives legitimacy to the state and its laws. For Rousseau, what gives legitimacy must be the original source and must be natural. The original source of the state must lie in the earliest stages of human history, and that must mean the emergence of human community from nature. The origin must be in nature, and therefore must be natural. Derrida approaches sovereignty with reference to other sources. The longest essay on sovereignty by Derrida from the

texts under consideration here is 'From restricted to general economy: a Hegelianism without reserve' (WD 9). What Derrida is
concerned with here is the dialectic of master and slave in Hegel,
and George Bataille's reading of that famous passage in Hegel. The
discussion is in the *Phenomenology of Spirit* (Hegel 1977), in a
section on 'Independence and dependence of self-consciousness:
lordship and bondage'. The standard translation at present (Hegel
1977) prefers lord and bondsman to master and slave; nevertheless
in general discussion 'master and slave' have stuck. Hegel's discussion of master and slave directly inspired important philosophical
work by Jean-Paul Sartre, in *Being and Nothingness*; discussions
in Karl Marx of the class struggle and in Nietzsche of master and
slave moralities, by accident or design engage with Hegel's theme
of master and slave. A brief summary of Hegel's original discussion is necessary for the exposition of Derrida. Hegel discusses
self-consciousness and its development into relations between two
consciousnesses. The development of consciousness itself requires
consciousness to be conscious of itself, but in becoming conscious
of itself it divides between consciousness that is just consciousness
itself and consciousness which exists as awareness of what consciousness is conscious of outside consciousness. The move from
simple consciousness to self-consciousness requires a consciousness, which can be conscious of itself as conscious of itself, and so is
conscious of a split between immediate consciousness and consciousness as an object of itself. The awareness of the duality of
consciousness brings us, in Hegel, to the situation where there is a
duality of two distinct consciousnesses, as it seems we cannot be
conscious of the relation between a duality of consciousnesses
unless there is already duality within consciousness. Consciousness can only regard another consciousness as a threat to itself,
because without another consciousness a single consciousness is
independent. Where there is another consciousness, recognition
becomes a disruptive presence. The discussion of recognition is
implicitly continuous with Rousseau's discussion of the self as a
self in society, which always imagines itself as it appears in the
imagination of other selves. In Hegel's discussion, consciousness
wants to be conscious of everything as part of itself. The existence
of another consciousness threatens that simple identity between

the world of a consciousness and the world of which it is conscious. The consequence is a conflict between the two consciousnesses as both consciousnesses try to force a complete recognition from the other. This is described, by Hegel, as a battle to the death in which the individual, who fears death the most, loses. That individual experiences negation and death as possibilities and avoids their realization by becoming the slave of a master. The slave labours and desires to serve the master, and the master is inactive. The consequence of the initial fear of death by the slave, and the subsequent product, labour, is that it is the slave who keeps the dialectic, consciousness and history in motion.

> The necessity of *logical* continuity is the decision or interpretative milieu of all Hegelian interpretations. In interpreting negativity as labour, in betting for discourse, meaning, history, etc., Hegel has bet against play, against chance. He has blinded himself to the possibility of his own bet, to the fact that the conscientious suspension of play (for example, the passage through the certitude of oneself and through lordship as the independence of self-consciousness) was itself a phase of play; and to the fact that play *includes* the work of meaning or the meaning of work, and includes them not in terms of *knowledge*, but in terms of *inscription*: meaning is a *function* of play, is inscribed in a certain place in the configuration of a meaningless play.
>
> (WD 260)

Bataille notes the victory of the slave in Hegel in order to criticize it. It is the triumph of negativity and limitation on the sovereignty of the individual. Some of this comes from Bataille's reading of Nietzsche, though Nietzsche himself does not say much directly about Hegel and may, or may not, have been responding to Hegel in parts of his work. Bataille discusses Hegelian sovereignty in the context of his own notions of expenditure. Through a mixture of Marxist influence, and research of anthropological sources, Bataille emphasizes the limits of an economy of exchange, including any economy in which commodities are produced in exchange for money. He points to evidence of gift giving, or potlatch, in premodern societies, where the economy operates through either giving away economic surplus, or even sacrificing it ritually. There can be an economy in which the surplus over what is necessary to maintain life is ritually destroyed, itself a gift to the gods, or is given away to other people in the community as a way of gaining status. This is an economy with no reserve, since the economic surplus is not saved or invested, which is interesting to Derrida for reasons other than Bataille's eagerness to find an alternative to capitalist commodity production. Derrida was not an outright Marxist during the time he was a well-known philosopher, though as a student he was connected with small revolutionary groups in Paris. Though always on the left, Marxism was an interesting source of analysis for Derrida, rather than a political orientation after his student years, and he had little to say directly about Marx until late in his career. There is an account of individual sovereignty in Bataille with strong ethical implications, and other uses. For Derrida, the idea of a general economy is a way of thinking about consciousness and language, which avoids reducing either to a limited set of concepts. There is an absolute production within consciousness and within language, which can in part be explained by the material forces at the origin of both. That is the material psychic forces, emerging from physiology, along with the material phonic and graphic content of language.

The ethical aspect, not thematized as ethics by Derrida, but clearly there, is that independence is preferable to dependence. The individual should be striving for absolute sovereignty, without subordination to death, desire and labour. The suggestion is not that it is a good thing to be the master of a slave, but that self-mastery is better than slavery. In Bataille, this also means a Nietzschean overcoming of an ethics of good and evil. Evil is referred to by Bataille in relation to any kind of transgression, any crossing of a social or psychological boundary, in which case evil can often be given a positive value as emancipation. Derrida does not get an explicit moral theory out of this, but he does always follow the suspicion of the polarity of good and evil. Sovereignty as a relation of the self with itself becomes the goal. That is there is a goal of the self, which affirms, gives and is independent, where death and negation as experiences of the limit can increase sovereignty, not restrict it.[2]

However, there are reasons for thinking that there is not a straightforward celebration of sovereignty and general economy in Derrida. He tends to oppose Nietzsche to Rousseau or Heidegger as one pole of Deconstruction. In Heidegger, there is nostalgia for Being; in Rousseau there is nostalgia for nature. In either case, we must consider the search for original Being or nature in their full presence, as necessary aspects of language and philosophy. Without the possibility of pure presence, it is not possible to conceive of meaning or communication. The approach of Bataille, or that way of using Nietzsche in general, is not adequate to death as a condition of consciousness, of non-communication as a condition of language. There cannot just be the pure gift, an economy with no reserve. The economy does require exchange, in the case of language and consciousness, as well as in the case of the money economy. Sovereignty can never be an absolute, since I cannot separate consciousness from its relations with others. Bataillean laughter and sovereignty is brought to bear against Hegel's negativity and labour on the dialectical road to the absolute. However, just as in the contrast of Nietzsche with Rousseau and Heidegger, there is no complete triumph over the negative, nostalgic and metaphysical. The two poles depend on each other, and include each other, while contesting each other.

> To laugh at philosophy (at Hegelianism) – such, in effect, is the form of the awakening – henceforth calls for an entire 'discipline', an entire 'method of meditation' that acknowledges the philosopher's byways, understands his techniques, makes use of his ruses, manipulates his cards, lets him deploy his strategy, appropriates his texts. Then thanks to this work, which has prepared it – and philosophy is work *itself* according to Bataille – but quickly furtively, and unforeseeably breaking with it, as betrayal or as detachment, dryly, laughter busts out. And yet, in privileged moments, that are less moments than the always rapidly sketched movements of experience; rare, discreet and light movements, without triumphant stupidity, far from public view, very close to that at which laughter laughs: close to anguish, first of all, which must not even be called the negative of laughter for fear of once more being sucked in by Hegel's discourse.

> (WD 252)

RELIGION

Consciousness must deal with limits and that is where we find the place of religion. Whatever may or may not be the case about the existence of God, or the reality of any religion, there is a limit to rationality. This is explained in relation to Descartes's deceiving demon in 'Cogito and the history of madness' (WD 2) in which Derrida is contesting Foucault's reading of the demon and insanity in Descartes's 'First Meditation' in *Meditations on the First Philosophy*. This was discussed in the last chapter in the context of knowledge, and certainly deserves to be looked at from the perspective of ethical value questions. There is a discussion of Foucault's *Madness and Civilisation* (Foucault 2001a), which explores the changing ways in which madness and sanity have been separated. Though Foucault suggests that oppositions between madness and sanity are constructed rather than natural, and change over history, Derrida claims he still makes an absolute separation between madness and sanity, taking the reading of Descartes as the key issue. The relevant discussion in Descartes is of the possibility that all my thoughts are the products of madness and are therefore imaginary, rather than real in reference; or that a demon is deceiving me so that all that I perceive in my mind refers to the impositions of the demon, rather than objects in the world. Derrida argues that the possibility of madness is always there in consciousness, and cannot be separated from the existence of consciousness. This is not because Derrida advocates an extreme scepticism, in which we should deny the reality of all our perceptions on the grounds that they may be fictions produced by madness or a demon. It is because the logical possibility of madness cannot be eliminated from consciousness.

The limit where we might find madness, or the diabolical, is further explored by Derrida with regard to God and religion. There is no suggestion that God exists, or that religion refers to objective truths. There is no discussion of the Devil or demons elsewhere in Derrida, though reference to the anxiety associated with a structure lacking a centre in 'Structure, sign and play in the discourse of the human sciences' (WD 10) has some overtones of the diabolical (WD 278–9). There is a clear echo of Pascal's anxiety that the individual human is lost in an infinite universe where God is absent, and which is like an infinite sphere with no centre. Derrida's philosophy does not exclude the possibility that God, the Devil or religion might be real, and it is a thoroughly agnostic philosophy. There is no attempt to discuss the validity of any claims of religion. What can be found is discussion of what it is like to be at the limit of rationality and law.

> If the centre is indeed '*the displacement of the question*', it is because the unnameable bottomless well whose sign the centre was, has always been *surnamed*; the centre as the sign of a hole that the book attempted to fill. The centre was the name of a hole; and the name of a man, like the name of God, pronounces the force of that which has been raised up in the hole in order to operate as a work in the form of a book. The volume, the scroll of parchment, was to have insinuated itself into the dangerous hole, was to have furtively penetrated into the menacing dwelling place with an animal-like, quick, silent, smooth, brilliant, sliding motion, in the fashion of a serpent or a fish. Such is the anxious desire of the book. It is tenacious too, and parasitic, loving and breathing through a thousand mouths that leave a thousand imprints on our skin, a marine monster, a *polyp*.
>
> (WD 297–8)

This discussion recurs in Derrida in various contexts (SP 104; WD 11), but its most overtly religious discussion can be found in two essays in *Writing and Difference*: 'Edmond Jabès and the question of the book' (WD 3), 'Ellipsis' (WD 11). Both focus on the French Jewish writer Jabès, with regard to the way in which he brings together poetry and the law as essential aspects of Judaic religious tradition. As ever, Derrida builds up a position by investigating texts. What he finds in the texts of Jabès is the strong tradition of law in Judaism going back to the Old Testament, particularly to the five books of Moses, known as the Torah or Pentateuch, which contain the Mosaic law. The Judaic tradition emphasizes law and interpretation of law. Interpretations require interpretation themselves. The oldest and most famous interpreters inevitably acquire a thick layer of their own interpreters. For Derrida's reading of Jabès, the interpretation of the interpretation is more than just interpretation. The interpretation of interpretation undermines any assumption that texts contain a single meaning that can be released in a single correct reading. If the interpretation itself requires interpretation, then the original interpretation itself must be unsuccessful in any claim to have released the naked truth of the text it is interpreting. What the doubling of interpretation, where interpretation itself is interpreting interpretation, does is show something necessarily true of interpretation. What it shows is that interpretation can always be doubled, can always be what is interpreted and that undermines any claim that there is an interpretation that gives us the original meaning of the text, including the texts of the law. There is no original meaning, in the sense that there is no meaning of the text that comes first and that there is no meaning of the text that dominates other possible meanings. All these comments apply to the interpretation of law, including religious law. The variability of the interpretation of law undermines a distinction, and opposition, which might be made between law and poetry. That distinction is continuous with distinctions deeply embedded in the history of philosophy, and all thought. That includes the distinction between the literal and the metaphorical with which we will be concerned, in more detail, in Chapter 7. The distinction between law and poetry refers to the literal-metaphorical distinction since the law claims to be a direct statement of rules and punishment, where these are all directly stated with as little ambiguity of interpretation as possible. Poetry is intrinsically metaphorical as it is constantly concerned with the non-literal meaning of words, with the ambiguities of meaning. The distinction between legal and poetic discourse looks like a very clear distinction. What Jabès dwells on is that, in the religious context, the law and poetry are intertwined, since both cannot be imagined without the other, and cannot exist without giving rise to the other. Poetry itself cannot float free from law; it must be limited in some way in its use of language, or its language will not be intelligible at all.[3] In the context of religion, poetry concerns itself with what law is concerned. They are both concerned with the word of God.

This remains the case even if we put aside the way in which religious scripture expresses the word of God through poetic language. That itself is the necessary consequence of the space occupied

by law and by poetry. Law in some respects is just a list of statements that enables some kinds of behaviour and institution, for-
bids other forms of behaviour and refers to punishments for
breaking prohibitions. However, law is never just a list of independent statements. They depend on each other and are in a hierarchy
since some laws essentially depend on other laws that are prior to
them. In the last instance laws rest on the general legitimacy of
law, what reasons we have for obeying laws and the authorities
that institute laws. The legitimacy of law cannot be some very pure
general law, since the question here is why law should be obeyed at
all. There is some point that is both very particular and very universal from which law derives legitimacy. It is a particular point
because there must be something very immediate and recognizable
about it; there must be something that is more concrete than the
abstraction of general laws. It is a universal point, because it does
establish the universality of law, which always claims unlimited
scope within its sovereign domain. The question here is also a
question of what sovereignty is. Poetry is concerned with words in
their very specific and particular meanings, and sensory character,
within the context of that poem. However, the words must be
meaningful in a universal way, or we will not be able to grasp the
words as meaningful. That tension within poetry, which could
serve as a definition of what poetry is, has the same characteristic
as law. Law's legitimacy must be universal in scope and particular
in that the legitimacy must be a particular thing.

One way in which we can ground both law and poetry is the
absolute. The absolute is what is more than universality and is a
particular thing. God can be defined as that absolute, and that
would be in line with the philosophical-theological discussion of
God as absolute being. The experience of poetry and the experience
of interpreting the law can both lead to a sense of the absolute. For
Derrida, the important thing here is not the subjective experience
of the absolute, though that must be taken into account in his
views of consciousness, but rather the absolute within poetic language and the language of the law. Looking for the meaning of a
poem, and its words, and the interpretation of laws both inevitably
bring up the issue of what the origin of law and poetry is: the
absolute possibility of the legitimacy of law and the meaning of

language. This can be explored without reference to God, but they have been explored in that way for a very long time, and continue to be explored in such a way. Therefore the questions of origin, possibility and the absolute cannot be fully explored without reference to the possibility of God, as a part of our culture. Even without the cultural legacy of religion, there is no possibility of considering these questions without considering the possibility of an absolute being at the origin.

Humanism

God can be regarded as a metaphysical idea, but then so can 'humanity', 'humanism' and 'human ideals'. Nietzsche the great critic of religion, who aimed to overturn the metaphysics of a supreme being giving purpose to the universe, referred to humanism as another metaphysical idea. If we establish 'humanity' as a single thing that provides the source of all values, then we just have another version of God. Derrida focuses on this issue, though mostly with reference to the three H's (Hegel, Husserl and Heidegger). He critically examines their attempts at avoiding humanism, which he finds are still open to Nietzsche's charge of creating a humanist metaphysics, and a religion of humanity. The major discussion of this is in 'The ends of man' (in MP), though related remarks can be found throughout the earlier texts. IOG emphasizes that, in Husserl, the Phenomenological approach is a reduction to pure ideas, which must be the product of human consciousness. Derrida finds a humanist metaphysics in Husserl, where the ideal contents of human consciousness orientate all knowledge and history. This humanist teleology, where philosophy becomes a discourse of the ends of humanity, or man, is itself a recurrence of Platonist metaphysics, where all visible reality contains the copies of ideas in a purely intelligible sphere. In this case, God has been replaced by man.

> The ambiguity of an *example* which is at once an undistinguished *sample* and a teleological *model* is still found here. In the first sense, in fact, we could say with Husserl that every community is in history,

that historicity is the essential horizon of humanity, insofar as there is no humanity without sociality and culture. From this perspective, any society at all, European, archaic, or some other, can serve as an example in an eidetic recognition. But on the other hand, Europe has the privilege of being the *good example*, for it incarnates in its purity the Telos of all historicity: universality, omnitemporality, infinite traditionality, and so forth; by investigating the sense of the pure and infinite possibility of historicity, Europe has awakened history to its own proper end. Therefore, in this second sense, pure historicity is reserved for the European *eidos*. The empirical types of non-European societies, then, are only *more or less* historical: at the lower limit, they *tend toward* non-historicity.

(IOG 115)

Derrida situates his criticisms of humanism, with regard to the three H's, though the positions most strongly attacked are those of the French interpreters of German philosophy. Jean-Paul Sartre is the most obvious target, as he at one time referred to his philosophy as Existentialist and humanist. Sartre's position was strongly influenced by his reading of Heidegger, though Heidegger himself criticized that reading in 'Letter on humanism' (in Heidegger 1993). Heidegger denied that his philosophical analyses put man at the centre, and distanced himself from any metaphysics of humanism. Derrida's position on humanism follows the example of Heidegger, but also turns it on Heidegger himself and his predecessors in German philosophy since Kant. Underlying that is a critique of humanism in Rousseau, which is dealt with in OG. Sartre's version of Heidegger and other German philosophers rests heavily on a strong tendency in French thought, which refers to Rousseau's view of humans as differentiated from all other animals by virtue of the infinite possibilities of consciousness, which cannot be reduced to any particular content and is free of all external determination. Derrida's critique is partly situated with reference to Foucault, who suggested that 'man' is an invention that is coming to an end (MP 111). What Foucault certainly did not mean is that the biological entity that we know as 'human' is going to disappear. The point for Foucault is that there is an idea of man and of humanism that comes from the Renaissance. The Renaissance refers to European culture from the fifteenth to the seventeenth centuries as it began to emphasize individual humans and man as the highest part of the universe, at the centre of all knowledge and art. Foucault claimed that 'man' is coming to an end as Marxist, psychoanalytic and Structuralist thought shifted the emphasis from individual intentions and rationality, to the way that consciousness and actions are the products of underlying forces and structures in the mind and society. Derrida does not endorse the most radical elements of Foucault's formulations, but does argue against any notion of autonomous transparent consciousness and of philosophy as directed towards a goal of ideal humanity.

In his commentary on humanism in German philosophy, Derrida looks at how humanity keeps appearing as the underlying presupposition of German philosophy, and as its goal, even as it tried to question the supremacy of a unified individual consciousness. Kant suggested that we should not be concerned with sympathy for humans; and that consciousness lacks transparent unity, since it is constituted by a split between its empirical self and its inner transcendental faculties. Instead, philosophy should be regulated by pure knowledge and pure ethics, which go beyond the contents of individual consciousness. Hegel strongly opposed any philosophy that puts inner individual conscience, and consciousness, at the centre, instead suggesting that we follow a pure logic and a pure Phenomenology devoted to pure being and absolute spirit. Husserl argued for a transcendental structure of Phenomenology, which goes beyond the contents of individual human consciousness in its exploration of pure ideas and pure structures. Heidegger began from an analysis of 'Dasein' (existence), and, though humans exist as Dasein, Dasein is more than human consciousness as it refers to a form of Being, the kind of being for which Being is a question. In all cases, Derrida argues that they have replaced human individuals and humanism with a form of metaphysical humanism, in which philosophy is directed towards a pure man beyond empirical examples of humanity, who becomes the ideal goal with regard to the conditions and objects of knowledge, and with regard to the rules of morality. This metaphysical humanism is regarded by Derrida as highly compatible with philosophical nationalism, something particularly clear for

Hegel and Heidegger, who claimed that the German language has uniquely philosophical characteristics and that the German nation has a uniquely philosophical spirit. In Heidegger's case, his Nazi orientation at one time in his life adds a particularly sinister twist and gives support to Derrida's criticisms of philosophical nationalism. Rather absurdly, the fact that Derrida defended Heidegger as a philosopher led to grotesque accusations of being soft on anti-Semitism and Nazism. Metaphysical humanism is compatible, and even supports, philosophical nationalism, because a particular nation is taken as embodying universal human values and goals, serving as the guide to the other nations.

Humanism takes a paradigm of humanity, which excludes large parts of empirical humanity. What Derrida is particularly concerned with is that the European philosophical tradition has taken the white Western male as the paradigm of all humanity. Philosophy has been embedded in ethnocentric, colonialist and patriarchal assumptions. In OG, Derrida points to phonocentrism as Occidentalist, since it defines non-European hieroglyphic languages, such as Ancient Egyptian, and ideogram-based languages such as Chinese as inferior because these languages are not written with alphabetic characters that represent sound. 'Plato's pharmacy' (in D) refers to the ways in which Plato dealt with Egyptian myths that both relies on them and dismisses them as pre-rational. 'White mythology' (in MP) includes the suggestion that philosophy is the mythology of the West as one of its themes. Derrida has very little to say about the particularities of colonial/post-colonial, Orientalist and gender studies. His ideas have been used by people in those fields; the translator of OG, Gayatri Chavravorty Spivak, is a notable example. Derrida is, however, often regarded with suspicion by the more radical workers in these fields as too liberal; and he certainly never endorsed any view in which the Oriental, or black or female perspective is necessarily preferable to the Occidental, or white or male perspective, though he always thought it should be recognized. His metaphysical position was very clearly that oppositions use a hierarchy that can be reversed for strategic purposes, so that we might use a reversed hierarchy to attack the initial hierarchy, but always recognizing that both the first hierarchy and the reversed hierarchy are metaphysical and both are to be overcome. Derrida could not therefore consistently argue that the Oriental, the black or the female could be placed above the Occidental, the white or the male, except as limited strategic gestures, on the way to the dissolution of the whole hierarchical way of thinking. Despite occasional rhetorical flourishes, Derrida's position is essentially that of a cosmopolitan individualist of a left-wing variety, committed to legality and universal human rights as the basis for addressing injustice between nations, genders and ethnicities. Both Derrida's philosophical texts and Derrida's comments on French, European and international politics make this very clear, and comments by the more left-wing and radical of Derrida's readers confirm this, though there are some for whom Derrida is to be taken as a totem of everything 'radical', and find any other reading rather shocking.

Derrida's criticisms of metaphysical humanism do not lead him to oppose the concept of human rights or universal values; he is essentially criticizing the way that metaphysical humanism abstracts from individual humans and even worse provides a support for philosophical nationalism. Part of his argument with Lévinas is that the Jewish perspective is not superior to, opposed to or even clearly distinct from the Graeco-German tradition in philosophy. Derrida would certainly be suspicious of any attempt to reduce the history of philosophy to an essence contained in Greek and German philosophy; and suggested that Lévinas's pro-Jewish arguments read European philosophy in the same way as the German nationalists.

7

METAPHOR, LITERATURE AND AESTHETICS

THE PLACE OF LITERATURE

In OG, Derrida does not focus on literature and aesthetics directly. He does focus on a rather personal and literary text by Lévi-Strauss, *Tristes Tropiques* (Lévi-Strauss 1992). The title is left in French in the English translation. It of course simply means the sad tropics, providing a memoir of Lévi-Strauss's fieldwork amongst 'primitive' Nuer people in tropical South America. The title is appropriate to a book that dwells on a nostalgia for Lévi-Strauss's time amongst 'natural' and 'primitive' people. It is the memory of leaving the tropics, and the experience of going away from them, which is sad, the conditions of nostalgia. In contrast to the Structuralist goal of universal, objective neutral history, Lévi-Strauss dwells on the ideal aspects of the primitive, as does Rousseau though never in an unambiguous way. The book not only situates Lévi-Strauss with Rousseau, but also implicitly with the sixteenth-century essayist Michel de Montaigne and the twentieth-century novelist Marcel Proust, both occasional but significant references in Derrida: for example Montaigne is cited at the beginning of 'Structure, sign and play in the discourse of the human sciences' (WD 10) while Proust features in 'Force and signification' (WD 1). Montaigne's masterpiece, the *Essays*, emphasizes: solitude, the comparisons between European peoples and 'cannibals', the variability of points of view and interpretation; while Proust's masterpiece *In Search of Lost Time* emphasizes memory, nostalgia, time and the redemptive qualities of pure art. Derrida's discussion of Lévi-Strauss, running throughout OG, is an implicit discussion of aesthetics, particularly in those areas of overlap between Montiagne, Proust and Lévi-Strauss. An implicit point of criticism that Derrida has with regard to Lévi-Strauss is that he essentially brought themes from Montiagne, Rousseau and Proust to the study of 'primitive' peoples, thereby impairing his anthropological goal of understanding those societies in their own terms. But there is also the implicit suggestion in OG of the inescapability of aesthetics and poetics in establishing a position in social science, or any other form of knowledge, as can be confirmed by his invocation of Gaston Bachelard's poetry of space when discussing Husserl's epistemology of geometry (OG XII 133). Derrida's philosophy is persistently aesthetic in that he expresses himself in a distinctive style of philosophical writing; and the various arguments for the irreducible presence of aesthetic questions in all branches of philosophy.

This emphasis on the aesthetic as a central part of philosophy goes to the beginnings of Continental European philosophy, in Kant as he included a theory of the beautiful and the sublime in the *Critique of the Power of Judgement* (Kant 2000), which provides a way of unifying the practical (ethical) and theoretical (epistemological-metaphysical) domains of philosophy. After Kant, Schelling, Hegel, Schopenhauer, Kierkegaard, Nietzsche, Heidegger, Adorno, Merleau-Ponty, Sartre, Lévinas, Gadamer and Deleuze all wrote major works on aesthetics, or at least gave it a major part in their major works, and gave aesthetics a major role in philosophy. The emphasis on the aesthetic is one thing distinguishing the Continental European tradition from Analytic philosophy, where aesthetics tends to be regarded as subordinate to the questions of ethics, language and mind, which determine most discussions of aesthetics. There is a large body of material by Analytic philosophers on aesthetics, but of the great figures in Analytic philosophy few have had even a little to say about aesthetics, and none of them established their reputation through work in aesthetics. This is reflected in a very different attitude to philosophical style, since Analytic philosophers regard style as a secondary adornment and potentially mystifying if it becomes a central concern of philosophical writing. The great exception is Wittgenstein, who still had very little to say directly about aesthetics. On the other side of the divide, Husserl is the exception as he had little to say about aesthetics and wrote in a very straightforward and technically precise way.

There is a route between Derrida's aesthetic concerns and more general philosophical concerns. That route, or at least it is the easiest route, is metaphor. Metaphor, along with analogy, is discussed in many places in Derrida, including his introduction to SP, which sets up Phenomenology as that which can never be successful in its attempt to escape from metaphor into pure description of phenomena. In 'Qual quelle: Valéry's sources' (in MP), there is a discussion of metaphor and poetry, but the longest exposition on this theme, by far, is 'White mythology: metaphor in the text of philosophy' (in MP), which is one of Derrida's most widely read texts. Chapter 3 above includes discussion of those aspects most relevant to general issues in philosophy of language, but there is a lot more going on that has been kept for this chapter, which will focus the discussion of metaphor on an explication of the more 'aesthetic' parts of the paper.

METAPHOR

Derrida argues from a position about what metaphor is to its role in philosophical texts. Metaphor involves all of philosophical language.[1] It is the usage of 'natural language' in philosophical discourse. Abstract notions always hide a sensory figure. There is doubleness in the abstraction of language, where the word abstracted from its sensory origin, and then a concept abstracts from all the sensory traces of the word. That is the concept has increased linguistic value because it can be used outside the strict sensory origin and taken into other concepts (MP 210). In the history of philosophy, the sensory image has been viewed as what is original and therefore of the higher value, and it has been assumed that there is a purity of sensory language in circulation at the origin of language, and that therefore the hidden sense of a word, behind the abstract concept, can always be determined (MP 211). That valuation of the origin is an etymological position that interprets the movement from the physical to the metaphysical as degradation, so that there is an urge for the recovery of the original figure. The primitive meaning is a sensory and material figure, which is not exactly a metaphor. The original is a kind of transparent figure equivalent to literal meaning, which becomes a meaning when philosophical discourse puts it into circulation. The meaning is taken for a proper meaning and its metaphoricity is overlooked, in the forgetting of the first meaning and the first displacement. Philosophy rests on a double effacement. There is an economy in philosophy, in which metaphysics use the words that have taken the double effacement furthest. Negation dissolves finite determination, breaking the tie of a concept to any particular entity and thereby concealing the metaphorical nature of the relation between a concept and a being. Metaphysics is a white mythology, the Indo-European mythology of *logos*, which is a mythos, as the universal form of reason (MP 213). The uncovering of the metaphoricity of concepts leads to a symbolist conception of language, which treats the signifier as analogically tied through resemblance and natural resemblance to the signified (MP 215). Metaphorical value invades even the most natural, universal, real, luminous exterior of things, because the concept is a substitution for the thing that can be no more than an analogy for what it substitutes. In this we find the synchronic (unchanging, structural forms of language) being displaced by the diachronic (changeable, time-conditioned aspects of language) reversing the priority Saussure gave to the synchronic over the diachronic, in a linguistics conditioned by metaphysical reduction of the presence of being.

There is no general classification of metaphor as an absolute, because any philosophy of metaphor has to rest on metaphor that is on what it is trying to explain. The philosophical treatment of metaphor has in practice tended to reduce metaphor to ornamentation of philosophical ideas. From this point of view, nothing in metaphor overburdens the natural development of the idea.

Identifying itself with the signified idea, metaphor cannot be distinguished from the idea, or distinguish itself at all, except by trying to establish itself as a superfluous sign, which necessarily fades away. This goes back to Plato's distinction between Platonic dialogue and the rhetoric of the Sophists. There is a persistent emphasis on inactive metaphors in philosophical discourse on metaphor. It is said that the author did not think of them, and therefore they are inactive since the author did not think of them, and metaphorical effect is in the field of consciousness. The movement of metaphorization is a movement of idealization, since it is the expansion of a word beyond its immediacy. All the regional discourses of philosophy lead back to the metaphorical content of the relation between the concept and the sensory content. While metaphor idealizes, it also incorporates time and space, so that the relation between the transcendental ideal and the conditions of perception in time and space are both present in metaphor. Any attempt to develop a philosophical account of sensory contents, in a transcendental and formal account of metaphor, must return to forms of space and time as what is necessary to sensory perception, and the metaphors that inhere in them.

The concept of metaphor is a philosophical theme. The consequences of this are double and contradictory. First, it is impossible to dominate philosophical metaphors from outside, in a concept of metaphor, which is philosophical rather than metaphorical. Second, philosophy is incapable of dominating the metaphors and figurative language that must exist within philosophy. It is from beyond the difference between the proper and non-proper that the effects of the proper and non-proper have to be accounted for. There is therefore no proper philosophical category to condition the metaphorical turns of fundamental, structural and original philosophical origins. Metaphor is less in the philosophical text, and the rhetorical text with it, than the philosophical text is within metaphor. Metaphor cannot be named by metaphysics except by catachresis, which retraces metaphor through its ghostly philosophical appearance as 'non-true metaphor', which is necessarily what metaphor always is. Being disappears in the metaphors of light, clarity and radiance in which metaphysical tradition has tried to bring it to presence. These come from the inevitable repeated return of that which subjects metaphysics to metaphors. It must be reduction to metaphors, not just metaphor. If there was only one possible metaphor, which is the dream at the heart of philosophy aiming to find a master metaphor for what being, the true, etc, are, if there could be reduction to one central metaphor there would be no more metaphor. If there is one metaphor, there is the legibility of the proper on the basis of the one true metaphor. However, metaphor is always bad metaphor, the failure to reveal what is said in metaphor as itself. As metaphor is always articulated into a plurality of parts, it does not escape syntax, rules that join individual parts into a whole. The necessity of that syntax allows metaphor to give rise to a text that is not exhausted by meaning: that is a text that cannot be reduced to a single proper signification.

Metaphor must be what erases itself, indefinitely constructs it own destruction because its syntax follows univocal rules of meaning that conflict with the plurality necessary for there to be metaphor, which finds more than one possible meaning within a word. There are two ways in which metaphors destroy themselves. They repeat and imitate each other while separating according to the same law. One way is what reduces metaphor to proper meaning; the second way explodes the distinction between the metaphorical and the proper.

The first way in which metaphors destroy themselves is when they follow the line of resistance to the dissemination, the plurality that cannot be reduced to univocity, of the metaphorical in a syntax that carries a loss of meaning within the metaphor, since it is the metaphorical absorption of metaphor in the proper meaning of Being. That is, in the meaning of Being, the meaning of metaphor is reduced to rules connecting names, in which one name substitutes for another name. However, the names are still metaphorical in nature, and Being itself comes from the metaphoricity of words. Metaphysics includes metaphor even as it generalizes from the word taken up in metaphysics so that it can be reduced to the non-metaphorical. The origin of the truth of metaphor is thought to be revealed, in metaphysics, by carrying it to a proper ground or a proper horizon of meaning. The carrying itself repeats metaphor, which means the carrying of a word. This is the circle of return to itself, and it has dominated the history of philosophy. Metaphor has appeared in the history of philosophy as a provisional loss of meaning, which is always recovered. Metaphor is resisted in philosophy as what obscures the clarity of intuition, concept and consciousness. However, metaphor appears as the resemblance necessary for the law of the same, for there to be unity of the concept, intuition and consciousness. The idea of resemblance is based on the dream of naming without syntax and linguistic rules, which trouble us because they are always abstract in relation to particular words.

The second way in which metaphor destroys itself resembles the first self-destruction and is often mistaken for it. Here metaphor passes through the syntactic resistance to pure naming, and thereby undermines the opposition of the syntactic and semantic including the philosophical hierarchy that subordinates syntactic rules to semantic meaning. The passing through undermines the opposition of proper and syntactic, since it shows that meaning cannot be reduced to exterior rules, which are supposedly non-metaphorical. Metaphor carries its own death within it and the death of the philosophy that aims to reduce the metaphor within it to the proper. That death never comes; it is the tendency of metaphor to try to obliterate itself in a pure unity of name and object, and it is the tendency of philosophy to try to eliminate metaphor from language, which always refers in a proper way.

This opposition is typical of the opposed elements of an unavoidable double in Derrida. There is always a repetition and doubling, which is also a contradiction and denial. Though both elements are necessary in order for there to be either one of elements, Derrida always has a preference and here it is for the metaphor over the philosophical law, because this is the resistance of the empirical fact of metaphors to transcendental law, and because Derrida always wants to preserve metaphor.

> From philosophy, rhetoric. That is, here, to make from a volume, approximately, more or less, a flower, to extract a flower, to mount it, or rather to have it mount itself, bring itself to light – and turning away, as if from itself, come round again, such a flower engraves – learning to cultivate, by means of a lapidary's reckoning, patience. . . . Metaphor *in* the text of philosophy. Certain that we understand each

word of this phrase, rushing to understand – to inscribe – a figure in the volume capable of philosophy, we might prepare to treat a particular question: is there metaphor in the text of philosophy? in what form? to what extent? is it essential? Accidental? Etc. Our certainty soon vanishes: metaphor seems to involve the usage of philosophical language in its entirety, nothing less than the usage of so-called natural language *in* philosophical discourse, that is, the usage of natural language *as* philosophical language.

(MP 209)

Derrida's discussion of metaphor in 'White mythology' is an implicit justification for his style of writing philosophy, and for putting the aesthetic at the centre of thought. If metaphor cannot be eliminated from philosophy, and the attempt to do so is necessarily metaphysical, then there is a reason for writing philosophy that emphasizes the forces of metaphorical play which are always necessary for there to be language, including the language of philosophical writing.

There have been attempts to exclude metaphor from the study of literature. Derrida identifies this as Structuralism in literary criticism, which he regards as a metaphysical tendency that has always existed in literary criticism. He investigates the problems of Structuralism, and its relation with the Symbolist ideal of pure poetry, in 'Force and signification' (WD 1).

STRUCTURALIST AND SYMBOLIST POETICS

Structuralism is inescapable in the discussion of literary texts, and has always been present in literary criticism. Structuralism is an ever-present tendency towards the relaxation of the attention given to force. The relaxation arises from a tension within force itself, because where force cannot understand itself forms come to attention. Forms come from the creation of force within force. Structuralism as a contemporary movement in literary criticism is criticism that has separated itself from force, and it can do so because force creates form in order to interpret itself. Structural analysis comes from the defeat of force and this gives it a great melancholic pathos despite the neutral objective stance of Structuralism. Structuralism is unavoidably the position in which emotions and all psychic forces have gone.

> *Form* fascinates when one no longer has the force to understand force from within itself. That is, to create. This is why literary criticism is structuralist in every age, in its essence and destiny. Criticism has not always known this, but understands it now, and thus is in the process or thinking itself in its own concept, system and method. Criticism henceforth knows itself separated from force, occasionally avenging itself on force by gravely and profoundly proving that separation is the condition of the work, and not only of the discourse on the work. Thus is explained the low note, the melancholy pathos that can be perceived behind the triumphant cries of technical ingenuity or mathematical subtlety that sometimes accompany certain so-called 'structural' analyses. Like melancholy for Gide, these analyses are only possible only after a certain defeat of force and within the movement of diminished ardour. Which makes the structural consciousness consciousness in general, as a conceptualization of the past, I mean of facts in general. A reflection of the accomplished, the constituted, the *constructed*. Historical, eschatological, and crepuscular by its very situation.
>
> (WD 4–5)

Structuralism also has a place as an aspect of consciousness. Structural consciousness is consciousness in general containing the conceptualization of the past, and facts in general. Despite the neutral objective pretensions of Structuralism, it has strongly eschatological and crepuscular aspects (WD 5–6). It is eschatological, because by reducing time in literature to an a-temporal set of relations, it has brought time to an end as happens in the eschatology of the apocalypse where temporal experience ends, suggesting that the past is grasped as a set of a-temporal relations. In a less religious aspect, it is crepuscular, referring to the twilight and the coming of night, because it is the end of the day. The light, which illuminates action in literature, has come to an end in the Structuralist night where actions have disappeared into static relations between elements. In Structuralist literary criticism, there is spatiality instead of temporality, because actions over time are reduced to relations between simultaneously present elements. This creates a schema, a word that suggests Kant's schematization of pure concepts so that they can apply to experience. For Derrida, any schematization will empty experience of force. A totality of form and meaning of the literary object becomes possible for the Structuralist by eliminating force. The Structuralist forms both abandon the forces of life and are haunted by them, in a way that joins the scientific claims of Structuralism with Symbolist aesthetics.

Symbolist aesthetics refer to the aesthetic positions associated with Romantic Symbolism in France, as the Romantic focus on poetry as self-expression through a pure aesthetic language developed into a focus on the pure word itself divorced from external representation and reference. Derrida does not write literary history, and does not explain the context directly, but 'The double session' (in D) explores the poetry and aesthetic thought of Stéphane Mallarmé. There is a less influential, but relevant, discussion of the later Symbolist Paul Valéry, in the earlier essay 'Qual quelle: Valéry's sources' (in MP). The relevance to Structuralism is that Structuralism looks at the word on the Saussurean model according to which its meaning is given by its place in a system of signs, not by the object that may be its referent; Symbolist poetry (and related prose work) is concerned with the word as an object in itself separate from any object to which it might refer. The interest of Derrida in Structuralism and Symbolism should in no way be taken as an advocacy of linguistic idealism, or some radically anti-realist perspective in metaphysics and epistemology. Derrida discusses Structuralism and Symbolism; he does not advocate them. In particular he does not advocate the immaterial denial of force in both tendencies, and while he suggests paradoxes in the relations between words and objects he never suggests that words lack external referents.

There is a general mode of the presence or absence of the thing itself in pure language. A work of literature is both open to Structuralist criticism and is more than an object of criticism, because the work must exist both as an articulated structure and as a unity in itself. The notion of the primary unity of the literary object leads Derrida to the operation of creative imagination. This requires us to turn ourselves towards the invisible interior of poetic freedom (WD 12). That leads us into a Romantic, or Symbolist, darkness paralleling the night of Structuralism, because poetic freedom that creates the unified object must be a pure freedom beyond law, which is therefore obscured from the illumination of any kind of articulation or explanation. This becomes a theme of literary work itself, the sense that the work rests on exile and separation. This is something that can be found in literature of any type in any era, but Derrida is picking up on the very dominant role of such issues in literature since the Romantic era, through Symbolism and on into 'Modernism' and 'Postmodernism'.

It is important to realize that Derrida never uses the terms 'Modernism' and 'Postmodernism', referring to more specific entities like Antonin Artaud's 'theatre of cruelty' (WD 6; WD 8) or briefly to James Joyce's novels (WD 3; WD 4). Derrida does not have a theory of literary periodization, but his comments on literature rather suggest that he does not find any point in distinguishing Modernism or Postmodernism from Symbolism, and that Symbolism can be taken as the defining term for innovative literary work ever since the mid-nineteenth century.

The aesthetics, which Derrida finds in Symbolism, and underlying Structuralism, is that of pure absence, the absence of everything that can be inspired by announcing all presence. It is the aesthetics of the pure book, which Gustave Flaubert called the 'book about nothing'. Flaubert was a nineteenth-century French novelist, one of the founders of the novel as we know it, particularly in *Madame Bovary* and in *Sentimental Education*. Flaubert is sometimes seen in terms of Realism, that is the literary tendency to contain an accurate picture of a society and its tensions. While Derrida does not deny such issues, evidently he sees the definition of the novel, and general literature, since Flaubert as most significantly Symbolist. The proper object of criticism is the way in which the nothing to which Flaubert referred, meaning the absence of objects in the pure aesthetic space of writing, is determined by disappearing. It must disappear because the work is more than the pure freedom of its origin: there is an object that is articulated in structures.

Derrida emphasizes the anguish of writing, which reflects the spirit in which writers have written about writing since the Romantic era, but Derrida is particularly following the spirit of Maurice Blanchot here, who was also a major influence on Michel Foucault and Emmanuel Lévinas. Derrida has little to say directly about Blanchot in his early texts, but the influence is clear enough. From the 1940s onwards, Blanchot wrote a series of essays and books on literature, and his own literary works, which are particularly concerned with the empty purity of literary writing; the place of nothingness, death and night; the anxiety of the writer encountering these limits. In this spirit, Derrida suggests that anguish is more than a state of mind of the writer: it is necessary in the blind freedom of literary creation, which explores words in an imaginary world.

Derrida emphasizes that Structuralist literary criticism continues from themes in philosophical metaphysics. We have already seen a link between Kantian schemata of the concepts of experience, and G.W.F. Leibniz is also invoked, as a philosophical Structuralist. In Leibniz's Rationalism, there is no anguish of choice between possibilities since the world is a system of elements, which are compatible with each other, just as the Structuralist literary critic sees the literary work as a system of elements rather than choices and actions. The Leibnizian metaphysics assumes a world reflecting the will of a perfectly rational God. The world is the World of God, as the world, which must exist as it is because God is perfectly rational and this is the most rational world possible. Writing, as opposed to Structuralist criticism, is to know that the Book does not exist and that there are only books, which undermines metaphysics as it cannot cope with the variety of subjective experience, except as elements contained within a totality. Writing must be more than the one text that is metaphysical truth, in a metaphysical system or in the world as conceived by metaphysics.

Derrida does not refer to Modernism or Postmodernism, but he does refer to a modernity and a modern aesthetics, though only defined in such a way as to make them synonymous with Symbolism. Modernity, including modern criticism and aesthetics, is defined by the sign that is absolute or divine, as what is either absent or haunts writing. Writing lacks absolute reference to an absolute world in a relation of absolute truth, though the desire for the absolute inevitably haunts writing. Modern writing confronts the impossibility of separating meaning from writing as there is no *logos*, absolute meaning, preceding writing. Meaning only comes from the forces and structures of writing. Modern aesthetics deals with this in 'inscription' that has the power to rise above the phonocentric and logocentric view that language is essentially spoken signs. Signs are also essentially what can be inscribed as writing; and they are more than a sign of something external to itself, or limited by a system of signs as totality.

Writing is conceived by Derrida as both resistant to metaphysics and caught up in metaphysics. There is never a simple escape from metaphysics in literature for Derrida, and in general there is never a simple escape from metaphysics. The urge to bring the absolute into presence, to have truth and being immediately before us, is necessary for there to be thought and for there to be language. Writing, itself, tries to become speech, as it is always caught up in the inescapable illusion that meaning is immediately present in speech, as opposed to its absence in writing. It is literature and poetics that make us aware of these aspects of writing, which are present in all forms of writing.

In Structuralist criticism, structure serves as a way of putting together related significations, recognizing themes, and ordering constraints and correspondences in the text. Structuralism attempts a scientific view of literature, but structure is itself part of a history of metaphor, on the basis that language can only determine things by spatializing and that language must spatialize when it reflects upon itself. The figures of Structuralism, which are the forms it finds in the literary work, cannot be regarded as fixed structures. They can only be referred to in the context of the metaphorical play, which allows the identification of forms. The forms can only be defined as metaphors, which organize the work into an order from the point of view of that metaphor. The trouble with the Structuralist schematization is that it excludes time, as it reduces time to spatial forms, which in the end can only be metaphors; the values and forces that make up the object are left as an enigmatic beauty which cannot be defined by Structuralist forms.

Derrida associates Structuralism with three metaphysical tendencies that undermine its claims to be non-metaphysical and scientific: preformationism; teleologism; and the reduction of force, value and duration. Preformationism is a word that most often appears in the history and philosophy of biology, sometimes in relation to philosophy of the seventeenth and eighteenth centuries. In the history of biology, it refers to the idea that the embryo of the animal contains its final form, which in the history of philosophy tends to coincide with Platonist recollection, the view that knowledge is recollection of ideas present in our mind from the earliest stages of our life. Preformationism is an issue in the study of Leibniz and Kant, though it is a particularly specialized area of study. It is not obvious quite what aspects of 'preformationism' that Derrida is most concerned with, but in the context of literary studies he uses it to refer to the idea that the work essentially copies something that exists before it and from which it grows. In Derrida's view, Structuralism reduces the literary work to a copy of pre-existing forms, leaving it unable to discuss the differences between different literary objects. Preformationism has a long history in literary criticism according to Derrida. It appears in the view that art is the imitation of nature, a view that can be taken back to Aristotle's *Poetics*. Despite the claim of Structuralist literary criticism to overcome a view of literature as imitation of nature, by concentrating on pure forms, it rests on a view of forms that are natural and naturally pre-exist literary works. This is all anticipated by Aristotle, for whom the arrangement of elements, in a plot, always imitates the order of nature. Structuralism clearly resists teleology on the surface, as it claims to deal with a-temporal forms. However, Structuralism is selecting forms in the reading of literary text, so that the literary text is about those forms and the text becomes dominated by a purpose that is the goal of realizing those forms. Again, there is an echo of Aristotle, for whom teleology is a dominant motif. The world, all humans, all actions, all substances can be defined most importantly with reference to their end according to Aristotle. The reductionism of Structuralism, which eliminates force, value and duration, is metaphysical, because metaphysics is what replaces force with static relations, replaces evaluations with pure descriptions, and is what replaces temporal duration with relations in space assuming a static view of reality. Structuralism is a demand for the flatness of literature and its horizontal orientation, which desires that every element of signification be spread out in the simultaneity of form. Derrida tries to link Structuralism with Phenomenology by pointing out that just as Phenomenology is orientated towards the horizon of the infinite at the limit of consciousness, where there are pure ideas, Structuralism is oriented towards pure forms that are infinite in relation to any particular forms. Both have shared metaphysical presuppositions, though Phenomenology is concerned with consciousness and Structuralism is concerned with structural forms.

Force is necessary to language, which cannot be language, without what is other to pure forms and systems of significations. Metaphor is an expression of the force of language, and is the only way in which language can pass from one existing thing, or meaning, to another. Metaphor is how we deal with differences between things because it is the force of displacement of meaning, which enables us to associate one thing with another, and therefore establish the differences between them. Force and metaphor in language are the anti-metaphysical parts of language, because through force and metaphor we see how language works as difference not as the appearance of, or submission to, an indivisible Being. Passion or force and structure or form are perpetual opposing elements in aesthetics, which Friedrich Nietzsche referred to as the Dionysian and the Apolline in *The Birth of Tragedy*. They are not parts of the history of literature; they are what is necessary for there to be a history of literature. In this case, Structuralism has a place in literary criticism, and always has, but it can never be the whole of literary criticism.

SYMBOLIST POETICS

The discussion of Mallarmé, largely staged in 'The double session' and 'Outwork, prefacing' (both in D), takes Symbolist poetry and poetics as a powerful criticism of Platonist metaphysics that displaces and does not reverse metaphysics (D 211). Reversal of metaphysics would just be metaphysics again. Mallarmé does what a deconstructive philosopher does by undermining metaphysics through writing, and so should be read together with Nietzsche and Heidegger. It is the syntax in Mallarmé that challenges Platonism rather than any explicit argument. Derrida focuses the discussion of the displacement of Platonism around the 'hymen' in Mallarmé. In French, hymen has the same physical meaning as in English, and also refers to marriage, which it used to in English as well. Derrida points to the use of 'hymen' in Mallarmé's writing as a moment of undecidability. He is playing on the contrary meanings of 'hymen' as a barrier to sexual desire, as a sign of female virginity; and 'hymen' as the consummation of sexual desire on the night of a marriage. It is the syntactical possibility of undecidability in language that Mallarmé explores through literature. This is not just a play with words within the field of literature, as it shows something essential about language. Language is not a set of meanings pre-existing words and fixing them in relation to the outside world. Language exists as rules for the combination of words, syntax, and that syntax does not exclude contradiction. There would be no syntax without contradiction. If it is possible to use words, it is possible to use the same word with contradictory meanings. Syntax restricts what kinds of combinations of words are possible, but it does not prevent contradiction, or undecidability, appearing in the meaning of sentences. The syntactic rules contain the possibility of undecidability and contradiction. The discussion of undecidability in Mallarmé is particularly important for Derrida, because it shows a way of handling contradiction, which is not to eliminate or to ignore it. It is an affirmation of the inevitability of undecidability, which is the other way of looking at contradiction. We simply cannot decide which of two conflicting interpretations is true, and that undecidability crosses the boundary between the semantic and the syntactic. Semantics is concerned with meanings, so the conflict of meanings is a semantic issue, while the possibility of formulating contradictions is a syntactic issue. Derrida emphasizes the syntactic over the semantic here, and in other places such as 'Signature event context' (in MP), because he wants to avoid the priority of meaning as an abstraction from the materiality of language and communication. Syntactical rules in themselves are general, but they refer to the manipulation of symbols rather than meaning content, so they are not complicit with the turning of meaning into a transcendental abstraction.

Derrida is also concerned with the way the contradiction is embedded in the fundamental experiences we have. Sexuality is such an experience, where we have a feeling that takes us towards the body rather than towards representation. Derrida connects this aspect of sexuality with death and with sneezing. Death is conventionally linked with sex and love, because intensity of love and sexual desire may take us to the limits of consciousness and therefore to the experience of death. That is a rather romantic theme of much literature and art. The sneeze has similar connotations but in a more burlesque way suggestive of physical humour, associated with the clown Pierrot, an archetype used by Mallarmé. In the sneeze as in the sexual act, at the climax we may feel a momentary loss of consciousness as if we have died for one instant. Both the sexual act and the sneeze are experiences where we are at the limits of experience because the body overwhelms our thoughts and conscious processes. This provides a counterpart to the Romanticism of Symbolism. The pure word, or the pure work of art, can be taken as an experience at the limit of consciousness of the same kind as the experience of intense physical actions such as the sneeze and the sexual climax. Derrida gives an important role to aesthetic Symbolism, but without accepting any version of it, which excludes the body, material reality and empirical forces. For Derrida, Symbolist aesthetics does not exist in a transcendence of the material world but as part of its physical forces, breaking through representationalism and abstract understandings of meaning in language.

He also sees in Mallarmé a paradigmatic alternative to Aristotelian aesthetics. Aristotle's *Poetics* refers to literature as the imitation of an action in nature, which is generally known as theory of mimesis. For Derrida, Mallarmé effectively displaces Aristotelian mimesis as effectively as he displaces Platonic metaphysics. In Mallarmé, mimesis appears in the miming of mimesis (D 224). The doubling of mimesis questions mimesis by unsettling any notion of the naturalness of the original mimesis. The miming refers to the physical burlesque of Pierrot, which is a comical approach to what mimesis in acting might be. The break with mimesis emphasizes the purity and nothingness of the artwork, and also the randomness of the artwork. There is no teleology of the artwork, as in the Aristotelian conception of plot as action with a purpose, and the final state of the substance as its highest cause. Poetry is an engagement with chance, with the throw of the dice mentioned in the title of one of Mallarmé's poems. Poetry is not pure chaos, but its form contains irreducible chance, and literature in general works through the accidental power of the combinations of words, themes and phrases that can be found in it. That is partly the product of the pure blind lawless freedom of imagination, Derrida discusses in relation to the poet.

> The adventurous excess of a writing that is no longer directed by any knowledge does not abandon itself to improvisation. The accident or throw of dice that 'opens' such a text does not contradict the rigorous necessity of its formal assemblage. The game here is the unity of chance and rule, of the program and its leftovers or extras. This *play* will still be called *literature* or *book* only when it exhibits its negative, atheistic face (the insufficient but indispensable phase of reversal), the final clause of that age-old project, which is henceforth located along the edge of the closed book: the achievements dreamed of, the conflagration achieved.
>
> (D 54)

The character of the poet, and the status of poetics as book that attempts to write the book as the book, which Derrida notes in Mallarmé, is also explored in Derrida's discussion of the work of the French-Jewish writer Edmond Jabès who mixes religious and aesthetic themes with questions of law and interpretation in 'Edmond Jabès and the question of the book' (WD 3) and 'Ellipsis' (WD 11), which were discussed with regard to their religious aspects in Chapter 6 above.

THE BOOK, LAW AND POETICS

There is a writing that begins history and which history begins, in the book as a book. In the book as book, there is a constant displacement of meanings in a metonymic series of substitutions. The poet is bound to language in the experience of freedom, and delivered from freedom by his or her own speech. The freedom of the poet, and the escape from the anxiety of freedom in a sovereign language, is the subject of the book, as book; and the book is the subject of the poet. In its representation of itself, the subject is shattered and opened. Writing is a representation of its own abyss, the rift that appears between the word and meaning. The book is an infinite reflection on itself, because of the impossibility of reducing writing to meaning, while the book must be concerned with the presence of meaning, so that it must question its own possibility. The poet has a freedom of the passion that translates obedience to the law in the word, into autonomy. Freedom depends on what restrains it, so it receives everything from a buried origin. The site is always elsewhere. The poet is not born anywhere but is always somewhere else, wandering, in a state of separation from true birth, in which the poet is born out of speech and writing, law and the book. The poem has its origin in law, because law exists in its broken fragments, where the text has an outlaw status. Commentary on the law is a form of speech in exile and separation, because it is now the law, but, as law always requires commentary, law only exists as broken fragments of itself, which require commentary in order to fit together. There has always been interpretation. There are two interpretations of interpretation. The Law becomes the Question because its own interpretation has to be interpreted.

> Between the fragments of the broken Tables the poem grows and the right to speech takes root. Once more begins the adventure of the text as weed, as outlaw far from '*the fatherland of the Jews*', which is a '*sacred text surrounded by commentaries*'. The necessity of commentary, like poetic necessity, is the very form of exiled speech. In the beginning is hermeneutics. But the *shared* necessity of exegesis, the interpretative imperative, is interpreted differently by the rabbi and the poet. The difference between the horizon of the original text and exegetic writing makes the difference between the rabbi and the poet irreducible. Forever unable to reunite with each other, yet so close to each other, how

could they ever regain the *realm*? The original opening of interpretation essentially signifies that there will always be rabbis and poets. And two interpretations of interpretation. The Law then becomes Question and the right to speech coincides with the duty to interrogate. The book of man is a book of question. . . . But if this right is absolute, it is because it does not depend upon some accident *within* history. The breaking of the Tables articulates first of all, a rupture with God as the origin of history.

(WD 67)

Writing is already the writing of the origin, and the concealment of the origin. There can be no truthfulness in the origin. Writing is separation from the origin, the following of traces of the origin. Writing is displaced onto a broken line between speech as lost speech and speech as promised speech. The writer is absent in a book, but the writing is always engaged in trying to make that absence present. The writer can never be in the book, but writing always refers to a point of unity. Things come into existence and lose existence by being named, so that language is the rupture with totality itself, since the totality is always disrupted by the equivocation of naming, which ensures that the fragment is the form of what is written. Interruption is necessary for there to be signification; it is the death of the self. Writing must be what goes beyond identity, because it goes towards the other but this can only happen within the book itself. Writing is where ontology and language are connected and confused, as meaning is always a question of Being, of what can have being, which can be taken as a definition of the central question Derrida addresses in OG. Writing is opposed to Being and the rationality of *Logos* for which writing is responsible. The Being of the world reveals its presence in illegibility. Original illegibility is the possibility of the book, and of the meaninglessness risked by the poem as the condition of its meaning. The book and writing enable us to understand speech and language as governed by the structure of absent origin, so overcoming the philosophical assumption going back to Plato's *Phaedrus*, according to which speech reflects the truth of the speaker's intentions and writing is a secondary displacement, discussed in 'Plato's pharmacy' (in D).

Writing designates the closure of the book and the opening of the text. The closure of the book is the theological encyclopaedia modelled on the book of man; the opening of the text is the network of traces marking the disappearance of exceeded God or erased man. The closure of the book allows the affirmative wandering of the written mark to become a wandering without return, an adventure of expenditure without the reserve of anything. However, it is only in the book that we can designate the writing behind the book. Repetition does not let itself be contained within the book. The passion of the origin in writing is not the origin, but the trace that takes its place. The trace is what replaces a presence that has never been present, an origin by means of which nothing has begun. The book claims that the return of the 'origin' that inspired it should be its complete presence. The mythical book preceding all repetition lives on the deception that the centre is irreplaceable, outside all play and figurative language. Once the book lends itself to representation, which is when it is written, the book is read as a book, an abyss of the infinite redoubling of origin and centre. The space of the centre calls to us as death and God, but it can only be a void, and a labyrinth. Without presence, writing is a beyond of the book.

Derrida presents an opposition and mutual inclusion of law and poetry. This kind of duality is very persistent in all of Derrida's philosophy. While there is a strict logic, for Derrida, according to which both members of the pair are equally necessary there is always a preference for one of the pair. In this case it is poetry. Derrida always prefers the empirical to the transcendental, and the law is transcendental, or trying to be so. He also prefers the metaphorical and poetic in every possible situation.

The book, and the law and poetry are engaged with the force of writing. There is a physicality of writing, which belongs to all law and all literature. In the discussion of Mallarmé, the physicality of poetry is the physicality of all art: an issue that Derrida discusses in the most sustained way in 'The theatre of cruelty and the closure of representation' (WD 8).

REPRESENTATION AND CRUELTY

The theatre of cruelty refers to the theatre of the dramatist and drama theorist Antonin Artaud discussed by Derrida in two essays from *Writing and Difference*: 'La parole soufflée' (WD 6) and 'The theatre of cruelty and the scene of writing' (WD 8). His practice and his theory aim to overcome theatre as a representational spectacle and transform it into an experience of the body. Derrida writes on it in terms of the criticism of metaphysics and humanism. Theatre as representation is its own disappearance as theatre as physical action. The dominance of theatre as representation is part of the humanist ideal of man, who rises above the body. However, there is always cruelty at work in the theatre at the limit of representation, where there is the body. Artaud follows Nietzsche in an attempted break with the Aristotelian conception of art as imitation, which established the metaphysics of Western art. The theatre of cruelty expels God and metaphysics from the stage, in a non-theological and non-metaphysical space. The stage is theological if it is dominated by speech that governs it from a distance, if it has an absent author-creator who regulates the meaning of representation from a distance so that it represents his intentions. In general, Western theatre has seen pictures, music and gesture as illustrations of a text, given the status of a *logos* pre-existing the performance. Western theatre has assumed the unity of word and concept, reducing words to concepts, which threatens the stage itself as it subordinated to abstract concepts at a distance. The staging (or *mise-en-scène*) is liberated when released from the author as God. In this case, the stage will not be a representation, if representation means the spectacle as a surface displayed for spectators. The stage will not even offer the presentation of a present, if the present is what is in front of me. The metaphysics of the stage turns what is presented on stage to a representation of something external.

> Inspiration is the drama, with several characters, of theft, the structure of the classical theatre in which the invisibility of the prompter ensures the indispensable *différance* and intermittence between a text already written by another hand and an interpreter already dispossessed of that which he already receives. Artaud desired the conflagration of the stage upon which the prompter was possible and where the body was under the rule of a foreign text. Artaud wanted the

machinery of the prompter spirited away, wanted to plunder the structure of theft. To do so, he had to destroy, with one and the same blow,
both poetic inspiration and the economy of classical art, singularly
the economy of the theatre. And through the same blow he had to
destroy the metaphysics, religion, aesthetics, etc., that supported
them. He would thus open up to Danger a world no longer sheltered
by the structure of theft. To restore danger by reawakening the stage
of cruelty – this was Antonin Artaud's *stated* intention, at very least.

(WD 176)

Cruelty in representation fills the body. In the theatre of cruelty
the archi-manifestation of force or life predominates as cruelty on
the body. The stage is a closed space that is produced from within
itself, so that it is not organized from another site that is absent.
The end of representation is also original representation; the end
of interpretation is also an original interpretation, which no mas-
ter-speech can permeate in advance. There is now representation as
the self-presentation of visibility and sensibility in themselves.
Speech and writing become gestures again, subordinating the logical and discursive aspects of speech. All speech contains gesture,
even as oppressed and denied. The gestures are unique movements
in conflict with the generalities of concept and repetition. In the
discussion of 'repetition', Derrida is playing on the double meaning of the word in French as repetition and as rehearsal. Rehearsal
is a metaphysical aspect of theatre, because it is the attempt to produce a perfect representation of the author-God's intentions, and
denies the uniqueness of the moment of the performance by subordinating it to the text as an abstract thing. This brings us to the
moment of the origin of language, when repetition is hardly possible, and language is emerging from gesture. Repetition, like
Structuralist forms, separates forces from themselves. Artaud
moves towards purity of the presence of life and force, which is
itself metaphysical in Derrida's terms, but may be preferable to the
Structuralist metaphysics as incorporating an empirical challenge
to transcendence. Repetition in both senses is inevitable. All words
are constituted by the possibility of repeating themselves, and it
must already have been divided by repetition in its 'first time',
since even the first time rests on the possibility of repetition. The

signifying referral must be ideal in order to refer to the same thing every time. The idea of a theatre without representation is an idea of the impossible, but it does enable us to conceive the origin and limits of theatre. Presence must have always already repeated itself. The pure affirmation that Artaud seeks in the theatre of cruelty must be open to repetition itself: the possibility of its repetition is necessary to the existence of the affirmation. Affirmation is not a self-contained event; it contains otherness in its possible repetition, in the logic of iterability.

Within this framework, we can see theatre as the cruelty and 'evil' of violence on the body. The evil of the theatre of cruelty is always in theatre, as what is a relationship with the body as a force that must be violent and therefore 'evil'. Tragedy can be conceived as essential to representation, before it is a form of representation, since theatre itself refers to the suffering of the body.

Philosophy for Derrida is always caught up in metaphor, literature and aesthetics. Philosophical language cannot eliminate metaphor, and therefore cannot eliminate its status as literature. There is reduction of philosophy to literary writing in Derrida; what he does argue for is that philosophy cannot eliminate the literary aspect. Philosophical language will always contain metaphors. The philosophical tradition of the West has tended to try to abstract from metaphor, but this can only be another mythology, another fiction. Philosophy contains metaphor and the interpretation of the laws it tries to establish. The interpretive activity will always lead towards the poetic and metaphorical status of language as free invention. That is not an argument for arbitrariness in argument; it is an argument for saying that there is no position in which arbitrariness has been eliminated, and that is why philosophy never comes to an end.

8

TOWARDS A DEFINITION OF DECONSTRUCTION

PHENOMENOLOGY, TRANSCENDENCE AND EQUIVOCATION

In Derrida's account of Deconstruction, the ideas of duality and equivocation are constant. This is the case from the earliest work. IOG does not use the word Deconstruction, but it does establish the constant themes of duality and equivocation. In IOG VIII, Derrida points to the difficulty of constituting history within Husserl's Phenomenology and suggests two possible solutions. The difficulty arises because Husserl is attempting a reduction of all experience and all consciousness to the univocal language of Phenomenology, which is concerned with establishing the world on the foundations of pure ideas. The two solutions that Derrida suggests are with reference to James Joyce and Husserl himself.

The invocation of Joyce confirms the importance of the literary and the aesthetic in Derrida's philosophy. Derrida is referring (without naming them in this context) to the two novels: *Ulysses* and *Finnegans Wake*. *Ulysses* had a profound impact on twentieth-century literature, partly through its extreme use of detail in the day in the life of some characters in Dublin, and the extreme variety of language used to give the impression of the total world of Dublin on that day. *Finnegans Wake* is not open to any account of its plot, setting or characters since it takes the play with different forms of language, and different languages, to the extreme, so that we experience the life of language in an endless variety of play, fragmented stories and cultural references. We can be sure that Derrida referred to both texts because he writes of the 'Odyssean repetition of Joyce's type' (IOG 103) and *'recollection (Errinnerung)'* (IOG 102). *'Ulysses'* is the Latin form of Homer's *Odyssey*, and Joyce's novel is concerned with the repetition of the Homeric epic, along with endless historical and literary narratives, in the context of early twentieth-century Dublin. *'Errinnerung'* is alluded to many times in *Finnegans Wake*, most famously on the first page as 'river run'. The Joycean solution to the problem of the science, or Phenomenology, of history is a complete absorption in the empirical facts of history, as they appear conditioned by language. In this case there would be no distance between historical discourse and the diversity of individual facts that make up history.

Husserl's solution to his own problem is simply to continue with the Phenomenological reduction. The variety of facts in history may, however, overflow the pure ideas of Phenomenology, which will never be able to account for every detail in the enormous variety of historical facts. In the Phenomenological solution, the diversity of facts will just have to be sacrificed, and the assumption is that they have no reality in relation to the infinite content of pure ideas. This approach will not just threaten the diversity of facts; it will obliterate time. Pure ideas do not exist in time, because they exist as transcendental entities, which necessarily transcend temporal and spatial conditions. This will leave history deprived of what seems like an essential aspect. History is concerned with events in time and the Phenomenological reduction may appear to obliterate history more than establish it on Phenomenological grounds.

Derrida acknowledges that the Joycean solution is just as much in contradiction with history. If historical discourse is completely lost in the extreme multiplicity of facts, then there will be no history. History results from a standing back from empirical material in order to select it and put it in a comprehensible discourse, where there are identifiable events. Both the Joycean and Husserlian solutions are inadequate, but Derrida has a preference. The Joycean solution is closer to the kind of philosophy he is doing. Whenever

Derrida refers to two types of Deconstruction, two types of solution to any problem, or two types of self-destruction, he always prefers one. In the last chapter we saw that Derrida prefers metaphor to the proper in language and poetry to law, as he always prefers the empirical and the poetic. In this context, we can predict that Derrida prefers Joyce. It is not so much because Derrida explicitly says he prefers one element in his doubles, but that the context of his work as a whole pushes clearly and strongly in that direction.

The overall view on the issue of Joyce and Husserl, on history, is that there is an irreducible equivocation between these two views when we talk about history. We cannot find a point that will harmonize the two views, or eliminate one of them. We are just inevitably caught in a contradictory, and undecidable, position between two alternatives. Any historical discourse must be empirical and it must abstract from empirical context in general ideas. Even the most apparently empirically oriented historical work will have to use language and language abstracts out of context to name things as examples of the same thing. The two alternatives contain each other, a situation that is tied up with what can be known as doubling, repetition and iterability. Iterability is the term that captures the argument most deeply. Iterability is the possibility of repetition that necessarily contains the possibility of difference and the possibility of sameness, because every repetition creates something different but something that is the same.

Let us quote the penultimate paragraph of IOG XI, which sets out the deconstructive project, after the build up of all the preceding paragraphs.

> The primordial Difference of the absolute Origin, which can and indefinitely must retain and announce its pure concrete form with a priori security: i.e., the beyond or the this-side which gives sense to all empirical genius and all factual profusion, that is perhaps what has always been said under the concept of '*transcendental*', through the enigmatic history of its displacements. Difference would be transcendental. The pure and interminable disquietude of thought striving to 'reduce' Difference by going beyond factual infinity toward the infinity of its sense and value, i.e. while maintaining Difference – that would

be transcendental. And Thought's pure certainty would be transcendental, since it can look forward to the already announced Telos only by advancing on the Origin that indefinitely reserves itself. Such a certainty never had to learn that Thought would always be to come.

(IOG 153)

Even by Derrida's standards this is an enigmatic paragraph, but there is an argument that sets up his philosophical position and which can be explained. The main concern is to show that Difference should not be transcendental. Derrida starts with an explanation of why the word 'transcendental' is used. The word is essentially used to deal with the origin as absolute. If the origin is absolute, it is undifferentiated and cannot connect with the manifoldness and diversity of empirical facts. In that case it needs a source of differentiation. If we start from the assumption of the absolute origin, then the only source of differentiation is a similarly absolute original difference. Derrida then says that the primordial difference is both a priori and concrete. This invokes a contradictory moment of what must be, as it is, without reference to experience since it is a priori, but which is a pure concrete form. The thing that is both pure and concrete is contradictory. Derrida is referring to the kind of contradictions Husserl gets into with the Phenomenological approach. If we take pure, infinite ideas as the ground then we are always going to get into contradiction applying them to experience, the finite and the concrete. This is the necessary consequence of all metaphysics. However, we cannot get beyond this just by having a non-metaphysical empiricism. Without the capacity for pure ideas, experience is just going to be a chaos of facts, which will not even be fully formed facts. This is a version of Kant's argument that concepts without intuitions are empty and that intuitions without concepts are blind. We must see Derrida in a Kantian lineage, since Kant argued that reason inevitably tends towards contradiction as it reaches beyond experience, and that is a necessary consequence of having reason. Reason is needed for there to be understanding, that is knowledge of objects, which strongly suggests that all experience is caught up in the necessary possibility of contradictions. Derrida takes a very similar line, and a line that must be considered as going back to

Kant, when he claims that there is a history of displacements under the concept of 'transcendental'. Here is a series of displacements because the transcendental is never able to harmonize with experience, a gap that is constantly covered over by finding ways of referring to the transcendental which apparently evade this problem. The problem of the transcendental is that it tries to understand the first difference as transcendental, which is a failure to deal with the question of what material, empirical differences are. The transcendental difference is trying to go beyond the 'factual infinity', by which Derrida must mean a transcendental infinity of the pure idea that goes beyond the infinity that appears in the empirical world. There is the infinity of material diversity, which should probably include the infinity contained in mathematical series, as opposed to the concept of an infinite pure idea in Husserl's Phenomenology, which refers back to ideas in Kant and ultimately to the ideas, or forms, in Plato. For Derrida, Husserl makes the unnecessary assumption that infinity in mathematics requires a pure idea of infinity, which confirms Husserl's assumption that the pure idea is infinite. Infinity does not exist as a pure idea for Derrida, the pure idea of sense and value assumed by Husserl. That conception of the idea is tied up with an absolute origin that acts as the metaphysical cause and goal of the transcendental difference. What is missing in the metaphysical assumption is the understanding that the thought concerned will never come. The metaphysical always refers to an absolute, which we cannot avoid assuming in some way, but which can never be present or arrive any way. That paragraph has established some key deconstructive issues: the transcendental must always be challenged by the empirical, the absolute is never present and the transcendental is concerned with the absolute.

PHENOMENOLOGY AND DECONSTRUCTION

The discussion of Husserl's Phenomenology carries on in SP, with a much more detailed account of the various aspects of Phenomenology, than can be found in IOG, tied together by the theme of signs. The issue of difference, which we have just discussed in relation to the end of IOG, continues with reference to time and representation. The moment in which we can grasp our own consciousness is subject to an analysis already referred to in Chapter 4 above. Not only does that analysis establish claims about mind and consciousness, it develops the question of difference that really gets to the question of what Deconstruction is, or what Derrida's philosophy is, however we might choose to name it. The discussion of the moment is concerned with the difference that enters into the instant itself. The instant cannot be abstracted from time and difference as if it were a transcendental absolute. Husserl's moment now looks like that pure concrete form that has a priori certainty, mentioned at the end of IOG. Not only does Husserl have pure ideas, he has things in the empirical world that look transcendental and absolute, because the Phenomenological reduction to pure ideas necessarily has that consequence. The instant is not indivisible; even the transcendental origin contains difference of some kind. The instant is never indivisible. Mathematically the instant can always be divided, and according to Derrida the instant in experience must contain duration, and therefore must contain difference. The instant lasts a period of time, however short that period of time is, therefore it contains difference. There is nothing that is before difference, separate from difference or abstracted from difference. Only metaphysics can make such a claim, though it is an inevitable claim because we always do transcend the empirical in language, which always contains a reference beyond the instant. It is differentiation, including temporal differentiation, that makes the transcendental inevitable. The empirical excludes the transcendental, but makes it necessary for language and consciousness to transcend the diversity of the empirical in order to cope with it in thought and language. The question of the instant connects with the question of the auto-affection of consciousness. The grasping by consciousness of something in an instant is an act of auto-affection since it is grasping some content of itself, and is therefore acting upon itself.

There is also an investigation of the difference contained in representation (SP 3, 4), with regard to the relation between the word in consciousness and the representation of that word in imagination (SP 43–4). From Husserl's point of view, the most real existence of the word is in pure consciousness, which should mean the word as imagined not as encountered empirically. The problem here is what the difference could be between the word as we encounter it in consciousness and the word as we imagine it. In both cases the word exists fully in our consciousness. The word may exist as a physical thing outside consciousness, but as a word with a meaning that communicates something, it only exists in consciousness. There should be a difference between the word as we imagine it and the word as it exists itself, but since both these kinds of existence are in consciousness the differentiation is a paradoxical one. For Derrida, this confirms a view of difference as repetition. The same thing can be repeated and can be different while the same, but not identical. This is a problem for Husserl, because for Husserl the contents of consciousness are completely transparent to consciousness, which therefore cannot recognize a difference between the word in consciousness as the word itself, and the word as imagined in consciousness. The problem continues into the issues of the relation of representation with what is represented and of the signifier with what is signified. Where is the difference between the representation of the word and the represented word? What is the difference between the sign as signifying and the sign as signified concept? These problems cannot be isolated as a specific puzzle of inner consciousness, because, once the distinctions are undermined in one context, the distinction as a whole is undermined and the existence of conceptual oppositions is under irresistible pressure (SP 50–2).

These questions continue in Derrida's investigation of the instant and of self-affection in Husserl. Derrida brings in a famous linguistic invention: 'différance', to deal with these paradoxical kinds of differences. It appears at the end of SP 5.

> But what we are calling time must be given a different name – for 'time' has always designated a movement conceived in terms of the present, and can mean nothing else. Is not the concept of pure solitude – of the monad in the phenomenological sense – *undetermined* by its own origin, by the very condition of self-presence that is, by

'time', to be conceived anew on the basis now of **différance** [my emphasis, BS] within auto-affection, on the basis of identifying identity and non-identity within the 'sameness' of the *im selben Augenblick* [the instant/blink of the eye itself, BS]?

(SP 68)

The discussion finds an expression for the problem of the absolute transcendental nature of consciousness in Husserl's Phenomenology by referring to a 'monad in the phenomenological sense'. This is a reference to Leibniz, who suggested that the universe can be best conceived of as a union of isolate points of perception. Each point is logically independent and only experiences its own world of perception, in the strong sense that it does not experience anything outside itself, so that it is experiencing its own world instead of an objective independent world. The idea of a solitary self-contained consciousness contains that of the self-contained instant, which Derrida finds to necessarily upset the monadic principle since it cannot be stated without reference to an auto-affection that introduces non-identity. That is a non-identity, or difference, that can be contained with the same. The same can contain difference, which is why there is no absolute presence of Being, or the origin, truth, *logos* and so on. Derrida uses a word for that kind of difference. It is 'différance', but the translator does not note the introduction of the new word, rendering it as 'difference'. It is only in a footnote in the next chapter (SP 82) that the translator notes that Derrida has introduced the neologism, 'différance'. It is not the purpose of the present book to get into the details of translation problems, but this anomaly is one that needs mentioning as it does have a major impact on the reading of SP. The English title is itself an odd translation choice, since the exact translation of the French would be *Speech and* **Phenomenon**, or possibly *The Voice and the Phenomenon*.

Despite the status of 'différance' as a new word invented by Derrida, it appears rather surreptitiously in SP without an explicit definition. It is only defined contextually, that is the definition has to be inferred from the context in which the word is used. In this context, it looks like a 'différance' means the kind of difference that indicates non-identity within the same, which suggests that the regular kind of difference distinguishes between things that are taken as the same. Within Derrida's work as a whole, this looks like 'différance' as difference in itself as the pure and transcendental difference, which nevertheless disrupts metaphysical assumptions about the transcendental and the pure. For Derrida, there is no transcendental law, or pure idea, that exists in separation from force and the empirical. Some readings of Derrida assume a transcendental structure in his philosophy (Rorty 1991a; Gasché 1986). This cannot be completely untrue, because Derrida himself is arguing that no philosophy, or thought in general, can step outside the transcendental. However, the basic Derridean terms should be seen as disrupting the structure transcendental law beyond empirical materiality. 'Différance' is a way of referring to how materiality itself disrupts identity, by showing that the 'same' in our ideas contains difference. Identity and non-identity are identical in the same. That claim might seem to reassert identity, since it says that identity and non-identity are joined by identity. However, the inclusion of non-identity within identity is a way of undermining the identity of identity, and is the movement of 'différance'. This is a way of trying to frame a well-established philosophical position, which is that change and the existence of multiple points of view overflow, and disturb, identity and system. Such thoughts go back at least to Heraclitus, and most obviously include Nietzsche, within an anti-transcendental tradition. There is an empiricist element to this, and Derrida himself gives himself the label 'radical empiricist'; nevertheless his position needs to be distinguished from the general sense of empiricism, which is why Derrida is a *radical* empiricist. The difference is that 'empiricism' takes the identity of the contents of experience as given. It does not ask the question what establishes the identity of empirical contents; it asks the question how we get from them to more abstract reasoning. In that way it has the same separation of the empirical and transcendental as the more overtly rationalist-metaphysical ways of thinking. The attempt to overcome that distinction goes back to Kant. In some ways Derrida is following Kant, though not in the most explicit way. Derrida's thought, including the idea of 'différance', has origins in Kant's discussion of dialectical illusion, reflective judgement, the synthesis of the productive imagination, and other issues where the intended architectonic unity of his system seems in trouble at those points where he is trying to deal with its limits and origins. Words like 'origin' and 'idea' are themselves brought into question by Derrida, but we can never avoid using such words; we can think about the difficulties within them after reading Derrida. What 'différance' refers to is the material differentiation that can never be contained by ideas, which are always intrinsically transcendental. The transcendental itself exists within the forces of materiality, as these forces act upon themselves. 'Transcendence' in words and language is always an empirical force, which assumes ideational form within the forces of consciousness.

The term 'deconstruction' also appears in SP; this time the English translator does not overlook the first occurrence, but the index of the English edition does. It first appears in Chapter 4 on 'Meaning and representation':

> With the difference between real presence and presence in representation as *Vorstellung* [presentation in the sense of an idea, BS], a whole system of differences involved in language is implied in the same deconstruction: the differences between the represented and the representative in general, the signified and signifier, simple presence and the reproduction, presentation as *Vorstellung* and re-presentation as *Vergegenwärtigung* [representation, BS], for what is represented in the representation is a presentation (*Präsentation* [presentation in the sense of being present, BS]) as *Vorstellung*.
>
> (SP 52)

Again the definition must be taken as contextual rather than as explicit. 'Deconstruction' just appears within a discussion of the difficulties Husserl gets into with the distinction between what is present in consciousness and representing it in consciousness. He goes on in the rest of the paragraph to deal with repetition and otherness. In this context, Deconstruction is not a theory Derrida applies, but a movement within philosophy and within the consciousness that Phenomenological philosophy is trying to describe. There is a sense here of Deconstruction as a material force, though Deconstruction does appear in other texts by Derrida as the conscious strategy of a philosopher. The reference to Deconstruction in the passage quoted is to *d*econstruction, emphasizing that what we have here is the name of a process, or movement, rather than a philosophical approach. Nevertheless, Deconstruction is the name for a specific philosophical approach, so we will keep referring to it as *D*econstruction. The process here is that of the difference between real presence and representation, which is a difference within the same, since they are the same event in consciousness. Deconstruction here comes at the same thing named by 'différance', but from a different direction. 'Différance' refers to the difference that the same contains; Deconstruction refers to the same that contains difference. The rest of the paragraph quoted brings in the ideas of otherness and repetition within the same, so we are clearly concerned with what arises in 'différance'. Repetition is necessary to any idea, particularly pure Ideas in Husserl, since the Idea comes from the repetition of a finite idea, and it is the intrinsic infinite repeatability of the finite idea. The repeatability, which Derrida generally refers to as 'iterability', is the otherness of the finite idea, since it exists as what can become something other than itself in repetition.

Further fundamental terms in Derrida appear at the end of SP 6 on 'The voice that keeps silence'. In the context of the close critical analysis of Husserl, again, Derrida brings in the 'trace' and the 'supplement'. The trace appears in the breakdown of a living present: 'The living present springs forth out of its nonidentity with itself and from the possibility of a retentional trace. It is always already a trace' (SP 85). Derrida is concerned with Husserl's assertion of a living present, which is the pure presence of the moment. That is a moment which is fully present in consciousness and which is completely separate from other moments in time. For Derrida, all metaphysics contains such an idea. That is one reason why standard Empiricism is caught up in metaphysics: it strongly relies on the idea of moments in experience, which can be isolated as pure moments, undivided within themselves, and unrelated with other moments. The rationalist and metaphysical philosophers rely on a moment of intuition of the a-temporal idea, isolated from the flow of time, which assumes in common with Empiricism that moments can be isolated from their place in time. This argument in Derrida is strongly conditioned by

Heidegger, who argued in different ways over a long time that time is not a series of moments that can be isolated from each other, and that metaphysics seeks an a-temporal view. The 'trace' comes in for Derrida as the way in which what we have now in consciousness always contains something retained from previous moments. There is no content of consciousness that can be abstracted from the content in the preceding moments. The present content is always a repetition. There is no content that does not retain earlier content. If that was not the case, there could be no language, since a sentence, and even a word, has duration over time that relies on the retention of the content of consciousness at the moment that the linguistic item began, so there is no expression that is not a trace. There would be no capacity for even simple actions without some elementary kind of memory that allows us to know what it is we are doing.

There is no idea in consciousness that is not a trace, so there is no complete self-presence in consciousness, which raises the question of what defines the identity of an expression in consciousness:

> If indication is not added to expression, which is not added to sense, we can nevertheless speak in regard to them of a primordial 'supplement': their *addition* comes to *make up for* a deficiency, it comes to compensate for a primordial nonself-presence.
>
> (SP 87)

The problem Derrida is considering in this passage is that, from Husserl's point of view, sense in language requires expression within consciousness, and expression in language requires indication, which is the materiality of linguistic expression. There is no intrinsic unity of these elements: Husserl who is aiming for such a unity is still faced with the different layers contained within sense that resist unity. The unity is decisively ruptured for Husserl by the necessity for the materiality of indication in order for there to be language and communication, even the language that we are using silently in consciousness. The materiality of indication must be added to the expression, and exist interlaced with it. Even in the interlacing, the indicative is still other than the expressive. The simultaneous otherness and necessity of the indicative for expression

is its status as a supplement, according to Derrida. Again the definition is more contextual than explicit. There is a general relation
here that is fundamental for Derrida, which is the relation between
supplement and origin. We have already seen how the origin can
never be completely present for Derrida, and the idea of supple-
mentarity is a consequence. The origin is never present, so what
we have is always a supplement, as an addition or replacement.
Sense in language cannot be the original expression as a pure idea
in pure consciousness; it always requires the supplement of the
indicative, of the word as spoken or written. The metaphysical
position is to treat the 'supplement' as unnecessary and inferior in
relation to the 'origin', but the origin in pure being, truth, inwardness and so on is dependent on non-being, deception, the external
and so on.

STRUCTURALISM AND DECONSTRUCTION

Another element of Deconstruction appears in WD, in the discussion of Structuralist literary criticism: 'Force and signification'
(WD 1). Early in the essay (WD 5–6), Derrida suggests that
Structuralism itself leads to destruction and destructuring; he
does not use the word 'deconstruction' in that context but clearly
this is what he is thinking of when he suggests that
Structuralism destructures and destroys in the act of establishing
structures. The reason that Structuralism destructures itself
comes from the discussion of melancholy and twilight in
Structuralism quoted in Chapter 7 above. The Structuralist analysis brings meaning, consciousness, life and time to an end in the
pure Structures, which are the ruins of meaning. The Structures
are always a destruction of themselves because they are not
brought in to obliterate the text subject to analysis. They are
brought in to clarify the text, but instead no text is left when it is
analysed into relations between pure a-temporal structures,
which do not contain meaningful content. They are an attempt to
uncover relations, which exist without reference to meaning content. This is always self-destructive since the Structures can only
be recognizable if they are preceded by a discussion of content in

the literary text, which is the starting point of the Structures. The Structures can only show relations between content of a kind that belongs to a literary work when read from the point of view of subjective consciousness, which is the only way it can be read. The self-destruction of Structure is not a simple error in critical method. There cannot be critical method without a Structuralist pole. The Structuralist approach is therefore a 'solicitation' that shakes structures, and which only shows structures in order to collapse them. The showing of structures is the destruction of structures, and that paradoxical movement is the movement of Deconstruction. Since Derrida refers to Structuralism as a metaphysical approach, embedded in the history of metaphysics, his comments on Structuralism must refer to metaphysics. In this case, metaphysics is what uncovers structures and destroys them. It can uncover structures, because they are an aspect of the world of experience, and we cannot have experience unless we have ways of structuring it. The metaphysical structures must be eschatological and crepuscular, to use the language that Derrida uses himself to describe the effects of Structuralist literary criticism. That is because the metaphysical structures empty the empirical world of all content. There is no life, movement, or change of time in a universe of pure structures. Since the pure structures have no content, they must be empty and must collapse. Another version of this thought can be found with reference to Lévi-Strauss in 'Structure, sign and play in the discourse of the human sciences':

> But in accordance with a gesture which was also Rousseau's and Husserl's, he must 'set aside all the facts' at the moment when he wishes to recapture the specificity of a structure. Like Rousseau, he must always conceive of the origin of a new structure on the model of catastrophe – an overturning of nature in nature, a natural interruption of the natural sequence, a setting aside *of* nature.
>
> (WD 292)

The Structuralist anthropology of Lévi-Strauss is placed in the historical context of Rousseau and Husserl, emphasizing that structuralism does not only occur within Structuralist theory. Rousseau's theories of society and language, which are informed by Descartes, and Husserl's Phenomenology, informed by Kant, are shown to share the same metaphysical assumptions as Structuralism in the strictest sense. Structure excludes facts and nature, in the purity of its form, and therefore can only encounter change as generalized violence. It cannot deal with the empirical process of change and can only represent it as a catastrophe. The structures fix nature in a certain way, so that nature itself is conceived as collapsing when there is change.

Deconstruction is an inevitable movement of thought, because we inevitably structure experience. Another way of explaining that is to say that the empirical forces turn upon themselves, in transcendental force, as consciousness experiences a world only through experience through laws, forms, ideas and structures if it is going to have a world of experience. The moment of instituting structures is the deconstruction of structure, in the movement of solicitation, which is another name for Deconstruction.

That moment is not a moment of detached theoretical reflection: it is a moment of encounter with madness and violence:

> From its very first breath, speech, confined to this temporal rhythm of crisis and reawakening, is able to open the space for discourse only by emprisoning madness. This rhythm, moreover, is not an alternation that additionally would be temporal. It is rather the movement of temporalization itself as concerns that which unites it to the moment of logos, but this violent liberation of speech is possible and can be pursued only in the extent to which it keeps itself resolutely and consciously at the greatest possible proximity to the abuse that is the usage of speech – just close enough to *say* violence, to dialogue with itself as irreducible violence, and just far enough to *live* and live as speech. Due to this, crisis or oblivion perhaps is not an accident, but rather the destiny of speaking philosophy – the philosophy which lives only by emprisoning madness, but which would die as though, and by a still worse violence, if a new speech did not at every instant liberate madness while enclosing within itself, in its present existence, the madman of the day.
>
> (WD 60–1)

The long quotation from 'Cogito and the history of madness' (WD 2) above gives a powerful suggestion of the way in which Derrida's philosophy is not just a detached theoretical reflection, and is certainly not just a game of 'deconstructive' tricks. Because Derrida refers to the need for constant Deconstruction, and sometimes refers to the play of the signifier, he is often regarded as an irresponsible game player. However, Wittgenstein in his later work, particularly the *Philosophical Investigations* (Wittgenstein 2001), frequently refers to 'language games' and constantly tries to demonstrate what he claims are the illusions of philosophical tradition. This does not lead most philosophers to claim that Wittgenstein was only interested in games and had no positive contribution to make to philosophy. Such a view of Wittgenstein would generally be regarded as an example of gross misreading. The same should apply to the reading of Derrida.[1]

The passage is from Derrida's discussion of Foucault's *Madness and Civilisation* (Foucault 2001a) with reference to Foucault's reading of Descartes, discussed in Chapter 6 above. For defining Deconstruction, the important points here are that speech comes from a rhythm of violent constraint on madness, and the liberation of speech in the appearance of madness. In the following paragraph (WD 61–2), Derrida puts this in terms of expenditure, excess and economy. The economy appears in the first paragraph as temporalization, in which Derrida suggests that there is a temporal rhythm that is not time as what contains experience. Experience, conceived in terms of language here, exists as the alternation between the containment and liberation of madness. The madness in the context of Foucault on Descartes refers to Descartes's demon: the possibility that the world of my experience is a world of demonic deception. There is no escape from what Derrida refers to as the 'demonic-hyperbole' (WD 61). Experience contains the possibility that my experience is unique to myself, though attempting to express such a view is contradictory and therefore mad. Any use of language, for Derrida, means taking a place in the intersubjective nature of communication. The statement of the demonic hypothesis is impossible and hyperbolic. It is a moment of absolute openness and excess expenditure that cannot be sustained. It is mad because at this point language, communication, rationality and thought will stop. Thought and language enable us to formulate the hypothesis, but the hypothesis drains everything out of thought and language. There will be no possibility of saying anything if the demon hypothesis remains. The possibility of an economy of language rests on excluding the possibility that language cannot refer to any stable meaning. At this point Derrida is going beyond the epistemological scepticism most obviously present in Descartes's demon hypothesis to the semantic scepticism that follows. If there is no limit to doubt about the reality of the objects of my ideas, there is also no limit to doubts about the meaning of my ideas. Unlimited doubt about meaning exhausts the energies of language, which needs some fixity and some binding to function. The demonic hyperbole removes all limits and bounds on language, in which case language cannot function. That hyperbolic possibility cannot be eliminated and therefore madness cannot be eliminated. Discourse and dialogue are only possible on the condition of the violence of madness and the violence that constrains madness.

The much misunderstood Derridean understanding of 'play' appears as a central issue in 'Structure, sign and play in the discourse of the human sciences' (WD 10). The point is very definitely not to celebrate arbitrariness and legitiman an anything goes attitude to interpretation, knowledge and philosophy. The attitude that 'anything goes' is more clearly celebrated by Paul Feyerabend in *Against Method* (Feyerabend 1993), a book rooted in 'Analytic' philosophy of science, which it argues can only be continued by recognizing the sceptical conclusions that follow from the constant fallibility of science. Despite the abuse of Derrida by some Analytic philosophers as an opportunistic and rhetorical sceptic, the most obvious place to look for a strongly worded and rhetorical scepticism is some of Feyerabend, and definitely not in Derrida.

Derrida is attempting to think through what the consequences are of a non-metaphysical position. Deconstruction means being at the limits of metaphysics, which can never simply be abolished. In this respect, Derrida is occupying a place comparable to that of Wittgenstein, when Wittgenstein talks about the limits of thought and what cannot be said in the *Tractatus Logico-Philosophicus*

(Wittgenstein 1961). Derrida points out that, if there is no totality with a centre to determine interpretation and meaning, then interpretation and meaning emerge from the equivocations and contextuality of signs within discourse. Discourse itself does not reflect a world of fixity and determinism; it emerges from the 'playful' equivocation and contextuality of the sign. Again this means that we are faced with madness, anxiety and unintelligibility. There is no way in which we can fix meanings absolutely, or find completely stable structures to contextualize them in a deterministic manner. There are corresponding affects in consciousness, in the affirmation that is associated with the autonomy of the signifier. The signifier found to be autonomous exists as affirmation of what meaning it has according to a particular context. The signifier is justified by the energy that is used in bringing it into Being, and is the affirmation of that energy. The expenditure of energy always has an affirmative force, as opposed to the negative force of what binds meaning, which Derrida finds in Structuralism and all other forms of thought affected by metaphysics. Play is the affirmation that metaphysics must limit:

> Play is the disruption of presence. The presence of an element is always a signifying and substitutive reference inscribed in a system of differences and the movement of a chain. Play is always play of absence and presence, but if it is to be thought radically, play must be conceived of before the alternative of presence and absence. Being must be conceived as presence or absence of play and not the other way around.
>
> (WD 292)

The play advocated by Derrida is not an irresponsible scepticism, or nihilism; it is the construction of a position in which reality does not exist in the stark oppositions of presence and absence, or being and nothingness. Reality is the constant equivocation between absence and presence, as everything constantly comes into and out of existence, changes, and exists only in relation to the context of other things. Being itself should be seen as this play, rather than as the opposite of nothingness. Derrida takes a linguistic model here, appropriate to Lévi-Strauss's anthropology, which he is discussing here. Language exists as signification because of the system of differences and the chain of substitutions, which means that signification only exists in the equivocal manner that arises from change and context. Play is the repetition, substitution and contextuality of the sign that can never be said to be simply absent or present, and the same applies to anything in the experienced world. That loss of an absolute origin is where Deconstruction arises.

> Turned towards the lost or impossible presence of the absent origin, this structuralist thematic of broken immediacy is therefore the saddened, *negative*, nostalgic, guilty, Rousseauistic side of the thinking of play whose other side would be the Nietzschean *affirmation*, that is the joyous affirmation of the play of the world and of the innocence of becoming, the affirmation of a world of signs without fault, without truth, and without origin which is offered to an active interpretation.
>
> (WD 292)

DECONSTRUCTIVE STRATEGIES

The thought of play has a double consequence, which is not surprising since doubling is a constant theme in Derrida; and it must be so because there is no origin, there is only the trace, repetition or supplement of the origin. The dominance of the trace, repetition or supplement means that there is no isolated singularity, but there is always a doubling that also allows for the difference within the same. The double consequence of the thinking through of play in Derrida suggests a duality in Deconstruction, a duality here named as Rousseau or Nietzsche. There is no explicit preference between the two and both must be taken as essential parts of the equivocation of Deconstruction, which has the same equivocation as any other idea or concept and exemplifies that duality. Nevertheless, Derrida's thought as a whole does suggest a preference for the Nietzschean perspective over the Rousseauistic alternative, though it is important to remember that they can never completely exclude each other. Derrida's exposition above makes clear that, though he likes to express his philosophical arguments in terms of language and the sign, he means those arguments to be also arguments about the world in every sense. Like

Wittgenstein, in all stages of his thought, Derrida cannot separate discussion of language from discussion of the world, but Wittgenstein is not normally taken as a linguistic idealist, and there is no more reason to attribute such a view to Derrida. The opposition between the two poles of Deconstruction is between the affirmative and the negative; the saddened and the joyous; guilt and innocence. Both rest on the collapse of immediacy, the impossibility of finding truth, Being, and reality in the immediate contents of consciousness, which is what distinguishes Derrida from most forms of Empiricist philosophy. The collapse of immediacy necessarily leads to the two deconstructive poles. The first pole is close to metaphysics, but is premised on the longing for the metaphysical absolute, which cannot be attained, a feeling that Derrida has sometimes said he shares. The second pole is the opposite of metaphysics, but this is an opposition that cannot be sustained as a simple opposition as there is no affirmation of difference, play and becoming without the capacity to think of the absolute, the metaphysical and the transcendental unities of thought.

The suggestion of two kinds of Deconstruction also appears in the final pages of 'The ends of man' (in MP). There is a distinction between two perspectives in Nietzsche's *Thus Spoke Zarathustra*[2] (MP 135–6): the perspective of the superior man (Nietzsche's German is also sometimes translated as the higher man) and the superman (Nietzsche's German is also sometimes translated as overman). The superior man has something like Rousseau's view as described above; and the superman has something like Nietzsche's view as described above. Derrida also suggests that Heidegger can be seen as like Rousseau. Heidegger is more clearly an example of one pole of Deconstruction than Rousseau, because, unlike Rousseau, Heidegger was concerned with overcoming metaphysics and used words such as 'destruction' and 'deconstruction', though in a less central way than Derrida when working through what thought could be after metaphysical philosophy. Heidegger was centrally concerned with the interpretation of Being, and linked terms such as Presence and Appropriation, in a way that emphasizes the priority of grasping being as Being, though recognizing that Being can never fully disclose itself. Derrida implicitly compares this pole of Deconstruction with Rousseau's view of nature.

The discussion of Heidegger and Nietzsche in the final pages of 'The ends of man' takes place in the context of a general discussion of Deconstruction, where Derrida lists its main points (MP 134–6). He refers to 'trembling' rather than 'Deconstruction', in a sense linked with 'solicitation' in 'Force and significance', but references to destruction and Deconstruction appear in the discussion. The first step is a reduction of meaning, which means the reduction to system or structure according to the most pure Structuralism in the metaphysical tradition, which counters anthropological, or humanist metaphysics, and all notions of meaning. The second step is a strategic bet from, a phrase Derrida is using to emphasize the supremacy of chance over necessity, which trembles the system in a violent relationship of Western thought with what is other to it. The trembling is divided into two strategies: exiting the system by making its basic assumptions completely explicit in repeating them, which risks staying within the system; exiting the system by going right outside it and opposing it completely, which risks repeating the system in a blindness, or naïveté, which ignores the likelihood of repeating the assumptions of a system in a complete attack on it. The third step is a discussion of the difference between the superior man and superman. That distinction, which is also the distinction between Rousseau/Husserl/Heidegger and Nietzsche, is clearly to be identified with the distinction between a trembling of the system from within, and the trembling of the system from outside. The suggested resolution of these two strategies is a solution according to Nietzsche, referring to Nietzsche's use of a plurality of styles and languages.

On the definition of Deconstruction, the most precise and explicit account in Derrida can also be found in 'Signature event context' (MP). Its unusually direct and explicit argument make it worth quoting at length.

> Deconstruction cannot limit itself or proceed immediately to a neutralisation: it must by means of a double gesture, a double science, a double writing, practice an *overturning* of the classical opposition *and* a general *displacement* of the system. It is only on the condition that deconstruction will provide itself the means with which to intervene in the field of oppositions that it criticises, which is also a field of

nondiscursive forces. Each concept, moreover, belongs to a systematic change and itself constitutes a system of predicates. There is no
metaphysical concept in and of itself. There is a work – metaphysical
or not – on conceptual systems. Deconstruction does not consist in
passing from one concept to another, but in overturning and displac-
ing a conceptual order, as well as the nonconceptual order with which
the conceptual order is articulated.

(MP 329)

What this discussion shows is that Deconstruction overturns a
hierarchy in the metaphysical oppositions in order to displace the
system as a whole. This is why it is a major mistake to think that
Derrida values writing over speech. His claim is that metaphysics
has traditionally opposed speech to writing and has usually put
speech above writing. There is deconstructive strategy in which
writing is given priority, as when 'archi-writing' is used to refer to
the basis of language, but this just serves a purpose in which the
opposites are shown to depend on, and include each other, so that
neither can be placed above the other, though they always remain
different as the repetition or doubling of the other. What is also
important is that Derrida refers to the 'nondiscursive forces' and
the 'nonconceptual order'. He is making it clear that his philosophy is not a linguistic idealism, or an idealism of any other kind,
because concepts and discourse only exist within empirical forces,
which must be taken into account by philosophical Deconstruction
as a counter to philosophical metaphysics. Just after the passage
quoted, Derrida introduces another deconstructive term, which is
the graft, referring to what is added to a concept in the metaphysical tradition in order to disrupt the system. The notion of a graft
itself rests on the assumption that there is no absolute origin, only
a series of traces or supplements that substitute for the origin in
our discourse.

Much more could be said about the way in which deconstructive strategies appear in Derrida, but apart from 'Dissemination',
to which we return soon, we have covered the main terms.
'Différance' is covered in an essay with the same title in MP, but
within the limits of this chapter it is enough to note that the discussion confirms what was said in SP, but developed at some

length to take account of deconstructive strategies, the nature of forces and signification, and terms such as trace. The idea of the supplement is discussed at considerable length in OG, in various contexts but particularly: writing and speech, the inside and the outside, ontological difference, the natural and the social. 'Dissemination' is the title of a book by Derrida, and of one of the chapters in that book. That chapter, however, is maybe the least valuable of the early texts of Derrida that we are considering. It dwells on Philippe Sollers, a novelist, intellectual polemicist and journal editor little known outside France except by association with Derrida and other figures whose work he published. 'Dissemination' appears in the first chapter 'Outwork' and the discussion continues in the succeeding chapter, 'Plato's pharmacy', with reference to related terms such as insemination. The purpose of the word is partly to align Deconstruction with psychoanalysis, as the word is used to introduce allusions to male insemination and the Freudian theme of castration anxiety. It also serves to name a version of the affirmative pole of Deconstruction (D 26). It is a way of referring to the irreducibility of plurality, which Derrida suggests unifies the two poles of Deconstruction in 'The ends of man'. It is where there is no presence, just a trace, where the law is blown up (D 26). Dissemination includes the pure and endless reflections and shadows that defy any metaphysical idea of appearances as the copy of forms, or any aesthetic concept of the work of art as mimesis of reality (D 40–1). It refers to pure writing, the openness of the moment before writing, the excess that cannot be absorbed into metaphysical concepts rupturing the distinction between the inside and the outside (D 41–2). The context within which it is introduced is the discussion of prefaces in Hegel's books. Hegel wrote prefaces and introductions on the impossibility of writing such things, on the grounds that the system of philosophy only exists as the whole system not as a summary. Derrida looks at the contradictions Hegel enters into when he writes a preface, or introduction, which must either include the whole of the system, or is completely outside the system. Either the system is empty, because its structure can be given as a preface, or introduction; or the system is so full of the meaning of the whole in its every part, which are all inseparable from the whole, that nothing which is not a part of the system can be part of that meaning of the whole, so there is nothing to say about the system from outside it in a preface, or an introduction. Dissemination tries to get round that dilemma by emphasizing chance in the text, and the lack of the identity of the text. A book, particularly as discussed by Mallarmé, is not identical with itself though it is the same as itself. This is an issue also considered in relation to Jabès in WD. 'Plato's pharmacy' serves as an exemplification of dissemination, since it deals with Plato's lack of control over his texts. Close examination shows a pattern of words and phrases which have a counter argument to the more overt argument.

'Dissemination' confirms the Nietzschean affirmative pole of Deconstruction as superior, and the aesthetic position of Derrida, who uses the literary text as a model for reading the philosophical text. There is still a philosophical argument, in which the strategies of writing philosophy and the status of philosophical writing are taken as the core issues in philosophy, which condition all the other questions.

NOTES

1 INTRODUCTION: DERRIDA'S LIFE AND THE BACKGROUND TO HIS PHILOSOPHY

1   Numbers in bold refer to chapter numbers in Derrida. Numbers in normal font refer to page numbers in Derrida.
2   Born in Austria but made his career in Germany.
3   Born in Lithuania but made his career in France.

2 METAPHYSICS

1   236e–241e in the standard pagination that appears in the margins of all academic Plato editions.
2   Discussed in more detail in Stocker 2000.
3   Derrida refers briefly to Chomsky in 'The linguistic circle of Geneva' (MP 139–40 and 152).
4   Notions of economy are explored in 'From restricted to general economy: a Hegelianism without reserve' (WD 9) and 'Différance' (in MP).
5   On Heidegger and language, see '*Ousia* and *Grammē*: note on a note from *Being and Time*' (in MP).

3 LANGUAGE: SENSE AND MEANING

1   *Philosophical Investigations* (Wittgenstein 2001) §§ 239–315, though the whole of what follows on the philosophy of mind, and philosoph-

ical psychology, could be seen as an extension of the private language argument.

2   For a position in French philosophy comparable with Derrida, see *Difference and Repetition* (Deleuze 1994).

3   See Chapter 1 of *Individuals*.

4   Frank B. Farrell draws attention to this comparison in 'Iterability and meaning: the Searle–Derrida debate' (Farrell 1998).

5   See Farrell 1998; Richmond 1996; Moore 2000. Also see discussion of this topic in Stocker 2003.

6   *Philosophical Passages* (Cavell 1995).

7   For an appreciative if critical Analytic reading of 'White mythology', see Morris 2000.

8   See note 1 above for Wittgenstein reference. A useful discussion can be found in 'A critique of pure meaning: Wittgenstein and Derrida' (Sonderegger 1997).

4 CONSCIOUSNESS: INTENTIONALITY AND PERCEPTION

1   Derrida emphazises Freud's 'debt' to Nietzsche and Freud's anxiety about this in *The Post Card* (Derrida 1987a).

2   An explicit discussion of Lacan can be found in 'Le facteur de la vérité' (in Derrida 1987a), which means something like 'The bearer of truth' but the title is left in French in the English edition for reasons that we cannot enter into here.

3   A claim made by Christina Howells (Howells 1998) and Thomas Baldwin (Baldwin 2000).

4   *Being-in-the-World* (Dreyfus 1991).

5   In particular, see *The Book to Come* (Blanchot 2002) and *The Space of Literature* (Blanchot 1982). Also *The Writing of the Disaster* (Blanchot 1986), which contains responses to Derrida.

5 KNOWLEDGE: ORIGIN AND STRUCTURE

1   See Stocker 2000 for a more detailed discussion.

2   See *For Marx* (Althusser 1990) and *Reading Capital* (Althusser 1997).

3   Useful and clear discussions of Internalism and Externalism can be found in the first part of *Subjective, Intersubjective, Objective* (Davidson 2001), where Davidson tries to find a middle way, which can usefully be compared with Derrida, and where he discusses

Putnam's 'Meaning of "meaning"' (Putnam 1975), discussed in Chapter 3 of the present book.

4   In the Preface to *Mind and World* (McDowell 1996), p ix.

6 VALUES: ETHICS, SOVEREIGNTY, HUMANISM AND RELIGION

1   The relationship between the questioning of the absoluteness of the self and questions can be found in recent Analytic philosophy. Derek Parfit questions the continuous existence of the self, which for him implies a greater sense of obligation to others than to myself (Parfit 1984). John Doris refers to 'postmodernism' in an argument largely derived from experimental psychology and cognitive science, which suggests that we do not have a strong independent continuous self, though his conclusions are less immediately optimistic morally than Parfit (Doris 2002). Despite joining the unconsidered and muddled polemical attacks on Derrida, Williams is probably closer when he suggest that the self can assume moral responsibility though it does not exist as an unchangeable metaphysical entity over time, particularly when we consider Williams's interests in Nietzsche and literature (Williams 1981 and 1985).

2   The attempt to find a position on sovereignty that is somewhere between mastery and slavery could be usefully compared with the work of the Analytic political philosopher Philip Pettit on 'non-domination' in politics (Pettit 1997).

3   Questions of law, the origins of law and fictionality exist at the heart of political and legal philosophy throughout the history of philosophy. For Analytic philosophy the most important example is the work of John Rawls on the foundations of justice with regard to the 'initial position' and the 'veil of ignorance' (Rawls 1999).

7 METAPHOR, LITERATURE AND AESTHETICS

1   For a discussion of Analytic aesthetics and Derrida's view of metaphor, see Novitz 1985, Fisher 1987 and Buechner 1987.

8 TOWARDS A DEFINITION OF DECONSTRUCTION

1   After Wittgenstein, there is the example of Donald Davidson, whose work looks at the metaphorical nature of language, and indetermi-

nacy of meaning in language (Davidson 2004 and 2005). His work to some degree follows on from W.V.O. Quine's discussions of radical translation, that is indeterminacy in translation along with holism in meaning (Quine 1960 and 1977), though, unlike Davidson, Quine joined the polemics against Derrida.

2 Nietzsche 1969.

BIBLIOGRAPHY

WORKS BY DERRIDA

(1973) *Speech and Phenomena and Other Essays on Husserl's Theory of Signs*, trans. David B. Allison and Newton Garver, Evanston, IL: Northwestern University Press.

(1976) *Of Grammatology*, trans. Gayatri Chakravorty Spivak, Baltimore: Johns Hopkins University Press.

(1977) *Limited Inc*, trans. Samuel Weber and Jeffrey Mehlman, Evanston, IL: Northwestern University Press.

(1978) *Writing and Difference*, trans. Alan Bass, London: Routledge.

(1979) *Spurs: Nietzsche's Styles*, English and French trans. Barbara Harlow, Chicago, IL: University of Chicago Press.

(1981) *Dissemination*, trans. Barbara Johnson, London: Continuum.

(1982) *Margins of Philosophy*, trans. Alan Bass, Hemel Hempstead: Harvester Wheatsheaf.

(1984) 'Two words for Joyce', in *Post-Structuralist Joyce: Essays from the French*, eds Daniel Ferrer and Derek Attridge, trans. Geoffrey Bennington, Cambridge: Cambridge University Press.

(1986) *Glas*, trans. John P. Leavey and Richard Rand, Lincoln: University of Nebraska Press.

(1987a) *The Post Card: From Socrates to Freud and Beyond*, Chicago, IL: University of Chicago Press.

(1987b) *The Truth in Painting*, trans. Geoffrey Bennington and Ian McLeod, Chicago, IL: University of Chicago Press.

(1989a) *Edmund Husserl's Origin of Geometry: An Introduction*, trans. John P. Leavey, Lincoln: University of Nebraska Press.

(1989b) *Of Spirit: Heidegger and the Question*, trans. Geoffrey Bennington and Rachel Bowlby, Chicago, IL: University of Chicago Press.

(1990) 'Force of law: the mystical foundation of authority', *Cardozo Law Review* 11 (5–6): 920–1056.

(1992) 'Ulysses gramophone: hear say yes in Joyce', in *Acts of Literature*, ed. Derek Attridge, London: Routledge.

(1995) *The Gift of Death*, Chicago, IL: University of Chicago Press.

(1996) 'Adieu', *Philosophy Today* 40 (3): 33–4.

(1997) *The Politics of Friendship*, London: Verso.

(2003) *The Problem of Genesis in Husserl's Philosophy*, trans. Marian Hobson, Chicago, IL: University of Chicago Press.

OTHER REFERENCES

Althusser, Louis (1990) *For Marx*, trans. Ben Brewster, London: Verso.

——(1997) *Reading Capital*, trans. Ben Brewster, London: Verso.

Austin, J.L. (1975) *How to Do Things with Words*, Oxford: Oxford University Press.

Baldwin, Thomas (2000) 'Death and meaning – some questions for Derrida', *Ratio* 13 (December): 405–7.

Benjamin, Walter (1996) *Selected Writings. Volume 1: 1913–1926*, eds Marcus Bullock and Michael W. Jennings, London: Belknap/Harvard University Press.

Blanchot, Maurice (1982) *The Space of Literature*, trans. Ann Smock, Lincoln: University of Nebraska Press.

——(1986) *The Writing of the Disaster*, trans. Ann Smock, Lincoln: University of Nebraska Press.

——(2002) *The Book to Come*, Stanford, CA: Stanford University Press.

Buechner, Jeffrey (1987) 'Radically misinterpreting radical interpretation', *The Journal of Aesthetics and Art Criticism* 45 (4): 409–10.

Canguilhelm, Georges (1991) *The Normal and the Pathological* (with an introduction by Michel Foucault), trans. Carolyn R. Fawcett, Cambridge, MA: Zone Books/MIT Press.

Cavell, Stanley (1995) *Philosophical Passages: Wittgenstein, Emerson, Austin, Derrida*, New York: Harvard University Press.

Davidson, Donald (2001) *Subjective, Intersubjective, Objective*, Oxford: Oxford University Press.

——(2004) *Inquiries into Truth and Interpretation*, Oxford: Oxford University Press.

——(2005) *Truth, Language and History*, Oxford: Oxford University Press.

Deleuze, Gilles (1988) *Foucault*, trans. Seàn Hand, Minneapolis, MN: University of Minnesota Press.

——(1994) *Difference and Repetition*, trans. Paul Patton, London: Athlone/Continuum.

Deleuze, Gilles and Guattari, Félix (2004) *Anti-Oedipus: Capitalism and Schizophrenia*, trans. Robert Hurley, Mark Seem, and Helen R. Lane, London: Continuum.

Doris, John M. (2002) *Lack of Character: Personality and Moral Behavior*, Cambridge: Cambridge University Press.

Dreyfus, Hubert (1991) *Being-in-the-World: A Commentary on Heidegger's Being and Time Division I*, Cambridge, MA: MIT Press.

Evans, Gareth (1982) *The Varieties of Reference*, Oxford: Clarendon Press.

Evans, John Claude (1991) *Strategies of Deconstruction: Derrida and the Myth of the Voice*, Minneapolis, MN: University of Minnesota Press.

Farrell, Frank B. (1988) 'Iterability and meaning: the Searle–Derrida debate', *Metaphilosophy* 19(1): 53–61.

Feyerabend, Paul (1993) *Against Method: Outline of an Anarchistic Theory of Knowledge*, London: Verso.

Fichte, J.G. (1982) *The Science of Knowledge*, trans. Peter Heath and John Lachs, Cambridge: Cambridge University Press.

Fisher, David H. (1987) 'Dealing with Derrida: a response to Novitz', *The Journal of Aesthetics and Art Criticism* 45(3): 297–9.

Foucault, Michel (2001a) *Madness and Civilisation*, trans. Richard Howard, London: Routledge.

——(2001b) *The Order of Things*, trans. Anonymous, London: Routledge.

——(2002) *The Archaeology of Knowledge*, trans. Alan Sheridan, London: Routledge.

——(2003) *The Birth of the Clinic: An Archaeology of Medical Perception*, trans. Alan Sheridan, London: Routledge.

Gasché, Rodolphe (1986) *The Tain of the Mirror: Derrida and the Philosophy of Reflection*, Cambridge, MA: Harvard University Press.

Glendinning, Simon (1998) *On Being with Others: Heidegger–Derrida–Wittgenstein*, London: Routledge.

Hegel, G.W.F. (1977) *Hegel's Phenomenology of Spirit*, trans. A.V. Miller, Oxford: Oxford University Press.

Heidegger, Martin (1962) *Being and Time*, trans. J. Macquarrie and E. Robinson, Oxford: Blackwell.

——(1972) *On Time and Being*, trans. Joan Stambaugh, New York: Harper.

——(1993) *Basic Writings*, ed. David Farrell Krell, London: Routledge.

Howells, Christina (1998) *Derrida: Deconstruction from Phenomenology to Ethics*, Cambridge: Polity.

Husserl, Edmund (1983) *Ideas Pertaining to a Pure Phenomenology and a Phenomenological Philosophy, Book 1*, trans. F. Kerslen, Dordrecht: Kluwer.

——(1990) *Ideas Pertaining to a Pure Phenomenology and a Phenomenological Philosophy, Book 2*, trans. R. Rojcewicz and A. Schwer, Dordrecht: Kluwer.

——(2001) *Logical Investigations*, 2 vols, ed. Dermot Moran, trans. J.N. Findlay, London: Routledge.

Kant, Immanuel (2000) *Critique of the Power of Judgement*, trans. Paul Guyer and Eric Matthews, Cambridge: Cambridge University Press.

Kierkegaard, Søren A. (1992a) *Concluding Unscientific Postscript to Philosophical Fragments*, 2 vols, trans. Edward V. Hong and Edna H. Hong, Princeton, NJ: Princeton University Press.

——(1992b) *Philosophical Fragments/Johannes Climacus*, trans. Edward V. Hong and Edna H. Hong, Princeton, NJ: Princeton University Press.

Kuhn, Thomas S. (1996) *The Structure of Scientific Revolutions*, Chicago, IL: University of Chicago Press.

Lévinas, Emmanuel (1998) *Otherwise than Being, Or, Beyond Essence*, trans. Alphonso Lingis, Duquesne, PA: Duquesne University Press.

——(1999) *Totality and Infinity: An Essay in Exteriority*, trans. Alphonso Lingis, Duquesne, PA: Duquesne University Press.

Lévi-Strauss, Claude (1992) *Tristes Tropiques*, trans. John Weightman and Doreen Weightman, Harmondsworth: Penguin.

McDowell, John (1996) *Mind and World*, Cambridge, MA: Harvard University Press.

Merleau-Ponty, Maurice (1962) *The Phenomenology of Perception*, trans. Colin Smith, London: Routledge.

——(1968) *The Visible and the Invisible*, trans. Alphonso Lingis, Evanston: Northwestern University Press.

Moore, A.W. (2000) 'Arguing with Derrida', *Ratio* 13 (December): 355–73.

Morris, Michael (2000) 'Metaphor and philosophy: an encounter with Derrida', *Philosophy* 75: 225–44.

Nietzsche, Friedrich (1969) *Thus Spoke Zarathustra*, trans. R.J. Hollingdale, Harmondsworth: Penguin.

Novitz, David (1985) 'Metaphor, Derrida, and Davidson', *The Journal of Aesthetics and Art Criticism* 44(2): 101–14.

Parfit, Derek (1984) *Reasons and Persons*, Oxford: Oxford University Press.

Pettit, Philip (1997) *Republicanism: A Theory of Freedom and Government*, Oxford: Oxford University Press.

Putnam, Hilary (1975) 'The meaning of "meaning"', in *Mind, Language and Reality: Philosophical Papers*, Cambridge: Cambridge University Press.

——(2004) *Ethics without Ontology*, Cambridge, MA: Harvard University Press.

Quine, Willard Van Orman (1960) *Word and Object*, Cambridge, MA: MIT Press.

——(1977) *Ontological Relativity and Other Essays*, New York: Columbia University Press.

——(1980) 'On what there is' in *From a Logical Point of View*, Cambridge, MA: Harvard University Press.

Rawls, John (1999) *A Theory of Justice*, Oxford: Oxford University Press.

Richmond, Sarah (1996) 'Derrida and analytical philosophy: speech acts and their force', *European Journal of Philosophy* 4(1): 38–62.

Rorty, Richard (1980) *Philosophy and the Mirror of Nature*, Oxford: Blackwell.

——(1991a) 'Is Derrida a transcendental philosopher?' in *Essays on Heidegger and Others: Philosophical Papers II*, Cambridge: Cambridge University Press.

——(1991b) 'Pragmatism, Davidson and truth' in *Objectivity Relativism and Truth: Philosophical Papers I*, Cambridge: Cambridge University Press.

Rousseau, Jean-Jacques (1980) *Rousseau on the Origin of Language/Johann Gottfried Herder On the Origin of Language*, trans. John H. Moran and Alexander Code, Chicago, IL: University of Chicago Press.

Russell, Bertrand (1992a) 'On denoting' in *Logic and Knowledge: Essays 1901–1950*, ed. R.C. Marsh, London: Routledge.

——(1992b) *The Principles of Mathematics*, London: Routledge.

Sartre, Jean-Paul (2001) *Sketch for a Theory of the Emotions*, trans. Anonymous, London: Routledge.

——(2003) *Being and Nothingness: A Phenomenological Ontology*, trans. Hazel E. Barnes, London: Routledge.

Saussure, Ferdinand de (1995) *Course in General Linguistics*, trans. R. Harris, London: Duckworth.

Searle, John R. (1977) 'The world turned upside down', *New York Review of Books*, 27 October.

——(1997) 'Re-iterating the differences: a reply to Derrida', *Glyph* 2: 198–208.

Sonderegger, Ruth (1997) 'A critique of pure meaning: Wittgenstein and Derrida', *European Journal of Philosophy* 5(2): 183–209.

Stich, Stephen (1996) *Deconstructing the Mind*, New York: Oxford University Press.

Stocker, Barry (2000) 'Pascal and Derrida: geometry, origin and discourse', *Symposium* 4(1): 117–41.

——(2003) 'Presence and immediacy in analysis and Deconstruction', *Yeditepe'de Felsefe* 2: 41–69.

Strawson, P.F. (1990) *Individuals: An Essay in Descriptive Metaphysics*, London: Routledge.

Williams, Bernard (1981) *Moral Luck: Philosophical Papers 1973–1980*, Cambridge: Cambridge University Press.

——(1985) *Ethics and the Limits of Philosophy*, Cambridge, MA: Harvard University Press.

Wittgenstein, Ludwig (1961) *Tractatus Logico-Philosophicus*, trans. David Pears and Brian McGuinness, London: Routledge.

——(2001) *Philosophical Investigations*, trans. G.E.M. Anscombe, Oxford: Blackwell.

INDEX